Achieving Our World

Achieving Our World

Toward a Global and Plural Democracy

Fred Dallmayr

ROWMAN & LITTLEFIELD PUBLISHERS, INC.
Lanham • Boulder • New York • Oxford

ROWMAN & LITTLEFIELD PUBLISHERS, INC.

Published in the United States of America
by Rowman & Littlefield Publishers, Inc.
4720 Boston Way, Lanham, Maryland 20706
www.rowmanlittlefield.com

12 Hid's Copse Road
Cumnor Hill, Oxford OX2 9JJ, England

British Library Cataloguing-in-Publication Information Available

Library of Congress Cataloging-in-Publication Data

Dallmayr, Fred R. (Fred Reinhard), 1928–
    Achieving our world : toward a global and plural democracy / Fred Dallmayr.
        p. cm.
    Includes bibliographical references and index.
    ISBN 0-7425-1184-7 (alk. paper) — ISBN 0-7425-1185-5 (pbk. : alk. paper)
    1. Democracy. 2. Human rights. 3. Pluralism (Social sciences) 4. Globalization. 5.
Identity (Philosophical concept) I. Title.

JC423 .D277 2001
321.8—dc21   2001019691

Printed in the United States of America

⊗™ The paper used in this publication meets the minimum requirements of American
National Standard for Information Sciences—Permanence of Paper for Printed Library
Materials, ANSI/NISO Z39.48-1992.

To Ilse,
wife, companion, friend

~

Contents

~

Preface

This book is the third step in a line of inquiry stretching back at least a decade. The first tangible way station along this road was a book titled *Beyond Orientalism* (1996), which was followed by *Alternative Visions: Paths in the Global Village* (1998). While the first book sought to critique and correct an aggressive and predatory worldview bent on subjecting non-Western societies to hegemonic Western standards, the second aimed to enlist and empower alternative voices and visions emanating from parts of our globe previously sidelined by dominant modes of discourse. Without abandoning these earlier accents, this book seeks to explore or uncover viable interconnections or linkages between elements of our world, linkages that might be conducive to some kind of mutuality, reciprocal recognition, and peace. The main emphasis of the book hence is on (what philosophers call) "mediations"—though this emphasis never forgets persisting forms of inequality and domination and hence real-life obstacles to recognition. The mediations examined here are arranged along two basic axes that are thematized under the labels of "local–global" and "self–other" trajectories. Although the two axes are closely linked and often overlapping, they can be distinguished at least for heuristic purposes as representing (loosely speaking) respectively vertical and lateral types of mediations.

The title *Achieving Our World* was chosen for a number of reasons. An immediate motivation was the attempt to profile the book's perspective against the backdrop of Richard Rorty's influential and widely discussed *Achieving Our Country*.[1] Although applauding Rorty's exhortation to his fellow countrymen to renew their active democratic commitments, I find it difficult to sympathize with his narrow focus on "our country"—that is, with his lingering ethnocentrism and Americanism (perhaps "America-firstism"). Without denying certain accomplishment of the American way of life, I consider it imperative to balance more judiciously praise and blame—that is, to acknowledge, alongside advances in individual freedoms, the egregious blemishes of "our country," including staggering inequalities of economic status together with persisting racial, ethnic, and gender inequities. In the international arena, the role of "our country" is even more deeply ambivalent: as the only remaining superpower, the United States is not only the leader of the "free world" (as Rorty maintains) but also the locus of global hegemony or domination in the military, economic, and technological fields (with foreign policies often dictated by sheer power politics rather than considerations of global justice). At this point, one of the trajectories previously mentioned comes clearly into new: the local-global axis. Precisely under democratic auspices favored by Rorty, people around the globe need to be encouraged and strengthened as public agents—which seems impossible to do from an ethnocentric perspective. This point underscores the importance of mediations. To phrase concisely a main thesis of this book: In our contemporary era of globalization, it is impossible to "achieve our country" without attempting to "achieve our world."

There are other motivations behind the choice of the book's title. Not long ago, Anthony Giddens published a text titled *Runaway World*, which was the outcome of his celebrated Reith Lectures in 1999. By choosing his title, Giddens meant to highlight certain centrifugal tendencies operating in the world today, tendencies that (in terms of his subtitle) determine "how globalization is reshaping our lives." Countering popular Enlightenment beliefs, according to which the world was to become steadily more rational and hence stable and manageable, his book points to very different developments. Here are some lines conveying the flavor of his argument:

> The world in which we find ourselves today, however, doesn't look or feel much like they [the Enlightenment philosophers] predicted it would. Rather than being more and more under our control, it seems out of our control—a runaway world. Moreover, some of the influences that were supposed to make life more certain and predictable for us, including the progress of science and technology, often have the opposite effect. Global climate change and its accompanying risks, for example, probably result from our intervention into the environment. . . . Science and technology are inevitably involved in our attempts to counter such risks, but they have also contributed to creating them in the first place.[2]

The notion of a "runaway" world, or a world placed in "fast forward," stands in contrast with the aspiration of "achieving our world"; at least, it indicates powerful obstacles on the road to such achievement. The image of "running away" suggests a world that increasingly escapes or slips from the range of human understanding and mediation; in aggravated form, it conjures up the dystopia of an increasingly mechanized, reified, or automated world. In moral and political terms, such a world would be one without political accountability and moral responsibility. This, however, is not the only possible form of world-slippage or human severance from the world. At a much earlier point, Hannah Arendt had examined a mode of slippage deriving not from centrifugal but from centripetal motives: from a retreat into radical interiority or a worldless subjectivism. In *The Human Condition*, Arendt portrayed this retreat under the label of "world alienation." Correcting some of Marx's assumptions (but sharing his edge against capital accumulation), she depicted the central thrust of Western modernity not as the plunge into worldliness but rather as the growing human exodus from the world. Contrary to some secularist readings of modernity, she wrote,

> modern men were not thrown back upon this world but upon themselves. One of the most persistent trends in modern philosophy since Descartes and perhaps its most original contribution to philosophy has been an exclusive concern with the self (as distinguished from the soul or person or man in general), an attempt to reduce all experiences, with the world as well as with other human beings, to experiences between man and himself. . . . World alienation, and not self-alienation as Marx thought, has been the hallmark of the modern age.

For Arendt, this severing process was bound to be intensified in the age of "runaway" globalization, an age marked by the "decline of the European nation-state system," the "economic and geographic shrinkage of the earth," and the transformation of humankind into a far-flung village "whose members at the most distant points of the globe need less time to meet than the members of a nation needed a generation ago."[3]

Both types of slippage—the centrifugal as well as the centripetal—put pressure on the title of this book. In fairness, one needs to add that both writers just mentioned are keenly aware of this pressure and seek to provide some remedies or antidotes—either through a revitalization of practical engagement (the *vita activa*) or through a strengthening of "civic culture" and a further "democratization of democracy" (on all levels, from the local to the global).[4] At this point, some additional semantic clarifications seem in order. For one thing, the notion of "achieving" does not suggest a form of technical construction or social engineering; rather, the term here has the connotation of practical labor or engagement—a labor in which the "achieving" agents are continuously challenged (or called into question) by what needs to be achieved. Far from designating a linear-strategic design, achievement hence carries a roundabout or mediating significance, operating steadily in the "middle voice" (between speaking and listening, moving and being moved). This significance carries over into the sense of "our"—which in no way should be taken as a possessive pronoun. If the goal of "achieving" involves the simultaneous transformation of achieving agents, then the world to be rescued from slippage cannot simply be the target of managerial appropriation. Despite the need to resist slippage into automatic self-regulation, the world can be "ours" only in a highly complex and mediated way—assigning to human beings only the task of responsible guardianship rather than mastery or possession. In a way, this aspect is recognized by Giddens when he writes, "We shall never be able to become the masters of our own history, but we can and must find ways of bringing our runaway world to heel."[5]

The preceding comments also throw light on the remaining, and most elusive, term of the title: *world*. As it happens, this term has been a prominent target of inquiry of philosophers throughout the ages (both in the West and the East). In recent Western thought, Martin Heidegger is justly famous (among other things) for having offered a concise formula or phrase pinpointing the sense of humane existence: the phrase "being-in-the-world." As Heidegger has explained, the term *world* in that phrase does not denote an external container (*res extensa*) into which humans accidentally or contingently happen to be placed; nor does it designate a subjective construct or arbitrary flight of fancy on the part of individual or collective agents. Rather, for Heidegger, the term was co-constitutive for, or intrinsic to, the meaning of "being human"; far from reflecting either an external mechanism or a private whim, *world* once again operated basically in the "middle voice," the voice of mediation correlating invention and discovery. As one should add, the use of *world* in Heidegger's formula did not imply a pre-judgment in favor of immanence over transcendence, or vice versa; nor did it involve a preference among the different levels—local, regional, and global—of world. The central issue for him was how human beings might properly "be" or achieve their status as "beings-in-the-world," without derailment into centrifugal or centripetal modes of slippage. In the course of his life, Heidegger became increasingly alarmed by the pressures and dangers of such slippage. As is well known, the later decades of his life were overshadowed by concern over the momentum of a steadily more automated and technological "runaway world" (famously stylized as "*das Gestell*"). At the same time, he remained deeply troubled by corresponding centripetal tendencies, manifest in growing solipsism, narcissism, world alienation, and "homelessness"; partly in response to these tendencies, his writings turned to the healing power of language, particularly the poetic language of Hölderlin, Trakl, and Rilke.[6]

In light of the above clarifications it is clear that this book is, or means to be, a study of mediations along several axes or trajectories (primarily the two mentioned before). In our time of rapid globalization, a major tension—eminently prone to slippage—exists between local and global dimensions of human life, between particular contexts and universal horizons. As we are told by historical sociologists and anthropologists, most people in earlier periods of history tended to live in small-scale communities clustered around extended families, clans, or tribes; despite their narrow confines, these local settings also provided people with a sense of "home" or refuge in the face of natural catastrophes and the constant threat of external invasions. Over the centuries, the lived horizons of traditional communities were steadily expanded—although even the older "empires" remained largely collections of small localities (precariously held together by a distant authority). A major change occurred with the onset of Western modernity when localities were forcefully integrated into larger nation-states—often at the price of severe disruptions of traditional life-forms and habituated modes of human identity or self-understanding. Similar disruptions or dislocations mark our current era—but are projected onto the global scale. In this situation of global turmoil, careful mediations or balancing acts need to be kept in place—to prevent people everywhere from slipping into radical forms of (centrifugal or centripetal) world alienation. This need is reinforced by the structural asymmetry of the global situation: the prevailing world hegemony (in military, economic, and technological fields) wielded by a few Western powers—an asymmetry that requires attentiveness to the legitimate local aspirations of peoples everywhere (freed from the blemish of xenophobia).[7] Along another trajectory, that of cross-cultural or (broadly) "self–other" relations, difficult mediations have to be maintained to obviate the deficits of recognition evident in predatory appropriation, "fundamentalist" retreat, and technical-global standardization.

This study is a book of mediations in another sense as well: by trying to bridge or reconnect a number of different academic disciplines or research agendas. In contemporary academia, the field of globalization and local–global interactions is basically the province—and virtual monopoly—of international relations and political economy experts. On the other hand, issues relating to self–other and cross-cultural relations fall basically in the competence of social philosophers and practitioners of various humanistic disciplines (from social psychology to cultural anthropology). This book deliberately seeks to transgress these disciplinary boundaries—for reasons having to do with the very topic of inquiry. In my view, our contemporary world cannot possibly be "achieved" in any significant way unless serious attention is given both to the vertical thrust of current developments—the (potential) integration of localities into an emerging cosmopolis—and to the cultivation of lateral, cross-cultural, or cross-societal sensibilities (discussed here under the label of "self–other" relations). In large measure, the achievement of the former integration depends or is predicated on advances in the latter domain—in the sense that genuine "universalism" or universality is possible only through the interaction and mutual transformation of sedimented particularities. Understandably, practitioners of existing disciplines may find uncongenial this correlation of fields, and hence may prefer to concentrate on aspects of the study germane to their specialty. Thus, philosophers and humanists may wish to focus entirely on part 2 of the study, while skimming lightly through the first part. Conversely, international relations specialists may prefer to devote attention chiefly to part 1, while treating the rest as *obiter dicta*. Still, my hope is that some readers will be sufficiently enticed by the general theme of the study to follow the complex mediations throughout their different dimensions.

Given the range of disciplines, my indebtedness extends to a broad array of writers. In the field of international relations, I owe a profound debt of gratitude to such authors as Richard Falk, James Buchanan, Anthony Giddens, David Held, and Raimo Väyrynen; Richard Falk, in particular, has opened my eyes to the domineering and "predatory" aspects of many forms of current globalization. Since, for me, globalization should proceed democratically and hence "from the ground up," I also am strongly indebted to a number of contemporary democratic theorists, including Sheldon Wolin, Claude Lefort, Ernesto Laclau, Chantal Mouffe—and, again, David Held for his arguments regarding a "cosmopolitan democracy." In the field of philosophy and the humanities, I wish to acknowledge my debt to such friends and/or esteemed colleagues as Paul Ricoeur, Jacques Derrida, Calvin Schrag, and Bernhard Waldenfels (to whom individual chapters in this book are devoted). Behind this array of contemporary thinkers, there are some more recessed voices whose influence is unmistakable. As attentive readers will no doubt perceive, this book is (again) a meditation on the multifaceted work of Martin Heidegger (the protagonist of the book's concluding chapter). Other more recessed voices are those of Charles Taylor, Michel Foucault, and Hannah Arendt.

These names, of course, are just the tip of the iceberg—only the solo instruments, so to speak—in a large orchestra comprising a great number of friends and acquaintances. Here I want to express my continuing gratitude to such steady friends as Hwa Yol Jung, Stephen White, Iris Marion Young, Jean Elshtain, Joseph Buttigieg, and Chris Ziarek—from whose interventions (often critical interventions) I have learned a great deal. This is also the place to acknowledge my debt to Stephen Wrinn, editor at Rowman & Littlefield, whose continued support and prodding helped me to persist in an endeavor whose complexities sometimes threatened to overwhelm me. My deepest thanks, however, go to my wife and our (now grown-up) children who, once again, supported and encouraged my far-flung peregrinations and provided me with a safe haven upon my return from voyages. Without their love and patience not a line of this book could have been written.

South Bend, Fall 2000

Notes

1. Richard Rorty, *Achieving Our Country: Leftist Thought in the Twentieth Century* (Cambridge, Mass.: Harvard University Press, 1998).

2. Anthony Giddens, *Runaway World: How Globalization Is Reshaping Our Lives* (New York: Routledge, 2000), 20–21. As Giddens acknowledges in the preface, the title was actually borrowed from an earlier Reith Lecturer, Edmund Leach.

3. Hannah Arendt, *The Human Condition: A Study of the Central Dilemmas Facing Modern Man* (Garden City, N.Y.: Doubleday Anchor Books, 1958), 230–31, 233.

4. Regarding the notion of the *vita activa* see Arendt, *The Human Condition*, 3–21. Regarding the emphasis on a "strong civic culture"—a domain differentiated from both the state and the marketplace—see Giddens, *Runaway World*, 95. Given the primary accent placed in contemporary globalization literature on political-structural and economic dimensions (state and market), this book shifts the main focus to this domain of civil society and civic culture. Regarding the "democratization of democracy" compare Gidden's comment, "But democracy today must also become transnational. We need to democratize above—as well as below—the level of the nation. A globalizing era demands global responses, and this applies to politics just as much as any other area" (93).

5. *Runaway World*, 23. The notion of human guardianship or custodianship was famously developed by Martin Heidegger in his "Letter on Humanism"; see David F. Krell, ed., *Martin Heidegger: Basic Writings* (New York: Harper & Row, 1977), 210, 221. The above observations clearly stand in contrast with Rorty's instrumentalist pragmatism or his fondness for social engineering.

6. Regarding "world" (*Welt*) see Heidegger, *Being and Time: A Translation of Sein und Zeit*, trans. Joan Stambaugh (Albany, N.Y.: State University of New York Press, 1996), 59–62 (par. 14); also "Letter on Humanism," in *Martin Heidegger: Basic Writings*, ed. Krell, 228–29. For his notion of *Gestell* consult, for example, Heidegger, *The Question Concerning Technology and Other Essays*, trans. William Lovitt (New York: Harper & Row, 1977);

also Michael E. Zimmermann, *Heidegger's Confrontation with Modernity: Technology, Politics, Art* (Bloomington, Ind.: Indiana University Press, 1990). Regarding the turn to poetry see, for example, Heidegger, *On the Way to Language*, trans. Peter D. Hertz and Joan Stambaugh (New York: Harper & Row, 1971); *Poetry, Language, Thought*, trans. Albert Hofstadter (New York: Harper & Row, 1971); also Véronique M. Fóti, *Heidegger and the Poets* (Atlantic Highlands, N.J.: Humanities Press, 1992) and my *The Other Heidegger* (Ithaca, N.Y.: Cornell University Press, 1993), esp. 132–80.

7. For an outstanding study of local–global relations, with specific reference to Latin America, see Walter D. Mignolo, *Local Histories/Global Designs: Coloniality, Subaltern Knowledges, and Border Thinking* (Princeton, N.J.: Princeton University Press, 2000). In a broad-ranging study of global trends, Benjamin R. Barber has examined the centrifugal and centripetal dangers of slippage under the labels respectively of "McWorld" and "Jihad"; see his *Jihad vs. McWorld* (New York: Random House, 1995).

~

Introduction

The adage "Know thyself" is both venerable and deeply perplexing. Its venerability derives not only from the fact that among all the things to be known nothing seems more intriguing than the "self," but also (and perhaps more crucially) from the realization that whatever is "known" at all, is predicated on some form of self-knowledge or self-awareness. The adage is perplexing, however, because of its apparent circularity. For clearly, the admonition to "know thyself" presupposes the very self that is addressed and exhorted to search for and thus know itself. The perplexity is not removed by a cancellation of circularity; for example, the stipulation of a radical gulf between the searching self and the target of its knowledge. For in this case, the self might well come to apprehend a radical otherness or externality (say, a distant planet), but it would not come to know "itself." As can readily be seen, thus, the admonition of self-knowledge or self-understanding—in all its venerability—opens up a whirlpool of agonizing questions having to do with the meaning of selfhood, the relation between self and "other," and the very status of self-"knowledge." It is this whirlpool of problems that long ago prompted the bishop of Hippo, St. Augustine, to exclaim in bewilderment, "*Quaestio mihi factus sum*" (I have become a question to myself).[1]

In our time, the bishop's exclamation echoes widely in the experiential awareness of humankind; what in his days may have been an individual puzzlement, has become today a near-universal agony. Several factors have contributed to this state of affairs. One factor can be traced to a curious "culture lag": a delayed reaction to the so-called Age of Discovery. As is well known,

1

modernity in the West was inaugurated, among other things, by the "Copernican Revolution" whereby Earth was dislodged from its central position and inserted into a web of planetary constellations. Apparently to compensate for this change, the fulcrum of the Earth was replaced by a new, more internalized pivot: the centrality of the ego (or Cartesian "cogito"), which became the linchpin of modern subjectivity and individualism. Only recently, in the twentieth century, was this linchpin in turn challenged by a number of developments supplementing the Copernican event. In the strictly philosophical domain, a prominent role was played by the "linguistic turn," that is, the discovery of language as the matrix and medium antedating human awareness in multiple ways. As a result of this discovery, human subjectivity—like Earth before—was increasingly "decentered" and embedded in a welter of texts, discourses, and symbolic meanings, a welter rendering dubious any notion of a pristine, uncomplicated selfhood. Add to this "turn" the role of cognate developments like post-structuralism, deconstruction, and hermeneutics, and one begins to see the reasons why, philosophically, human existence in our time is profoundly problematized, and hence forced to discover itself in ever more circuitous ways and detours.[2]

Philosophical developments are not self-contained, however, but nurtured by real-life experiences, especially the collapse of traditional forms of stability and continuity in the twentieth century. In the course of that century, two world wars together with a host of other calamities dislodged Europe (or European culture) from its centrality in world history, ushering in an era of "superpower" conflicts and new forms of political and technological hegemony. The same wars brought to an end the legacy of colonial empires, leading to the upsurge of a multitude of newly independent and "developing" societies around the world. All these events combined triggered large-scale population movements, evident in collective migrations and a staggering number of refugees and displaced people in many parts of the globe. Willingly or unwillingly, many people in our time thus have been constrained to undergo an experience that in earlier periods was reserved mostly for travelers or explorers: the experience of intense cross-cultural, interethnic, and interfaith encounters—encounters that are bound to unsettle customary conceptions of self-identity, often in traumatic and agonizing ways. In the latter part of the century, these experiences were further intensified and generalized by one of the most distinctive trends of our time: the process of "globalization" whereby traditional national boundaries are steadily crisscrossed by webs of technological, economic, and communication networks.

Although undeniable in its effects, the process of globalization is ambivalent and amenable to multiple interpretations. There is general agreement on the steady expansion of cross-societal contacts, an expansion spearheaded by technology transfers, global market forces, and the Internet; dispute, however, rages over its assessment. For some observers, devotees of ultimate unity, globalization means the progressive homogenization of all cultures and traditions, that is, the erasure of time-honored differences in favor of a higher synthesis or global "melting pot." In this vision, as one can see, the problems associated with local–global and self–other relations are not so much resolved, or even honestly tackled, but rather bracketed or sidelined as an obstacle to global unity and uniformity. What vitiates this vision, however, is not only its obtuseness to such problems but its basic deceptiveness; on closer inspection and under political auspices, the envisaged unity turns out to be not so much a higher synthesis but the supremacy of a distinct national culture superimposed hegemonically on other cultures—a practice well known from the history of colonialism and imperialism. Typically, the consequences of imperial unity have been devastating for suppressed or marginalized populations. For example, Lama Bataa Mishigish offers a lively account of the fate of Mongolian Buddhists under the Soviet empire (a particularly ambitious form of global internationalism):

> In the 1970s, it was common for monks walking in the street, dressed as monks, to be attacked by small kids who threw rocks and yelled at them. . . . Every individual was forced to be either antireligious or nonreligious at that time. Therefore, whoever went to a temple or was involved in religious activity was considered uneducated, or nationalist, or anti-Communist. They were pressured by the Communist party and were condemned and criticized publicly. They had no place freely to exercise their religious practice in society. The only way they could practice was secretly getting together in an isolated safe place and burning a few butter lamps to have a religious service.[3]

The Lama's account, no doubt, could be duplicated or multiplied by many similar stories taken from other imperial settings. What is surprising, however, is the fact that the demise of traditional empires (including the Soviet empire) has not really eliminated pressures for global uniformity—although such pressures now operate in more covert or subterranean ways. Even (or precisely) under liberal-economic auspices, global market forces and technology transfers tend to produce a standardization of production and consumer tastes—a process accompanied widely by a standardization of opinions and worldviews. Under the impact of these standardized views—largely replicas of Western modernity—recalcitrant cultures or populations are liable to be stigmatized again and to be treated (in the Lama's words) as "uneducated, or nationalist, or anti-Communist" (read now: anti-Western). In terms of interhuman relations, such

standardization amounts again to a bracketing of the complex mediations operating in global–local as well as self–other relations. As is well known, homogenizing policies of this kind have produced, and continue to produce, a backlash
or countermovement in many parts of the world, a reaction sometimes erupting
into violent xenophobia and always bent on salvaging (or congealing) indigenous modes of collective self-identity. Taking note of this backlash, the literature on contemporary global politics employs dramatic language. Thus, Benjamin Barber in one of his books depicts the global scene as dominated by the
rift between "Jihad versus McWorld," while Samuel Huntington—in a justly famous (or notorious) text—speaks of an impending "clash of civilizations,"
which basically amounts to a struggle between "the West and the Rest."⁴

To be sure, great care must be taken to avoid stereotypes or excessive sim-
plifications. Not every form of globalization or universal aspiration is necessarily imperialistic or unilaterally hegemonic; by the same token, not every
type of local or regional recalcitrance can be reduced to xenophobia or an incipient mode of ethnic cleansing. As Benjamin Barber observes, with considerable evidence, aggressive local self-assertion (which he terms *Jihad*) is only
a derivation or aberrant variation of popular self-determination, just as the
latter is only a derivation of the principle of democratic self-government.⁵
Precisely from the angle of an expanding or globalizing democracy, local or
cultural counter-moves to a standardizing globalism (Barber's "McWorld") enjoy a prima facie legitimacy—although they surely need to be seasoned and
cleansed of tendencies toward self-enclosure (preferably through internal critique). The same holds true of national self-government and struggles for national independence. In an important recent book, the American philosopher
Richard Rorty has placed before his compatriots an imposing task expressed
in the book's title, *Achieving Our Country*. In his study, Rorty challenged fellow Americans to commit (or re-commit) themselves to the goal of building
a stronger and more democratic society at home—instead of, or prior to, being continuously preoccupied with global or international developments.
Countering a tendency during recent decades to overindulge in theoretical
constructions, the same book exhorted American intellectuals to re-shoulder
the work begun by American pragmatism and progressivism: the work of liberating political praxis or practical engagement—without bothering lengthily
about theoretical warrants or "foundations."⁶

As mentioned in the preface, this book is in many ways a continuation of,
and response to, Rorty's study. Following Rorty, the volume seeks to rekindle
or reinvigorate the democratic agenda in the United States, an agenda that
has in large measure been sidetracked by public complacency and the self-
serving pursuit of private interests. Together with the pragmatist philosopher,

the author of this book also believes that democracy has to be built first of all at home and "from the ground up," rather than being promulgated from on high in the form of abstractly universal principles. There are two main points, however, where this book departs from, or seeks to rechannel the thrust of, Rorty's argument. The first point is highlighted instantly by the title: *Achieving Our World*—a title that preserves the emphasis on practical engagement or achievement but seeks to enlarge the scope of this engagement. In large measure, the title is a reflection of the globalization process in our time, a process the author believes is not an optional happening one is free to ignore. Given the relentless technological compression of the globe, the only available choice is between being a passive victim or a reflective participant in the process. That the latter option is preferable is confirmed by passages in Rorty's study, which acknowledge the high fluidity of the global labor market. If it is true, as he notes, that employers today are always ready and able to abandon (or "immiserate") local labor forces in favor of cheap labor abroad, then the only way to protect fair living standards is through a global extension of democracy.[7] This means that the "achievement" of one country today is possible only via the achievement of many or all countries.

The other point of departure has to do with the issue of antifoundationalism. Faithful to pragmatist teachings, Rorty asserts the "primacy of the practical over the theoretical" and proceeds to denounce or impugn many or most of the theoretical preoccupations of American intellectuals during the past half-century. As he notes, many of these preoccupations are of Continental European origin, and thus not properly germane or indigenous to the American experience (an argument not free of ethnocentric leanings). More important in the current context is a certain obtuseness of pragmatism narrowly construed. Clearly, the asserted "primacy of the practical over the theoretical" is itself a theoretical pronouncement, and thus can hardly be used to dislodge or delegitimate reflective theorizing as such. Moreover, as Rorty himself recognizes, theoretical initiatives during recent decades—even when of European origin— have greatly helped in raising social consciousness or sensitivity in the United States, in the sense of rendering Americans more sensitive or attentive to ethnic or cultural "otherness," to the problems of identity-formation, and hence to the complexity of self–other relations in a multicultural society.[8] As this author believes, again, the strengthening or reinvigoration of democracy is impossible without a heightened awareness of this complexity—a point largely ignored in old-style socialism and progressivism.

Valorizing theory in this manner does not amount to an endorsement of "foundationalism." In the author's view, theory does not constitute the premise or a priori foundation of action, a preamble from which practice could be deduced through logical entailment, nor does it furnish a mere cloak or *post-hoc* rationalization to practical conduct. Contrary to such construals, theorizing simply means a careful vigilance or reflective mindfulness, a certain way of "minding one's business"—where "business" includes what is happening in the world and how people behave toward each other. Differently put, theory is not the servant or handmaiden of practice (in a means-ends relation), nor its master or omnipotent dictator, but rather simply its custodian or attentive companion.[9] Viewed against this background, theory can only with great difficulty be separated from practice, and then only for limited heuristic purposes. This book adopts such a heuristic device, in the sense that part 1 ("Globalization and Democracy") focuses more on practical-political issues involved in the tension between global and local trajectories, while part 2 ("Pluralism: Variations on Self–Other Relations") shifts attention to more recessed theoretical problems having to do with the liaison between selfhood and otherness, identity and difference. One should note, however, the division is one of emphasis only and not of "primacy" in either direction; hence, overlaps are multiple and in principle unavoidable. As readers of chapters in both parts will quickly detect, practical-political concerns constantly invade and permeate "philosophical" deliberations, just as theoretical concerns impinge on discussions of globalization and the promotion of global democracy.

Part 1 is devoted to globalization, a crucial, even dominant, political and socioeconomic feature of our time. Although uncontested as a factual occurrence, this globalizing process is surrounded by intense controversy regarding both its overall direction and its normative and existential significance. This controversy is the topic of the opening chapter, which explores both the perils and potential benefits of the emerging cosmopolis. Beginning with descriptive-empirical accounts, chapter 1 finds broad agreement among social scientists concerning the close link between globalization and (Western-style) "modernization," a link that has led Anthony Giddens to characterize the former as one of the "consequences of modernity" exemplifying modern tendencies to disaggregate traditional communities and to redistribute symbolic meanings across widening dimensions of time and space.[10] Given this close linkage, normative and political assessments of globalization share the conflictual character marking discussions of modernity.

In the eyes of many Western observers, the process is equivalent to the dawn of a global "enlightenment," that is, the liberation of people everywhere from ignorance, oppression, and economic backwardness. Following the collapse of the Soviet Union, neoliberal economists in particular have come to celebrate the new global scenario as the emergence of a "borderless world," triggered by the triumphant "unleashing" of capitalism where market forces are finally "unbound."[11] More sober-minded observers point to the darker side of globalization—especially the growing rift between North and South, rich and poor, and hence to the rise of a new international class division. Faced with intensive hegemonic pressures, nonhegemonic or marginalized people sometimes seek refuge in radical self-enclosure or a retreat into nativist xenophobia (Barber's "Jihad"); under extreme provocation, such people may castigate globalization as a "curse" and Western modernity as a "Satanic plot" corrupting humankind. Sensitive to the dangers of such retreat—evident in "ethnic cleansing" and multiple forms of violence—the chapter endorses an alternative path of globalization, which (following Richard Falk) may be termed *globalization from below* and which relies on democratic, nondomineering interactions between peoples and societies. Apart from being backed up by grassroots social movements, the "promise" of this kind of globalization is nourished by hermeneutical-philosophical initiatives as well as by the longstanding universalist aspirations of the major world religions.

In the normative as well as cultural arenas, globalization heralds a number of difficult challenges and a plethora of both theoretical and practical conundrums. One such conundrum has to do with the relation between globalism and localism or the respective legitimacy of universal and particular claims. Chapter 2 examines this issue under the rubric of "global governance and cultural diversity." Taking its departure from Kantian cosmopolitanism, the chapter raises the question how the goal of cosmopolitan unity or a global "bonding" of nations (*Völkerbund*) can be accomplished in the face of the "crooked timber" of humanity evident in power contests and struggles for global hegemony or domination. After reviewing different conceptions of global governance—from the "idealism" of Stephen Toulmin to the "realism" of Samuel Huntington—the discussion shifts to various "antisystemic" or counter-cultural strategies resisting the imposition of global unity "from above"; special attention is given in this context to David Held's formulation of a "cosmopolitan democracy," which, seeking to build globalism "from the ground up," valorizes the beliefs and aspirations "generated by people themselves" as they are spread out in local cultural settings (thus mediating universalism and particularlism). By way of conclusion, the chapter finds hope for global "bonding" not so much in global power structures—despite the need for institutional restructuring—but in the growth of a global "civil society," especially the cultivation of a "global civic culture" (as advocated urgently by Elise Boulding, Anthony Giddens, and others).[12] Such a civic culture would be "cosmopolitan" neither in a standardizing nor a strictly

Kantian sense, but would reflect at best an overlapping and cross-fertilization of multiple cultures or ways of life.

The preference for grassroots globalization or globalism "from below" resurfaces in chapter 3, devoted to the relation between "global human rights and Asian values." Here the discussion starts from the opposition between "foundational" universalism (from classical "natural law" conceptions to Alan Gewirth) and "antifoundational" skepsis or relativism (from Jeremy Bentham to Rorty). Steering a path beyond this dichotomy, the chapter inquires into the "rightness" of rights-claims, a question that calls for a situated, carefully weighted, prudential judgment regarding their justice or equity. With specific reference to "Asian values" (or "Islamic values"), the chapter follows Henry Rosemont's emphasis on the need to differentiate between "concept clusters" reflecting different forms of human flourishing— clusters that are neither radically incommensurable nor blandly uniform or exchangeable. What this emphasis suggests is that the globalism or universalism of human rights is not a pre-given premise but rather a challenge and practical task—a challenge requiring intensive inter-human and cross-cultural learning and (what Tu Weiming calls) the ongoing "humanization" of humankind.[13]

The next two chapters shift attention to the status and meaning of democracy, particularly as seen in a neoliberal and globalizing context. Chapter 4 takes its departure from Sheldon Wolin's complaint about the increasingly "fugitive" character of democracy in our time, that is, the steady retreat of public-democratic commitments behind the upsurge of rampant consumerism and the cultivation of private self-interest under neoliberal auspices. Following a narrative sketch of the history of democracy—in both its liberal-individualist and republican-communitarian variants—the chapter turns to late modern or "postmodern" discussions that challenge such modernist premises as "sovereignty" and a constitutive "subjectivity" (lodged either in "microsubjects" or a collective "macrosubject"). Among recent and contemporary thinkers, attention is given primarily to such writers as Ernesto Laclau, Claude Lefort, and Jacques Derrida—the combined effect of whose teachings is the "decentering" of human agency and the deconstruction of all forms of totalizing collectivity or "we-community." Taking some cues from Richard Rorty, the chapter asks about the political costs of radical deconstruction—especially in an era dominated by liberal-individualist ideology. Without dismissing the importance of postmodern attacks on "totalization," this questioning points to an alternative political path, a path partially inspired by arguments of Chantal Mouffe and Iris Marion Young. The gist of this alternative is that, to retain its meaning, democracy should be neither substantialized nor "virtualized." Differently put, the "people" in that regime should be seen neither as empty ciphers nor as totalitarian masters, but as competent agents engaged in a continuing process of self-discovery and transformation. Properly energized, democracy in this transformative mode can still be a source of popular empowerment and thus escape the plight of being "fugitive" or "on the run" in Wolin's sense.

Chapter 5 places the same issue specifically in the broader context of globalization. In many ways, the central political problem of our time revolves around the possibility of preserving and strengthening democracy or democratic aspirations around the globe. The issue is explored in that chapter in the form of a "response to Richard Rorty," particularly Rorty's stirring plea to his fellow Americans to participate again in the task of "achieving our country." The chapter starts by offering an overview of Rorty's argument, focusing on his periodization of American "Leftism" during the twentieth century, a division opposing the older pragmatist or "reformist Left" to the later (post-Vietnam) "cultural Left" preoccupied with "identity" or the "politics of difference." In Rorty's presentation, the newer type of Leftism is characterized by its tendency to privilege theory over practice and hence to adopt a purely "spectatorial" stance in preference to practical-political engagement; his recommendations to its supporters are basically two: namely, first, to "put a moratorium on theory," and next, to "mobilize what remains of our pride of being Americans" and to shed any form of "anti-Americanism." Taking up Rorty's challenge, the chapter initially applauds his call for renewed practical engagement and a strengthening of social solidarity. Deviating from Rorty, however, credit is also extended to the recent "cultural Left," mainly for two reasons salient for democratic politics: its emphasis on respect for cultural difference and its support for incipient forms of democratic cosmopolitanism (along David Held's lines). The chapter concludes with a plea for a reconciliation between older "reformist" and newer "cultural" democrats—a reconciliation ably thematized by Nancy Fraser as the combination of the politics of "recognition" with the policy of "redistribution."[14]

Part 2 of the volume turns to the preconditions and underpinnings of a cosmopolitan democracy attentive to the need for viable cross-cultural or societal self–other relations. Chapter 6 addresses a crucial issue in this respect— namely, the possibility of a tenable conception of "self" or selfhood in our time. In their theoretical thrust, postmodernism and post-structuralism are sometimes associated with such mottoes as the "death of the subject" or "end of man," implying the obliteration of traditional modes of identity. Countering postmodern hyperbole, Calvin Schrag—in an instructive and elegantly written study—has taken up this issue, trying to determine what, if anything, is left of "the self after postmodernity." The result of his inquiry is ambivalent, although hardly discouraging. Without endorsing a foundational or "self-constituting" subject, Schrag discovers the footprints of the self—now a finite, concretely situated self—in a multitude of contexts, particularly the contexts of discourse, embodied action, social community, and religious striving for transcendence. While following closely the exposition of these modalities of self-display, the chapter raises the question whether Schrag's account of selfhood is not unduly restorative in character, thereby shortchanging the complexity of self–other relations. What the chapter strongly endorses, however, is Schrag's emphasis on "transversality": the aspect that genuine universalism can emerge only from the interactions of concretely situated, individual, or collective agents. In his words: "Transversal unity [also termed 'convergence without coincidence'] is an achievement of communication as it visits a multiplicity of viewpoints, perspectives, belief systems, and regions of concern."[15]

Transversal interaction might also be described as a form of "dialogue"—but one where neither partner is primary or fully self-constituting and where participants continuously undergo a difficult "decentering" process. Dialogue of this type has long been a hallmark of the German philosopher Bernhard Waldenfels. In a string of publications—including *Ordnung im Zwielicht* (1987), *Der Stachel des Fremden* (1990), and *Antwortregister* (1994)—Waldenfels has explored the complex border zone or crossroads between self and other, self and foreign or alien. Chapter 7 concentrates on a more recent text, titled *Deutsch-Französische Gedankengänge* (German-French Paths of Thought, 1995), which probes the multiple intersections and cross-fertilizations between German and French philosophy in the course of the twentieth century. Ranging over a broad field of ideas, the study examines such prominent figures as Edmund Husserl, Maurice Merleau-Ponty, Jacques Derrida, and Emmanuel Levinas, with additional side-glances devoted to a host of other thinkers (including Michel Foucault and Cornelius Castoriadis). The main focus of the analysis, however, rests on two important students of Husserl whose writings developed the insights of their teacher in radically different directions: Merleau-Ponty and Levinas. In the case of Merleau-Ponty, detailed attention is given to such key notions as "*entre-monde*," reversibility, chiasm, and "lateral universalism"—the latter term closely corresponding to Schrag's "transversality"; in the case of Levinas, the discussion properly accentuates the themes of singularity, exteriority, radical alterity and "other-responsibility" (*Fremdverantwortung*). In comparing the two thinkers, Waldenfels juxtaposes Merleau-Ponty's preference for self–other "interlacing" to Levinas's emphasis on self–other "separation" (or relation through nonrelation). In this connection, the chapter takes issue with Waldensfels's repeated prioritizing of separation over correlation, and also with the linkage between separation and irruptive forms of violence (*Gewalt*).

The issue of self–other separation recurs—in a still more dramatic way—in the work of Jacques Derrida. Although initially a critical student of Husserl with distinct Heideggerian leanings, Derrida subsequently underwent the strong influence of both Nietzsche and Levinas; particularly under the impact of Levinasian teachings, his writings increasingly came to accentuate the notions of asymmetry, nonreciprocity, and radical "alterity." This accent is clearly evident in his treatment of friendship, which is the topic of chapter 8. To bring out this point, the chapter concentrates on Derrida's discussion of the "politics of friendship" and also on a rejoinder formulated by Thomas McCarthy (along Habermasian lines). As the chapter tries to show, Derrida's discussion inserts friendship into a long-term trajectory ranging from antiquity to the present, a trajectory pointing to the progressive problematization of self–other relations and the growing "distantiation" of self from "other"—with the latter increasingly being equated with a radically asymmetrical alterity. In terms of the role of friendship, this development implies the progressive cancellation of amicable "bonding" and communitarian notions of social concord—with Derrida finally endorsing or postulating a "community without community" or else an "anchoritic community" predicated on mutual disjunction and solitude.[16] On these points the chapter registers a cautious dissent. Although the aim of disjunction is to ward off the appropriation/assimilation of the other by self-aggrandizing or predatory schemes, the drawbacks are glaring. First of all, the stress on disjunction resonates too well with contemporary liberal individualism and its celebration of private interest; more importantly, disjunction undercuts the very meaning of friendship, which evaporates in the absence of shared practices.

Not all contemporary French philosophers are equally willing to privilege distance over proximity. To illustrate a more balanced (and more Aristotelian) approach to these issues, chapter 9 turns to Paul Ricoeur and especially his magisterial study *Oneself as Another*, a study comprising both a detailed analysis of the modalities of selfhood and an impressive endeavor to formulate a contemporary "ethics" based on viable self–other relations. In his analysis of selfhood, Ricoeur traverses a terrain that in many ways resembles Schrag's travelogue, passing successively in review the different modes of self-display: those of the speaking, the acting, the narrating, and the moral-ethical self. Although none of these modes are egocentric in character, it is chiefly in the final stage, that of ethical life, that the relation between self and other becomes the central theme. At this point, Ricoeur develops a novel conception of ethics (modestly termed "little ethics") that carefully seeks to balance the modern accent on individual freedom with the need for ethical responsibility and community bonds. More specifically (and in line with Hegel), his study vindicates both "morality" and "ethics"—where morality stands for the (Kantian-style) task of moral self-legislation and ethics for the recognition of shared public standards (partly reminiscent of Aristotle). Transposed into the idiom of contemporary philosophy, this approach steers a difficult course between the alternatives of "egology" and "exteriority": that is, between Husserl's constitution of the other by self-consciousness, and Levinas's constitution of the self by the other (or alterity).[17] The chapter basically applauds Ricoeur's strategy—although tempering applause with some critical reservations, having to do mainly with the patchwork blending of morality and ethics, freedom and the common good, and still more importantly with a certain half-hearted construal of "oneself *as* another."

One of the noted shortcomings of Ricoeur's work is his treatment of Martin Heidegger, including the latter's conception of co-being (*Mitsein*). In the literature, Heidegger's thought is frequently interpreted as endorsing either a radical individualism or a pliant communalism, that is, as prioritizing either private "authenticity" or a surrender to the "powers that be." Neither of these readings, however, is tenable in light of his key formulation of human existence in terms of "being-in-the-world"—an expression whose hyphens imply neither separation nor fusion but a tensional involvement in multiple networks (including local–global and self–other relations). To be sure, misreadings of this kind are not entirely unprovoked given ambivalent statements in Heidegger's texts and his (at least temporary) support of Nazi totalitarianism. Nevertheless, there is still a great need to sift through the evidence. To show the untenability (or high implausibility) of a "totalitarian Heidegger," chapter 10 concentrates on a series of recently published writings—dating from the later 1930s—in which the philosopher with growing vehemence distanced himself from totalizing "worldview-ideologies," subsuming the latter under the broader umbrella of "*Machenschaft*" (a term designating the modern bent to organize, engineer, and dominate everything from the angle of calculable outputs). As the chapter shows, the same writings contain increasingly outspoken attacks on the reigning Nazi ideology—thus putting a dent into the claim of permanent complicity—while simultaneously holding open the possibility of nonmanipulative or "power-free" interhuman relations. In many ways, the notion of a nonmanipulative social-political order can be seen as an antidote to contemporary dangers of "totalization," especially the peril of a totalizing uniformity and standardization on the global scale.

The conclusion seeks to bring together and reconnect the different themes of this book. In their combination, the chapters in the two parts illustrate and elucidate the central concern of the entire study, which is the cultivation of a genuine global and pluralist civil society and "civic culture" as the only viable or promising path toward the goal of "achieving our world" democratically in the new millennium. This book unabashedly endorses a renewed practical-political commitment. After the immense atrocities of the twentieth century no one can any longer afford to be a passive bystander or to enjoy the luxury of public disengagement and irresponsibility. However, praxis cannot (or should not) be unreflective. Although inevitably nurtured by deeper existential motives, practical engagement needs to be critically vigilant and hence to be suffused and tempered by practical-prudential judgment. As stated before, this study champions neither the priority of theorizing over praxis nor the "primacy of the practical over the theoretical," but rather a kind of intertwining or companionship, whereby theorizing is always a thinking about praxis and lived experience, while praxis allows itself to be seasoned by a reflective mindfulness, by caring attentiveness to ourselves, to fellow-beings, and our "world"—a world comprising both nature and culture and immanent as well as transcendent horizons. Only through such attentiveness, the author believes, can our "crooked timber" be bent in the direction of social equity and a genuine "bonding" in a democratic *cosmopolis*.

Notes

1. St. Augustine, *Confessiones*, ed. J. Gibb and W. Montgomery, 2nd ed. (Cambridge: Cambridge University Press, 1927), Book X, 33. The passage is cited by Hannah Arendt in *The Human Condition: A Study of the Central Dilemmas Facing Modern Man* (Chicago: University of Chicago Press, 1958), 12.

2. Regarding this problematization of selfhood see my *Twilight of Subjectivity* (Amherst, Mass.: University of Massachusetts Press, 1981); also Michael E. Zimmerman, *Eclipse of the Self* (Athens, Ohio: Ohio University Press, 1981).

3. Venerable Lama Bataa Mishigish, "The Oppression of Buddhists in Mongolia," in *Buddhist Peacework: Creating Cultures of Peace*, ed. David W. Chappell (Somerville, Mass.: Wisdom Publications, 1999), 62.

4. Benjamin R. Barber, *Jihad vs. McWorld* (New York: Random House, 1995); Samuel P. Huntington, "The Clash of Civilizations?" *Foreign Affairs* 72 (Summer 1993), 22–49. Compare also Huntington, *The Clash of Civilizations and the Remaking of World Order* (New York: Simon & Schuster, 1996), and Mark Juergensmeyer, *The New Cold War? Religious Nationalism Confronts the Secular State* (Berkeley: University of California Press, 1993).

5. *Jihad vs. McWorld*, 8-12.

6. Richard Rorty, *Achieving Our Country: Leftist Thought in Twentieth-Century America* (Cambridge, Mass.: Harvard University Press, 1998).

7. *Achieving Our Country*, 85–86, 98. The adage "Think globally, act locally" hence needs to be modified in our time by the acknowledgement that we need to think and act both globally and locally.

8. *Achieving Our Country*, 75–76.

9. For a discussion of this mode of theorizing see the chapters "Political Philosophy Today" and "Praxis and Experience" in my *Polis and Praxis: Exercises in Contemporary Political Theory* (Cambridge, Mass.: MIT Press, 1984), 15–46, 47–76; also Michael Oakeshott, *Rationalism in Politics, and Other Essays* (New York: Basic Books, 1962) and *On Human Conduct* (Oxford: Clarendon Press, 1975).

10. Anthony Giddens, *The Consequences of Modernity* (Stanford, Calif.: Stanford University Press, 1990).

11. See Kenichi Ohmae, *The Borderless World: Power and Strategy in the Interlinked Economy* (New York: Harper, 1990); Lowell Bryan and Diana Farrell, *Market Unbound: Unleashing Global Capitalism* (New York: John Wiley, 1996).

12. See Daniele Archibugi and David Held, eds., *Cosmopolitan Democracy: An Agenda for a New World Order* (Cambridge, UK: Polity Press, 1995); Elise Boulding, *Building a Global Civic Culture: Education for an Interdependent World* (Syracuse, N.Y.: Syracuse University Press, 1990); and Anthony Giddens, *Runaway World: How Globalization is Reshaping Our Lives* (New York: Routledge, 2000).

13. See Tu Weiming, *Humanity and Self-Cultivation: Essays on Confucian Thought* (Berkeley: Asian Humanities Press, 1979); also my "Humanity and Humanization: Comments on Confucianism," in *Alternative Visions: Paths in the Global Village* (Lanham, Md.: Rowman & Littlefield, 1998), 123–44.

14. See especially Nancy Fraser and Axel Honneth, *Redistribution or Recogniton? A Political-Philosophical Exchange* (London: Verso, 2000).

15. Calvin O. Schrag, *The Self after Postmodernity* (New Haven: Yale University Press, 1997), 129. For an account by a political theorist pointing in a similar direction see Seyla Benhabib, *Situating the Self: Gender, Community and Postmodernism in Contemporary Ethics* (New York: Routledge, 1992).

16. Jacques Derrida, *Politics of Friendship*, trans. George Collins (London: Verso, 1997), 37, 42–43.

17. Paul Ricoeur, *Oneself as Another*, trans. Kathleen Blamey (Chicago: University of Chicago Press, 1992), 284.

PART ONE

Globalization and Democracy

CHAPTER ONE

~

Globalization: Curse or Promise?

In May 1996, Czech President Václav Havel delivered a lecture at Harvard University with the title "A Challenge to Nourish Spiritual Roots Buried Under Our Thin Global Skin." In that lecture, Havel pointed to prominent signs of our time, but above all to what he called "an almost banal truth: that we now live in a single global civilization." Although factually, to be sure, humankind has always inhabited a single globe, it is only in our time that this factual cohabitation is coalescing into, or taking the shape of, a common civilization. Among the factors contributing to this development, Havel accentuated the "modern idea of constant progress," the rapid "evolution of science" closely linked with this idea, and finally the so-called information revolution happening before our eyes—a revolution that has enmeshed (and continues to enmesh) our world in "webs of telecommunication networks" that not only transmit information of all kinds at lightning speed but also convey "integrated models of social, political and economic behavior." As a result of this battery of factors, he observed, our time is in the grip of a triumphant globalism or globalization—a process whereby, "for the first time in the long history of the human race," our planet is transformed in a few short decades into "a single civilization, one that is essentially technological."[1]

Havel's assessment of the signs of our time seems on the mark. Despite a rich welter of diverse, often conflicting, strands and tendencies, our age does indeed seem pervaded by a relentless and near-providential force or momentum, a momentum carrying humankind forward toward a kind of global destiny or cosmopolis. Yet, despite the undeniable strength of this force, globalization is by no means beyond controversy. Although widely acknowledged as a factual occurrence, intense dispute rages over the meaning or significance of globalization as well as its deeper (political and cultural) implications. This chapter attempts to explore or unravel this controversy by proceeding in three steps:

1. The first section looks at the process of globalization as seen and interpreted by prominent Western intellectuals and social scientists. The emphasis here will be mainly on empirical-descriptive accounts, while moral-evaluative criteria are held in abeyance.
2. The second section shifts the focus of attention to evaluative assessments proceeding from a deeper experiential level—especially the experience of people in "developing" societies who have been in large measure the passive targets or victims of Western-style globalization in our century.
3. To conclude, the third part explores the possibility of a new and different kind of globalization—what Richard Falk has called "globalization from below"—as an antidote or counterweight to strategies of global domination.

What Is Globalization?

Given its dramatic effects, globalization could not and did not escape the attention of Western social scientists. As one may recall, it was the communications analyst Marshall McLuhan who first coined the phrase "the global village"—although his comments were limited to somewhat aphoristic impressions. In the meantime, the process supporting McLuhan's phrase has become the target of a vast academic literature seeking to determine its basic causes and characteristic features.[2] Among Western scholars pursuing this line of inquiry, probably the most prominent is the sociologist Roland Robertson, well known for a string of writings devoted to the topic. In articles of 1987, Robertson basically followed McLuhan's intuitive lead by arguing that globalization might best be understood as "the crystallization of the entire world as a single place" or as the emergence of a "global human condition." The more concrete features of this conception were spelled out in greater detail in subsequent writings. In his book *Globalization: Social Theory and Global Culture* (1992), Robertson distinguished between the objective-empirical and the subjective-experiential dimensions of the process. As a concept, he wrote, globalization refers "both to the compression of the world and the intensification of the consciousness of the world as a whole." Amplifying this statement in the light of recent sociological theory, he added that globalization is "best understood as indicating the problem of the form in terms of which the world becomes 'united,' but by no means integrated in a naive functionalist mode." The term hence might be seen as "a conceptual entry to the problem of 'world order' in the most general sense."[3]

In the same book, although acknowledging the recently gathering momentum, Robertson also reflected on the more recessed origins and historical unfolding of globalization. In terms of this broader historical trajectory, the book passed in review various stages of global evolution, extending basically from the (Western) Renaissance to the present time. This evolutionary sketch moved from the rise of the modern European nation-state and the dissemination of European culture (through the vehicle of colonialism) to the formation of the League of Nations and the United Nations in our century, and finally to the Cold War of superpowers and the ensuing post–Cold War period characterized (in Robertson's view) by the rise of "multiculturality and polyethnicity." Given this evolutionary background in Western modernity, Robertson perceptively views globalism or global politics as intimately linked with the issue of "the interpretation of and the response to modernity." In recent times, this linkage has been complicated by a certain intellectual questioning of modernity itself. To this extent, Robertson emphasizes, globalization must be seen as closely related "to modernity and modernization, as well as to postmodernity and 'postmodernization.'" In its acute and presently most relevant sense, the concept appears to him "most clearly applicable to a particular series of relatively recent developments concerning the *concrete structuration of the world as a whole*" (where "structuration" is a term borrowed from the conceptual arsenal of Anthony Giddens).[4]

A slightly different account of the historical trajectory of globalization has been advanced by political economists who view the entire process as basically rooted in the cycles of growth and stagnation of the unfolding capitalist world economy. In this account, globalization—whose roots again are traced to the Renaissance or "Age of Discovery"—is not so much a smoothly continuous growth but rather a process punctuated by upward and downward movements, that is, by periods of expansion and decline or stagnation. Some economic analysts apply to these movements the theory of the "Kondratieff cycles," which are said to last roughly half a century and to be subdivided into roughly equal periods of accelerated and decelerated or shrinking growth. Most political economists place the real "take-off" phase of globalization in the nineteenth century, an era marked by the stability of the gold standard and international high finance and, in Karl Polanyi's famous formulation, by the economically spurring effects of "a hundred years' peace." According to Angus Maddison, globalization in the sense of capitalist expansion prior to

World War I was supported and guaranteed by the continuing economic pres-ence of Great Britain as well as the rising economic power of the United States. Although interrupted or decelerated during the interbellum period, the process of globalizing growth resumed after World War II at a rapid pace, ushering in the "golden age of capitalism" (Maddison's phrase) underpinned by the undisputed economic hegemony of the United States. More recently this golden age has not so much come to an end, but been muted or blurred by the end of the Cold War, the rise of new quasihegemonic actors, and the unstable conjunctures of the world economy.[5]

Despite the stronger accent on cycles of growth, most political economists agree with Robertson regarding the linkage between globalization and mod-ernization or the unfolding and dissemination of Western modernity. In fact, this linkage is a widely shared assumption of social scientists across discipli-nary boundaries. In the words of international relations specialist Raimo Väyrynen, the dominant interpretation of globalization in the social sciences today is "moored in the theory of modernization," with the result that glob-alization is viewed basically as "but a part of the larger social movement to-wards modernity, and, ultimately, reflexive modernization or postmodernity." Among contemporary social theorists, this interpretation is prominently en-dorsed by Anthony Giddens who views globalization as one of the intrinsic "consequences of modernity," an assessment based on the premise that the gist of modernity consists in the process of distantiation, dislocation, or "dis-embedding" whereby traditional symbol systems are lifted out of their local contexts and redistributed across new dimensions of time and space. Elabo-rating on this premise, Giddens defines globalization as "interaction across distance" or as "the intensification of worldwide social relations which link distant localities in such a way that local happenings are shaped by events many miles away and vice versa." This account is not far removed from the argument of James Rosenau, who presents globalization as a "boundary-eroding" process, and especially as a movement jeopardizing the "domestic-foreign frontier." Elements of the same account can also be found in the writings of sociologist Mike Featherstone, who postulates the emergence of something like a global or transnational culture, that is, a synthetic system of symbolic meanings transcending local contexts at least in the field of legal and commercial rules and procedures.[6]

Although innovative and informative in many ways, contemporary social science literature exhibits a notable shortcoming (which, perhaps, is the re-sult of a "*déformation professionnelle*"). Despite a wealth of empirical data and explanatory schemes, contemporary studies of globalization—with some ex-ceptions—tend to be marked by a kind of bland descriptivism, that is, by a tendency to observe and meticulously analyze empirical occurrences while studiously endeavoring to remain ethically neutral and politically disengaged. Yet, in this particular field of inquiry, the option of neutral disengagement appears to be unavailable—except at the price of naiveté or complicity. As most observes will agree, globalization is not simply an accident or fortuitous happening. Although fueled by a powerful momentum, its trajectory is neither automatic nor akin to a natural *force majeure*: overtly or covertly, its movement is backed up by hegemonic political stratagems as well as by intellectual preferences of a distinct cultural provenance. Here again, most social scientists will not simply ignore such strategies or preferences, but report them in a seemingly matter-of-fact way. An instructive case in point is the work of Lucian Pye, a spokesman of mainstream American political science and an expert on "development" (an earlier stand-in for globalization). Writing in 1966, in his book *Aspects of Political Development*, Pye noted, without further commentary, that the process of development or modernization

> might also be called Westernization, or simply advancement and progress; it might, however, be more accurately termed the diffusion of a world culture—a world culture based on advanced technology and the spirit of science, on a rational view of life, a secular approach to social relations. . . . At an accelerating rate, the direction and the volume of cross-cultural influences has become nearly a uniform pattern of the Western industrial world imposing its practices, standards, techniques, and values upon the non-Western world.[7]

Judged by the usual canons of academic neutrality (or circumlocution), Pye's comments are surprisingly candid and revealing—notwithstanding his failure to elaborate on their implications. It would be quite misleading and unfair, of course, to suggest that Western social scientists have been uniformly bland or noncommittal on the globalization issue. Both during the Cold War and in more recent years, a number of social analysts and intellectuals in the United States have been troubled by and openly critical of the asymmetry of global relations and the reality of Western hegemony in the postcolonial world. An important example is Immanuel Wallerstein, whose "world-system theory" has for several decades exposed and critiqued the inequities besetting global economic and cultural relations.[8] The persistence of Western hegemony in the postcolonial era is also the central theme of Edward Said's *Culture and Imperialism*, published in the aftermath of the Cold War. As Said observes in that study, imperialism did not become a thing of the past with the dismantling of the "classical [European] empires"; on the contrary, the emergence of the United States as the last superpower suggests "that a new set of force lines will structure the world." Traditional empires have always been characterized by a "twinning of power and legitimacy," that is, the juncture of domination in the political and cultural spheres. This juncture, Said notes, has not changed in our time. What is different in the "American century" is the "quantum leap in the reach of cultural authority," due in large measure to "the unprecedented growth in the apparatus for the diffusion and control of information." He adds, "Rarely before in human history has there been so massive an intervention of force and ideas from one culture to another as there is today from America to the rest of the world."[9]

As it happens, postcolonial hegemony is not only the topic of intellectuals critical of Western domination but also—more surprisingly—of U.S. policy analysts and strategic global theorists like Samuel Huntington. Huntington's work is often cited and attacked for his provocative thesis of an impending "clash of civilizations," first formulated in essay-form in 1993—a thesis that transfers the traditional rivalry or enmity between states into the arena of cross-cultural relations. Although dubious in many respects, passages in his work can also be invoked as providing a candid exposé of strategic realities in the "American century." Here are a few lines from his famous essay of 1993, titled "The Clash of Civilizations?"—lines that hardly require elaborate commentary:

> The West is now at an extraordinary peak of power in relation to other civilizations. Its superpower opponent has disappeared from the map. . . . It dominates international political and security institutions and with Japan international economic institutions. Global political and security issues are effectively settled by a directorate of the United States, Britain and France, world economic issues by a directorate of the United States, Germany and Japan, all of which maintain extraordinarily close relations with each other to the exclusion of lesser and largely non-Western countries. Decisions made at the U.N. Security Council or in the International Monetary Fund that reflect the interests of the West are presented to the world as reflecting the desires of the world community. The very phrase "the world community" has become the euphemistic collective noun (replacing "the Free World") to give global legitimacy to actions reflecting the interests of the United States and other Western powers.[10]

Given his indisputable expertise and academic prestige, Huntington's observations carry considerable evidential weight; they can surely not be dismissed as the ramblings of a marginalized dissenter.

Divergent Assessments

In its overall effects, globalization or the emergence of a "one-world" scenario is a gripping historical drama saturated with promises and risks. Moral as well as practical-political assessments of this drama vary greatly—depending in large measure on the observer's respective position or location in the globalizing process. In the eyes of many—though surely not all—Western observers, globalization is almost entirely synonymous with progress or civilizational advance. The spreading of industry, science, and technology, coupled with the expanding reach of media and market forces, tends to be greeted as a glorious panacea, perhaps even as the dawn of a worldwide "enlightenment" liberating people everywhere from the shackles of ignorance, oppression, and economic backwardness. It is hard to deny a certain kernel of truth in this acclaim of liberal modernity, especially when the accent is placed on such features as democratization and the dissemination of human rights. Although hardly an uncritical modernizer, Václav Havel finds it important to acknowledge the positive or life-enhancing and enriching aspects of globalization. In his assessment, the global networks and "capillaries" that are integrating humankind also "convey information about certain modes of human coexistence that have proven their worth, like democracy, respect for human rights, the rule of law, the laws of the marketplace." These features of liberal modernity, he notes, give people "not only the capacity for worldwide communication, but also a coordinated means of defending themselves against many common dangers," thus making "life on this earth easier" and open to "hitherto unexplored horizons."[11]

Havel's nuanced assessment stands in stark contrast with a fashionable kind of liberal euphoria or triumphalism that, disdainful of subtleties, erects Western modernity into an ideological blueprint. In the eyes of some Western observers, the collapse of the Soviet Union and of East European Communism has ushered in the prospect of a near-eschatological dénouement: the prospect of the culmination and perhaps even "end" of history (in the sense of the resolution of historical antagonisms). While political theorists and intellectuals find evidence for this prospect in the spreading of individual rights and freedoms, neoliberal economists focus their attention on the unleashing of capitalist production and initiative. A brief glance at neoliberal literature corroborates this focus. Thus Kenichi Ohmae celebrates in his writings the emergence of a "borderless world"—more specifically of a borderless world economy transcending and even erasing traditional political boundaries. In Ohmae's view, the true engines of globalization today are giant businesses and transnational corporations that increasingly dictate the pace of economic production and trade; under the impact of these steamrolling engines, traditional nation-states as well as local forms of management and production are progressively dwarfed and swept aside. In a similar vein, Lowell Bryan and Diana Farrell speak explicitly of the "unleashing" of

global capitalism where market forces are finally "unbound." In their account, economic globalization is closely linked with cultural transformation,
in the sense that global capitalism is paralleled and undergirded by the rise of
transnational media and communications networks effectively bent on standardizing global consumer tastes.[12]

Needless to say, (neo)liberal euphoria has not gone unchallenged or unop-
posed; given the deep traumas and agonies afflicting the contemporary global
scene, heady celebrations of capitalism "unbound" are empirically dubious as
well as morally and politically inappropriate and offensive. The dubious and
lopsided character of economic triumphalism has been exposed by numerous
political economists and other global experts. Thus, pointing to the convergence or complicity of market practices with political and military forms of
hegemony, economists Andrew Hurrell and Ngaire Woods have critiqued the
persistent and even deepening strains of "inequality" fostered, as well as cov-
ered up, by the process of globalization. Likewise, using in part Foucauldian
language, Stephen Gill speaks of a "disciplinary neoliberalism," meaning by
that phrase a grand ideology seeking to legitimate the unchecked sway of
transnational capital around the world. Pushing the critical edge of his analysis, Gill perceives this ideology also as the engine of global cultural streamlining and adaptation, that is, as the harbinger of a "market civilization" coer-
cively instilling habits of consumerism, political apathy, and dependence
(especially in nonhegemonic societies). Although attempting to steer a middle course, Raimo Väyrynen's study on *Global Transformation* is equally explicit about global disparities. In his view, economic globalization has a "dual
character" in terms of its consequences; while mobilizing new resources, opening up new markets, and fueling economic growth, its pursuit also diminishes
the "social and political control of capital," thereby increasing "inequalities"
both within and between societies and thus contributing to "social marginalization within nations and economic gaps between them." Relying on a large
set of economic indicators, Väyrynen draws this conclusion:

> The present world is characterized by the growing polarization between rich and
> poor countries. Empirical evidence on the world income distribution by countries
> shows that it is becoming increasingly bimodal or "twin-peaked." . . . In other
> words, the international middle class has been shrinking at the expense of the up-
> per class or, alternatively, the upper class has disappeared and all well-off countries
> belong to the middle class.[13]

This emergence of an international class structure—the division between
middle-class and underclass societies—is paralleled and intensified by a cul-

tural divide: that between hegemonic and nonhegemonic cultural frameworks and traditions. While the former are largely compatible and aligned with globalization, the latter undergo a process of dislocation and marginalization—an experience that is prone to lead to resentment and perhaps countercultural resistance. In his address at Harvard, Havel clearly perceived this cultural division or asymmetry (though without in any way endorsing Huntington's scenario). As he noted at the time, the much belabored rise of the "global village" actually harbors an internal fissure, in the sense that so-called global civilization is today no more than "a thin veneer over the sum total of human awareness, if I may put it that way." To a considerable extent, this veneer or "single epidermis" of globalism is deceptive, because it "merely covers or conceals the immense variety of cultures, of peoples, of religious worlds, of historical traditions and historically formed attitudes, all of which, in a sense, lie 'beneath' it." Havel speaks in this context of the "underside of humanity" overshadowed by globalization, a "hidden dimension" of humankind that "demands more and more clearly to be heard and to be granted a right to life." Seen in this light, our age appears inhabited by a dual and even "contradictory" process. In the same measure as the world at large increasingly accepts the "new habits" of globalism, a countermovement or resurgence of localism is occurring: "Ancient traditions are reviving, different religions and cultures are awakening to new ways of being, seeking new room to exist, and struggling with growing fervor to realize what is unique to them and what makes them different from others."[14]

Assessments of this cultural (or countercultural) revival vary, depending again in large measure on the observer's location. From the vantage of many Western "development" experts and policy analysts, local or indigenous cultural traditions appear mainly as roadblocks or obstacles hampering the path of modernization and global progress. In his 1993 essay, Huntington offered a culture-dependent gradation of obstacles to globalism. As he pointed out, "the obstacles to non-Western countries joining the West vary considerably"; they are "least for Latin American and East European countries," somewhat "greater for the Orthodox countries of the former Soviet Union" and "still greater for Muslim, Confucian, Hindu and Buddhist societies."[15] More philosophically trained Western observers are prone to detect in cultural revival a theoretical (perhaps even metaphysical) problem: the danger of the upsurge of cultural "relativism" in opposition to the yardsticks of global "universalism" (embodied in science and progress). Inhabitants of non-Western or nonhegemonic societies are less likely to share this view; for most of them, globalization is not so much a theoretical as a social, economic, and existential problem, accompanied often by marginalization, economic misery, and social and cultural alienation. This does not necessarily mean a wholesale opposition to Western modernity. Open- and fair-minded intellectuals in non-Western countries will often be ready to grant the benefits of modernization. The fact that the latter *can* generate a new dynamism in traditional societies, which, in turn, may release untapped social energies, especially among previously silenced or oppressed strata. Yet, as long as they have not yet completely "joined" or been assimilated into the West, the same intellectuals cannot fail to be attentive to prevailing political and economic disparities in the global arena. They can hardly forget that, in large measure, the benefits of globalizing modernity have come—and continue to come—to non-Western societies through the vehicle of colonialism or else postcolonial forms of Western hegemony. To this extent and from that angle, globalization is liable to be experienced as a mode of foreign intervention and manipulation, that is, as a "globalization from above" promoted (in subtle and not-so-subtle ways) by colonial and neocolonial masters.

Sometimes, under circumstances of extreme provocation, reaction to Western globalism or universalism may take the form of a radical self-enclosure or self-encapsulation, a retreat into an indigenous life-form coupled with a complete rejection of foreign (especially Western) influence. In such situations, leaders of indigenous movements may brand Western globalism as a curse, perhaps even as a Satanic plot designed to undermine or destroy cultural autonomy, including traditional religious beliefs and practices. This, in a nutshell, is what one means today by such terms as *fundamentalism* or *communalism*, especially their militant and xenophobic varieties.[16] Given their often destructive or devastating effects—sometimes culminating in "ethnic cleansing"—no one can be indifferent to the grave dangers signaled by these terms. To be sure, condemnation of these movements comes easily from the lips of neoliberal globalizers, especially those unperturbed by the implications of Western (economic, technological, and military) hegemony. However, global ideologues are not, and should not be, the only critics of a reactionary fundamentalism. More compelling and persuasive in this domain are critical voices otherwise friendly or sympathetic to nonhegemonic peoples. One of these voices is again that of Edward Said, hardly suspect of neoliberal euphoria. In his *Culture and Imperialism*, Said has eloquently castigated contemporary tendencies toward self-enclosure:

> All those nationalist appeals to pure or authentic Islam, or to Afrocentrism, *négritude*, or Arabism had a strong response, without sufficient consciousness that those ethnicities and spiritual essences would come back to exact a very high prize from their successful adherents. [Frantz] Fanon was one of the few to remark on the dan-

gers posed to a great sociopolitical movement like decolonization by an untutored national consciousness. Much the same could be said about the dangers of an untutored religious consciousness. . . . National security and a separatist identity are the watchwords.[17]

Whither Globalization? A Promising Path

While it is relatively easy—though no less necessary—to criticize reactionary or fundamentalist movements, it is much more difficult to chart a course able to avoid the pitfalls of both nativist localism or separatism and neocolonial hegemony or domination. The perils of the former are readily apparent to globalizers—who prefer to turn a blind eye to the second danger. The reverse situation obtains in the case of the marginalized or oppressed. Yet, the drawbacks of self-enclosure should be evident even to its fervent devotees. For one thing, retreatism is clearly only a reactive or negative mode of behavior, with stifling effects even on what it seeks to affirm. Moreover, even if stubbornly pursued, fundamentalist retreat can hardly fully succeed in our time—given that it is only the flip-side of, and hence largely parasitic on, what it rejects. As Havel observed, many groups or movements today are struggling against modern Western civilization and its proponents by "using weapons provided by the very civilization they oppose"; thus, they sometimes employ "radar, computers, lasers, nerve gases, and perhaps, in the future, even nuclear weapons—all products of the world they challenge—to help defend their ancient heritage." Apart from noting internal contradictions, these comments also point to the most ominous and perilous corollaries of self-enclosure: the bent toward destruction in the form of both domestic violence and external aggression.[18]

So, how can one find another way, an alternative global path leading between and beyond culture clashes and global domination? A shorthand formula for this path might be "grassroots globalization" or (with Richard Falk) "globalization from below," meaning the attempt to forge or build up the global city through the interaction of cultures and peoples around the world. In many ways, this seems to be the only fruitful and promising path today, that is, a path preserving the promise contained in the movement of globalization. Here again, Havel can serve as an insightful mentor. In terms of his address, world civilization should not blithely be equated with European or Western civilization, which in any case forms only a thin veneer or epidermis covering the globe. The real challenge facing humankind today, he stated, is to "start understanding itself as a multicultural and multipolar civilization," as a complex and densely textured fabric whose meaning lies "not in undermining the individuality of different spheres of culture and civilization but in allowing them to be more completely themselves." What this understanding brings into view is a global city bent neither on internecine warfare nor on uniformity or unilateral domination. In Havel's words, the global city

> must be an expression of the authentic will of everyone, growing out of the genuine spiritual roots hidden beneath the skin of our common, global civilization. If it is merely disseminated through the capillaries of this skin, the way Coca-Cola ads are—as a commodity offered by some to others—such a code can hardly be expected to take hold in any profound or universal way.[19]

Once universalism is seen no longer as a hegemonic tool nor as a target of abuse, it becomes clear that the path to the global city can proceed only from the ground up, that is, through the labor of cross-cultural interaction, critical engagement, and reciprocal learning. This travail necessarily has to start from local traditions and historically sedimented practices and beliefs; by moving from this core and opening themselves up to cross-cultural interrogation and testing, local traditions are likely to shed their dogmatic crust and become available again as rich resources of human and social transformation. As it happens, there are grassroots movements today operating across boundaries and pointing in the direction of a global civil society: movements such as interfaith alliances, ecological and feminist networks, and intersocietal labor coalitions. These movements are corroborated by developments in contemporary philosophy and literature. While traditional Western philosophy has tended to posture as blandly universal or absolute, recent philosophical initiatives have contributed to a fuller appreciation of the role of interhuman and cross-cultural dialogue. Most prominent among contemporary writings in this domain are the works of Hans-Georg Gadamer, Raimundo Panikkar, Mikhail Bakhtin, and Tzvetan Todorov. As is well known, Gadamer has portrayed both textual reading and intersubjective encounter as forms of dialogical exchange where initial assumptions first serve as launching pads of questioning, only to be called into question in turn by the demands of the encounter.[20] In the writings of Panikkar, what is particularly intriguing is the notion of an "imparative philosophy" (from Latin *imparare*, to learn) seen as a philosophy dedicated to learning through dialogue. What Panikkar has in mind is not simply a "comparative" approach or procedure—if the latter denotes the collection of comparative data by a neutral observer or spectator. This view closely resonates with the perspective of Todorov, who often draws on insights garnered from Bakhtin. In his epilogue to *The Conquest of America* (recounting one of the cruelest episodes of genocide), Todorov discloses his own normative stance or commitment—a commitment to "communication" or "dialogue," specifically a "dialogue of (or between) cultures." As he writes, somewhat hopefully, it is this dialogue of cultures that "characterizes our age" and that is "incarnated by ethnology, at once the child of colonialism and the proof of its death throes."[21]

As one should realize, however, the path of dialogue and "globalization from below" is charted not only by academic philosophers and scholars; it is also the course recommended by all or most of the great world religions and cultural traditions around the globe. This aspect can readily be documented. As Muslims surely will acknowledge, Islam cannot be tied to a particular country or locality but is linked with the "*umma*"—which is potentially global in character. This nonlocal character of Islam is repeatedly stressed in the Qur'an, including the first surah where God is called "*rabbi alamin*," which means lord and sustainer of the entire universe. In a similar way, Buddhists and Confucianists cannot limit their concerns to a narrow region or ethnic nationality without forfeiting the depth dimension of their beliefs— just as little as Christians can afford to remain ethno- or Eurocentric. Devoid of empirical identity, the notion of buddhahood resists any attempt at parochial or status-related fixation. Although taking its bearings from circumscribed "relationships," Confucianism ruptures or transcends confining boundaries through its emphasis on "*ren*" (humaneness) which is not regionally nor ethnically specific. Even Hinduism—which seems so closely rooted in the Indian soil—confounds and transgresses national borders in many ways, especially through its core notion of "*brahman*," which (as articulated by Advaita Vedanta) links or integrates human beings everywhere with the divine. To this extent, Havel seems to be on firm ground when he speaks of an "archetypal spirituality" pervading humankind (even beyond the limits of organized faiths), adding that "lying dormant in the deepest roots of most, if not all, cultures" there is a common bond that is not so much jeopardized by, but rather "anchored in the great diversity of human traditions."[22]

To be sure, great care must be taken in this domain to avoid every kind of triumphalism, that is, to screen "globalization from below" from the temptation of global hegemony and imperialism. One way to guard against this temptation is to distinguish between globalization and a doctrinaire globalism treating the global village as a *fait accompli*. From the vantage of grassroots globalization, universality and global unity can only be seen as a pledge or promise, not as anyone's privilege or secure possession. Although it is important to affirm and not to relinquish universal hopes, prudence dictates attention to critical questions like these: Who or which human agency genuinely embodies universalism, or who can legitimately speak "in the name

of" the universal (that is, Who is universal)?[23] For the sake of their own integrity, world religions (and cultural traditions) might do well to be mindful
of these questions, and thus avoid the confusion of *umma* or catholicity with
global-imperial ambitions. In sacred scripture, Christians (for example) are
exhorted to spread the "good news" around the world—but that news is one
of grace and charity and not of empire. This distinction clearly requires that
one also differentiates between teaching and hegemonically sanctioned conversion. In this context, members of all faiths—especially missionaries—
might usefully recall a passage in the Qur'an that states "No coercion in matters of faith" (*la ikhra fid-din*), a saying not too far from the Buddhist principle
of nonviolence and the Confucian emphasis on humaneness. A saying of the
prophet Muhammad is worth remembering here. As reported by Ibn Majah:
"A man once asked the Prophet if bigotry is to love one's tribe. 'No,' replied
the Prophet. 'Bigotry is to help your tribe to tyrannize others'."[24] This *hadith*,
in my view, can serve as the motto of intercivilizational dialogue today, il-
lustrating the meaning of "globalization from below."

Notes

1. Havel's address was presented at Harvard at a convocation during which he received
an honorary doctoral degree. The text is cited from *Just Commentary*, no. 28 (July 1996): 1.

2. See Marshall McLuhan, *The Gutenberg Galaxy: The Making of Typographic Man*
(Toronto: University of Toronto Press, 1962); also his *The Global Village: Transformation
in World Life and Media in the 21st Century* (New York: Oxford University Press, 1989).
According to Jan Aart Scholte, globalization has in recent decades become a "buzzword,
a term as ambiguous as it is popular." See Scholte, "Beyond the Buzzword: Toward a Critical Theory of Globalization," in *Globalization: Theory and Practice*, ed. Eleonore Kofman
and Gillian Youngs (London: Pinter, 1996), 44–45.

3. Roland Robertson, *Globalization: Social Theory and Global Culture* (Newbury Park,
Calif.: Sage, 1992), 8, 51. See also Robertson, "Globalization and Societal Modernization:
A Note on Japan and Japanese Religion," *Sociological Analysis* 47 (1987): 38; "Globalization Theory and Civilization Analysis," *Comparative Civilizations Review* 17 (1987): 23;
also Marshall McLuhan, *Explorations in Communication*, ed. E. S. Carpenter, (Boston: Beacon Press, 1960).

4. Robertson, *Globalization*, 8, 50, 53, 105. See also Anthony Giddens, *The Constitution of Society: Outline of the Theory of Structuration* (Berkeley: University of California
Press, 1984).

5. Angus Maddison, *Phases of Capitalist Development* (Oxford: Oxford University Press,
1982), 85–95, 248–53. See also Karl Polanyi, *The Great Transformation: The Political and
Economic Origins of Our Time* (Boston: Beacon Press, 1957); and Raimo Väyrynen, "Economic Cycles, Power Transitions, Political Management and Wars between Major Powers," *International Studies Quarterly* 27 (1983): 389–418.

6. See Väyrynen, *Global Transformation: Economics, Politics, and Culture* (Helsinki: Sitra, 1997), 32; Giddens, *The Consequences of Modernity* (Stanford, Calif.: Stanford University Press, 1990) 21–29, 64; James N. Rosenau, *Along the Domestic/Foreign Frontier: Exploring Governance in a Turbulent World* (Cambridge: Cambridge University Press, 1997), 81–82; Mike Featherstone, "Localism, Globalism, and Cultural Identity," in *Global /Local: Cultural Production and the Transnational Imaginary*, ed. Rob Wilson and Wimal Dissanayake (Durham, N.C.: Duke University Press, 1996), 60–65. Compare also Featherstone, ed., *Global Culture: Nationalism, Globalization and Modernity* (Newbury Park, Calif.: Sage, 1990), and Featherstone, *Undoing Culture: Globalization, Postmodernism and Identity* (Newbury Park, Calif.: Sage, 1995).

7. Lucian Pye, *Aspects of Political Development* (Boston: Little Brown, 1966), 44–45.

8. See Immanuel Wallerstein, *The Modern World-System*, 2 vols. (New York: Academic Press, 1974); *The Capitalist World-Economy* (Cambridge: Cambridge University Press, 1979); and *Geopolitics and Geoculture: Essays on the Changing World-System* (Cambridge: Cambridge University Press, 1991).

9. Edward W. Said, *Culture and Imperialism* (New York: Knopf, 1993), 282, 291, 319.

10. Samuel Huntington, "The Clash of Civilizations?" *Foreign Affairs* 72 (Summer 1993): 39. In the meantime, Huntington has fleshed out and greatly expanded his argument in book form (whose title omits the question mark of the earlier essay). See *The Clash of Civilizations and the Remaking of World Order* (New York: Simon & Schuster, 1996).

11. Havel, "A Challenge," *Just Commentary*, 1–2.

12. See Kenichi Ohmae, *The Borderless World: Power and Strategy in the Interlinked Economy* (New York: Harper, 1990); Lowell Bryan and Diana Farrell, *Market Unbound: Unleashing Global Capitalism* (New York: John Wiley, 1996). Compare also John H. Dunning, *The Globalization of Business: The Challenge of the 1990s* (London: Routledge, 1993); Saskia Sassen, "The Spatial Organization of Information Industries: Implications for the Role of the State," in *Globalization: Critical Reflections*, ed. James Mittelman (Boulder, Colo.: Lynne Rienner, 1996), 33–52; and Chris Farrand, "The Globalization of Knowledge and the Politics of Global Intellectual Property: Power, Governance and Technology," in *Globalization: Theory and Practice*, ed. Eleonore Kofman and Gillian Youngs (London: Pinter, 1996), 175–87. The eschatological reference is to Francis Fukuyama, *The End of History and the Last Man* (New York: Free Press, 1992).

13. Väyrynen, *Global Transformation*, 3, 15. See also Saskia Sassen, *Globalization and Its Discontents* (New York: New Press, 1999); Richard Falk, *Predatory Globalization: A Critique* (Cambridge, UK: Polity Press, 1999); Andrew Hurrell and Ngaire Woods, "Globalization and Inequality," *Millennium* 24 (1995): 447–70; Stephen Gill, "Globalization, Market Civilization, and Disciplinary Neoliberalism," *Millennium* 24 (1995): 399–442; further David Loy, "The Religion of the Market," *Just Commentary*, no. 30 (August 1996): 1–10. (I am indebted to Väyrynen for alerting me to some of these texts).

14. Havel, "A Challenge," *Just Commentary*, 2.

15. Huntington, "The Clash of Civilizations?" *Foreign Affairs*, 45. As an astute policy analyst, Huntington quickly added that countries that for some reason "do not wish to, or cannot join the West compete with the West by developing their own economic, military

and political power" and "by cooperating with other non-Western countries." The most ominous cooperation, in Huntington's view, is the "Confucian–Islamic connection."

16. In their book titled *Fundamentalism Observed*, Martin Marty and R. Scott Appleby state that "religious fundamentalism has appeared as a tendency, a habit of mind, found within religious communities and paradigmatically embodied in certain representative individuals and movements, which manifests itself as a strategy or set of strategies by which beleagured believers attempt to preserve their distinct identity as a people or group. Feeling this identity to be at risk in the contemporary era, they fortify it by a selective retrieval of doctrines, beliefs and practices from a sacred past." See *Fundamentalism Observed* (Chicago: University of Chicago Press, 1990), 8. Compare also Abdel Salam Sidahmed and Anoushiravan Ehteshami, eds., *Islamic Fundamentalism* (Boulder, Colo.: Westview Press, 1996).

17. Said, *Culture and Imperialism*, 307.

18. Havel, "A Challenge," *Just Commentary*, 2. In fairness one should grant that not all forms of self-enclosure are violence-prone; counter-examples would be Amish and Mennonite communities.

19. Havel, "A Challenge," *Just Commentary*, 2. For the notion of "globalization from below" see Richard Falk, "The World Order between Inter-State Law and the Law of Humanity: The Role of Civil Society Institutions," in *Cosmopolitan Democracy: An Agenda for a New World Order*, ed. Daniele Archibugi and David Held (Cambridge, UK: Polity Press, 1995), 163–79; and "Cultural Foundations for the International Protection of Human Rights," *Human Rights in Cross-Cultural Perspectives: A Quest for Consensus*, ed. Abdullahi Ahmed An-Na'im (Philadelphia: University of Pennsylvania Press, 1992), 44–64.

20. See Hans-Georg Gadamer, *Truth and Method*, 2nd ed., trans. Joel Weinsheimer and Donald G. Marshall (New York: Crossroad, 1989); and *Dialogue and Dialectic*, trans. P. Christopher Smith (New Haven: Yale University Press, 1980). Relying in part on Gadamer's writings I have articulated a perspective termed *differential hermeneutics* or *hermeneutics of difference*, applicable especially to cross-cultural encounters. See my *Beyond Orientalism: Essays on Cross-Cultural Encounter* (Albany, N.Y.: State University of New York Press, 1996), 39–62.

21. See Tzvetan Todorov, *The Conquest of America: The Question of the Other*, trans. Richard Howard (New York: Harper & Row, 1984), 250; Mikhail M. Bakhtin, *The Dialogical Imagination*, ed. Michael Holquist (Austin: University of Texas Press, 1981); Raimundo Panikkar, "What Is Comparative Philosophy Comparing?" in *Interpreting Across Cultures: New Essays in Comparative Philosophy*, ed. Gerald J. Larson and Eliot Deutsch (Princeton: Princeton University Press, 1988), 116–36. Compare also my "Toward a Comparative Political Theory," in *Border Crossings: Toward a Comparative Political Theory*, ed. Dallmayr (Lanham, Md.: Lexington Books, 1999), 1–10.

22. Havel, "A Challenge," 3. Regarding the universalizing tendency in Confucianism see "The 'Moral Universal' from the Perspectives of East Asian Thought," in *Confucian Thought: Selfhood as Creative Transformation*, ed. Tu Weiming (Albany, N.Y.: State University of New York Press, 1985), 19–34. Compare also Lionel M. Jensen, *Manufacturing Confucianism: Chinese Traditions and Universal Civilization* (Durham, N.C.: Duke University Press, 1997).

23. In this connection, one would do well to remember the words of Michel Foucault: "Nothing is more inconsistent than a political regime that is indifferent to truth; but nothing is more dangerous than a political system that claims to lay down the truth. The function of 'telling the truth' must not take the form of law, just as it would be pointless to believe that it resides by right in the spontaneous interplay of communication. The task of telling the truth is an endless labor: to respect it in all its complexity is an obligation which no power can do without—except by imposing the silence of slavery." See Lawrence D. Kritzman, ed., *Michel Foucault: Politics, Philosophy, Culture; Interviews and Other Writings 1977–1984* (New York: Routledge, 1988), 267.

24. See *Words of the Prophet Muhammad: Selections from the Hadith*, compiled by Maulana Wahiduddin Khan (New Delhi: Al-Risala Books, 1996), 95.

CHAPTER TWO

∽

Global Governance and Cultural Diversity: Toward a Cosmopolitan Democracy

"There is hope," Immanuel Kant writes at one point, "that after many revolutions and transformations the highest purpose of nature, namely a universal cosmopolitan condition, will finally emerge as the seedbed allowing the unfolding of all human endowments." The phrase appears in Kant's "Idea for a General History with Cosmopolitan Intent" (1784). In this essay, the philosopher is by no means unaware of the difficulties and obstacles obstructing the path leading to the "highest purpose of nature." A major obstacle resides in a certain cunning of nature itself, its tendency to pursue goals only through detours—particularly through the detour of the "unsociable sociability" of humans whose striving for selfish aims yields social benefits only indirectly or seemingly by accident. Hence, civility and just governance are arduous achievements requiring the progressive taming of the "crooked timber" of humanity. In an acute manner, the problem surfaces on the global level. Here again, nature's cunning uses human unsociability, evident in the relations between societies and states, as a means to reach "through their inevitable antagonism a condition of peace and security"; thus, through incessant armaments, wars, and devastations of all kinds, nature guides humankind to its purpose: to exit from the lawless condition of savages and to enter into a global "league of nations" (*Völkerbund*) governed by common laws. Although the latter step is the most difficult task facing human ingenuity, Kant declares it a plausible and instructive philosophical enterprise "to portray general world history according to a plan of nature aiming at the perfect cosmopolitan community of humankind."[1]

Kant's vision of global or universal governance is stunning and appealing—although its achievement is perhaps more remote than his essay suggests. Regarding nature's providential course, the past (twentieth) century offers starkly conflicting testimony. World wars, holocaust, genocide, ethnic cleansing, "killing fields"—all provide grim support to Kant's notion of the "crooked timber" of humanity. On the other hand, partly in response to these haunting experiences, efforts have been made—for the first time in history—to move in the direction of a truly cosmopolitan "bonding" of nations (Völkerbund), and these efforts have succeeded in establishing at least rudimentary forms of global governance. To be sure, both procedurally and substantively, that governance is still far removed from the global community envisaged in "Idea." For one thing, most of the global institutions and accords were created by national governments—whose competence to represent peoples or the masses of humankind is often in serious doubt. More important, the actual performance of global institutions has in many respects been "hijacked" or monopolized by a limited number of nation-states or powers, especially the hegemonic states of the Western (or Northwestern) hemisphere. Hence, the "crooked timber" noted by Kant is liable to afflict global institutions as well.[2]

In our contemporary setting, global governance balances precariously on the horns of this dilemma. Propelled by market mechanisms and advances in science and technology, humankind rushes headlong in the direction of globalization or the establishment of the "global village." Moved by the grim experiences of persecution and exploitation marking our age, peoples everywhere sense a longing for universal justice, security, and peace. At the same time, however, nation-states most eloquent in espousing global ideas and most instrumental in fashioning global institutions often display their all-too-human "timber" by mixing cosmopolitanism with selfish national (or regional) interest and with the lust for wealth and power. Faced with massive hegemonic pressures, the yearning of global "under-classes" for justice and equity is put severely to the test, sometimes prompting them to embrace xenophobia (or Western-phobia).[3] What these considerations bring into view is that the vision of global governance cannot just be a political stratagem nor a philosopher's blueprint, but has to be endorsed by the masses of humankind around the globe. Differently phrased: global justice and the meaning of "commonality" or common global norms cannot just be determined in Washington or in Königsberg but require attention to the vast patrimony of humankind manifest in the great diversity of cultures, traditions, and aspirations. The following discussion explores the intertwining or interpenetration of globalism and cultural or local diversity:

1. The first section examines the notion of global governance as it appears from a variety of prominent contemporary perspectives.
2. In the next part, the focus shifts to the dimension of cultural diversity, with an eye to the issue how diverse cultures and societies respond to the process of globalization.
3. To conclude, an effort is made to show the correlation of globalism and diversity by concentrating on some salient features of the emerging global "civil society."

Global Governance: Some Views

The goal of global governance—of some kind of "bonding" among countries and peoples—has been a long-standing human aspiration. Apart from Kant, the goal has been articulated and practically promoted by a host of intellectuals and statesmen, from the Abbé de Sainte-Pierre to Woodrow Wilson and beyond. As one should note, *global governance* in this connection does not necessarily mean a global government patterned on the model of the nation-state, that is, a state writ-large or a global empire. Conscious of the pitfalls of empire—evident in the long history of imperialism from ancient times to modernity—proponents of global bonding (*Bund*) usually stop short of endorsing the construction of a super-state that would accumulate or amass all the powers traditionally vested in individual states. Typically, articulations of global governance thus occupy a spectrum stretching from the traditional "anarchy of states," on one side, through various forms of association and federation all the way to global government, on the other end. A further factor needs to be taken into account: Discussions of global governance tend to oscillate between normative and empirical-descriptive accounts, that is, between accounts treating such governance as a yardstick (perhaps) guiding future developments, and accounts depicting (and perhaps endorsing) a prevailing state of affairs. Despite unclear boundaries and frequent overlaps between approaches, international relations literature tends to distinguish in this regard between normative or "idealist" and empirical or "realist" perspectives.[4]

Among contemporary philosophers, a strongly normative and future-oriented vision of global governance—though one not severed from past developments—has been advanced by Stephen Toulmin. In Toulmin's account, the expectation of global governance, or what he calls "cosmopolis," has actually been the secret longing or "hidden agenda" of Western modernity, a longing that can serve as a guidepost in the new millennium. As he writes, the beliefs that shape our historical foresight represent (what

German philosophers call) "our *Erwartungshorizont* or horizon of expectation"; such horizons delimit our "field of action" in which, at the moment, we see it as possible or feasible "to change human affairs, and so to decide which of our most cherished practical goals can be realized." As we move into the third millennium, a reasonable horizon of expectation (reasonable in light of all the forward-looking experiences of modernity) is the strengthening and steady unfolding of cosmopolitan institutions—provided we do not shrink from this task in fearful "trepidation" or out of nostalgia for the past. If we are ready to move ahead, he notes, we may welcome the new millennium as an arena that offers "new possibilities" but also demands "novel ideas and more adaptive institutions." For Toulmin, the road ahead requires a normative sea change, the development of a new moral vision and political practice:

> From now on, the overriding concern of administrators and politicians can no longer be to enhance the scope, power, and glory of those centralized national institutions that took shape and worked unfettered in the heyday of the nation-state, when sovereignty was its own reward. Rather we need to disperse authority and adapt it more discerningly and precisely: on the one hand, to the needs of local areas and communities, and on the other, to wider transnational functions.[5]

In contrast to Toulmin's normative horizons of expectation, some other contemporary thinkers consider cosmopolis a *fait accompli*. Thus, for Francis Fukuyama the agenda of Western modernity requires no further sea changes, but is basically accomplished or completed in our time: namely, through the triumphant ascent of Western "liberal democracy" and the worldwide acceptance of liberal-capitalist market principles. As he writes in *The End of History and the Last Man*, the collapse of communism and other nonliberal or totalitarian regimes has brought about a virtual "end" of historical developments and aspirations in the traditional sense, ushering in an era of global governance under Western liberal auspices. Undaunted by critiques of capitalism pointing to a growing gap between rich and poor, and North and South, Fukuyama ventures the opinion that the prevailing economic (and political) world system is "arguably free from fundamental inner contradictions" and, hence, self-perpetuating. In terms of social and political aspirations, his book presents our time as virtually the terminus or "end point of mankind's ideological evolution," demonstrated by the "remarkable consensus concerning the legitimacy of liberal democracy" around the globe.[6] In its triumphal language, one should add, *The End of History and the Last Man* is not an isolated phenomenon but forms part and parcel of a broader mood gripping many Western intellectuals in the aftermath of the Cold War. The mood is particularly pronounced among neoliberal economists who view global governance in terms of capital flows and international corporate markets. Thus, some economists speak of the emergence of a "borderless world" governed or guided by the power of the "interlinked" global market, while others herald the "unleashing" of global capitalism as the harbinger of a world system directed by neoliberal market principles.[7]

Needless to say, Fukuyama's globalism does not satisfy the vision of cosmopolis put forward by Toulmin and others. Nor does his celebration of Western-style liberal democracy (and neoliberal economics) measure up to the goal of a "cosmopolitan democracy" as formulated by David Held and others. For Held, democracy in the global arena (or "with a cosmopolitan intent") has to involve a far greater participation of peoples—especially the underprivileged masses of humankind—than exists in the contemporary world system; in other words, democracy (both domestically and globally) has to be basically a "bottom-up" enterprise transgressing the narrow limits of liberal-representative government endemic to Western countries. He writes that democracy today can only be fully sustained through agencies that "form an element of and yet cut across the territorial boundaries of the nation-state" (fashioned on the European model). This means that democratic institutions and practices must be linked to an "expanding framework" of societies and agencies, that is, to a "cosmopolitan model of democracy" involving a "system of governance which arises from and is adapted to the diverse conditions and interconnections of different peoples and nations."[8]

In advancing their global framework, Held and his associates are by no means unaware of the formidable obstacles standing in the way of cosmopolitan democracy. In this respect, Fukuyama's *The End of History* can be chided not only for its democratic deficit (its insufficient conception of democracy), but also for its insufficient realism (its neglect of the deep fissures marking contemporary global governance). In contrast to the "remarkable consensus" (under Western-liberal auspices) stressed by Fukuyama, more realistic observers detect a pervasive dissensus dividing the global community along ethnic, cultural, and religious lines. Thus, in his famous or notorious essay of 1993, Samuel Huntington depicted the end of the Cold War not as the gateway to global harmony but as the inauguration of an impending or imminent "clash of civilizations." In Huntington's portrayal, this clash is not a haphazard or fortuitous prospect but the (predictable) outcome of a stark fissure afflicting the global community: namely, the rift between "the West and the Rest"—between the West as the hegemonic world center and non-Western societies pushed into the periphery. As a result of this situation, global politics witnesses a counterpoint or backlash, that is, a "return to the roots phenomenon" among non-Western cultures that increasingly have "the desire, the will and resources to shape the world in non-Western ways." According to Huntington, this desire is present in all non-Western societies taken individually, but it sometimes also surfaces collectively. Threatened by hegemonic military and technological power, some countries have entered regional rallying movements or alliances, a strategy designed to foster "civilizational commonality" (according to the "kin-country syndrome") and prone to sow conflict in the world.[9]

Although couched in stirring language, the preceding account is not troubling to Huntington (and many other global realists); as a strategic policy analyst, his concern is basically with the preservation and promotion of Western hegemonic interests, not their critique (in favor of more equitable global arrangements). This aspect brings into view a division in the camp of "realists." Confronted with the evidence of humankind's "crooked timber," some analysts prefer to fasten on the notion of "crookedness" seen as a preordained, ineluctable fate, while others take the same feature as a summons to moral and political struggle (without necessarily expecting a successful outcome of their labors). Thus, in his *Culture and Imperialism*, Edward Said took his departure from the same global scenario depicted by Huntington—but presented it as a moving political indictment of global domination and inequity. For Said (as we noted in chapter 1), imperial domination has not been abolished with the dismantling of the "classical [European] empires"; rather, the rise of the United States as the last superpower indicates "that a new set of force lines will structure the world." While traditional empires pitted Europeans against a limited number of non-European societies, the "force lines" today have become global in extent. With the "American ascendancy" to hegemony, we witness a global confrontation between development and underdevelopment, between North and South, rich and poor. What is distinctive of the current "American" or Western-dominated period is not only the geographical extension of control but also its qualitative intensity. In the face of this global hegemony (or hegemonic form of global governance), *Culture and Imperialism* counseled a countermovement or kind of counterglobalism on the part of nonhegemonic societies and peoples—though a movement that must stay clear of xenophobia or nativist fundamentalism:

> If you are part of a Philippine, or Palestinian, or Brazilian oppositional movement, you must deal with the tactical and logistical requirements of the daily struggle. Yet I do think that efforts of this kind are developing, if not a general theory, then a common discursive readiness or, to put it territorially, an underlying world map. Perhaps we may start to speak of this somewhat elusive oppositional mood, and its emerging strategies, as an internationalist counter-articulation.[10]

Counterhegemonic Resistance

The arguments of Huntington and Said are liable, and meant, to shatter global illusions. Although proceeding from different, even opposite, perspectives, their accounts of the global scenario concur in their effect by rendering suspect the assumption of a smoothly harmonious cosmopolis or a "global governance" devoid of conflict or contestation. In his discussion of counterglobalism, Said refers approvingly to Immanuel Wallerstein's notion of "antisystemic movements" developed by the latter in a string of writings. Although the meaning of that term was initially restricted mainly to the economic domain, Wallerstein more recently has extended its scope to encompass nonhegemonic cultures or countercultures, thereby underscoring the role of cultural diversity as a resource in the struggle against global uniformity. Even prior to the appearance of Huntington's essay, his *Geopolitics and Geoculture* pointed to the growing importance of culture or cultures as the "intellectual battleground" in the emerging global system. Contrary to Huntington's "essentializing" tendency, Wallerstein (following Clifford Geertz) presented "cultures" as fluid, historically sedimented but open-ended meaning patterns bent on resisting the double lure of global absorption and local seclusion. In the literature on globalization, he noted, Western culture is often identified with universalism and progress, while non-Western cultures stand for particularism, localism, and stagnation—an opposition that is part of modern Western metaphysics and debunked by the long-standing collusion of universalism with particular power strategies (evident, for example, in France's "*mission civilisatrice*" and, more recently, the "American century"). In Wallerstein's view, universalism has always been "dear to the Western heart." In our own time, however, this agenda has come under attack, both for its uncritical faith in science and technology and its imperialist cultural strategy. Together with Said, Wallerstein hence stresses the need for cultural or countercultural "articulation"—again not as a ploy to sanction parochialism, but as an avenue encouraging a critical encounter between "the West versus the Rest" and also a mutual (dialectical) contestation between universalism and particularism.[11]

The importance of cultural or countercultural resistance is also emphasized—perhaps even more eloquently—by voices emanating from nonhegemonic cultural settings. Thus, Chandra Muzaffer, the prominent Malaysian Muslim intellectual, deplores the division of our globe into North and South (developed and underdeveloped regions) and its basically undemocratic consequences. What has emerged in recent decades, he observes, is a global system "in which the poor and powerless who constitute the overwhelming majority of the human race have very little to say over their own destiny"; but a system that "virtually disenfranchises the majority" of humanity "cannot be democratic." Global economic and military-political domination by the North (or West) is accompanied and aggravated by cultural hegemony and a relentless process of global assimilation. This process reaches deeply into non-hegemonic cultures. In Muzaffer's words, what has occurred and is occurring is "a massive 'taste transfer' from the West to non-Western civilizations—a taste transfer which is unprecedented in human history, both in terms of its magnitude and its impact." As a result of this transfer, non-Western cultures are literally under siege and sometimes nearly erased. Although, for Muzaffer, there is no problem with cross-cultural learning, the situation is different when "learning" is forced and a one-way street. When sound and viable local habits and practices are destroyed simply because of external pressure and the "psychological subservience of the dominated," then there are ample grounds "to defend the right of indigenous cultures to survive" (without abstaining from internal critique when needed). What is at stake here, however, is not only the survival of local traditions but the preservation of the diversity of global culture and, by implication, the vibrancy of democracy:

> The elimination of what is good and valuable in non-Western cultures could lead eventually to the destruction of cultural diversity and variety which has always been one of the worthier attributes of human civilization. Western culture masquerading as a global culture might then superimpose a sort of cultural homogeneity upon the diminishing cultural diversity of non-Western societies. . . . This is yet another reason why Western cultural domination is a danger to cultural democracy and human rights.[12]

Similarly, speaking from an Asian-Confucian vantage point, Tu Weiming critiques the lopsidedness in the relations between North and South (or West and East) in our contemporary world. Like Muzaffer, he notes a steady "taste transfer"—evident in "the receptivity of East Asian youth to U.S. popular culture and the susceptibility of the East Asian general public to U.S. consumerism"—trends that validate complaints about cultural hegemony and Westernization. Although these trends also bring unquestionable advances in some domains (such as political freedom, human rights, and due process), their benefits are offset by notable drawbacks in modern Western culture, especially the accent on self-serving individualism and a merely contractual construal of public life. For Tu Weiming, the point is not to discard Western modernity in favor of East Asian "nativism," but rather to promote a mutually beneficial contestation and learning process. Reviving Confucian legacies, he writes, cannot amount to endorsing "fundamentalist representations of nativist ideas"; rather, the issue is how Asian intellectuals can be "enriched and empowered by their own cultural roots in their critical response" to Western modernity—an enrichment that it is hoped will be reciprocal. The result may be a change or transmutation of the modernization-as-Westernization model presently dominating the world.[13]

As one should note, critical rejoinders to cultural hegemony are prompted (in the above cases) not by opposition to democracy, but rather by a desire to strengthen democracy both domestically and on the global level by bringing politics more closely into the reach of ordinary people. This latter aspect is recognized and fully appreciated by defenders of global governance in the sense of "cosmopolitan democracy." Thus, proceeding from the side of global democratic aspirations, David Held stresses the significance of cultural diversity for global politics. As he writes, the envisaged cosmopolitan community "does not require political and cultural integration in the form of a consensus about a wide range of beliefs, values and norms"—the main reason being that part of democracy's appeal lies precisely in its refusal to accept "any conception of the political good other than that generated by people themselves" (and these people are spread out in a variety of cultural settings around the globe). As a result, he adds, "distinctive national, ethnic, cultural and social identities are part of the very basis of people's sense of being-in-the-world," providing them with "deeply rooted comfort and distinctive social locations for communities seeking a place 'at home' on this earth." For his part, Daniele Archibugi invokes the existence of cultural diversity to challenge the desirability of a "world federal state"—precisely because of its intrinsic democratic deficit. For most of the world's peoples, he writes, the norms of such a state

> would seem alien to their particular historical and cultural traditions, and would be considered as authoritarian impositions. The creation of a world state, even in the remote future, can only imperfectly take into account the historical, cultural and, in the widest sense, anthropological peculiarities of the inhabitants of our planet. . . . [F]or this reason a world federal state becomes an aspiration which jeopardizes democracy.[14]

Adding a sharp political edge to these considerations, Richard Falk perceives the hope of a global or cosmopolitan democracy in the activation of peoples' initiatives drawing on a variety of cultural and countercultural resources. In Falk's account, a kind of global governance is already in place— one deriving from a process he describes as "globalization from above." "There are strong market-driven tendencies," he observes, "to constitute an effective system of global dimensions that operates to promote world trade and investment, and that protects the flows of strategic resources from South to North and that guards the North from threats mounted by the South." Relying on hegemonic power, globalization-from-above establishes a global normative network of rules—but one that is at odds with a genuine "law of humanity" or "law of peoples" (*ius gentium*). In Falk's view, only transnational or cross-national social forces and movements can provide the vehicle for such a law of humanity, that is, for a normative framework that is "animated by humane sustainable development for all peoples, North and South, and seeks to structure such commitments by way of humane global governance"—a governance "protective of the earth and its peoples" and "democratically constituted." To characterize this kind of governance—one not yet accomplished but normatively projected into the future—Falk uses the phrase "globalization from below," a phrase meant to identify (as he notes) emergent transnational and cross-cultural democratic forces and their dedication to "the creation of a global civil society that is an alternative scenario of the future to that of the global political economy being shaped by transnational market forces."[15]

Toward a Cosmopolitan Democracy

Falk's argument spotlights an important point: to be congruent with the diversity of cultures and peoples, democratic global governance needs to be built "from the ground up" through lateral interactions and transnational or cross-cultural movements. In the language of traditional political philosophy, such governance has to be anchored in a viable global "civil society" as the groundwork nurturing public institutions. The meaning of "civil society" in this context must be extended beyond market exchanges to encompass voluntary associations, cultural and religious formations, as well as transnational agencies (sometimes called "new social movements"). In Falk's usage, the term points mainly to two dimensions, both with global implications: first, to voluntary nongovernmental agencies, such as Amnesty International and various regional watch groups, where the focus is on the protection of individual freedoms and aspirations; and second, broader movements of peoples pursuing their emancipation from oppressive structures of (local or national) government. Global civil society, from this perspective, appears as a complex network of criss-crossing agencies and interactions, a network that, though still reflecting the persisting influence of nation-states, also exhibits "the effects of voluntary associations and social movements that are motivated by the law of humanity [*ius gentium*] and situated in civil society."[16]

In commenting on the role of international civil society, Falk does not limit himself to broad speculations, but offers a series of concrete recommendations designed to strengthen both cross-cultural cooperation and the viability of global governance. Some of these recommendations are structural or legal, others more political and moral in character. In the structural domain, his argument points to the weak popular grounding—or the democratic deficit—of existing international institutions, especially the United Nations. What is needed here are efforts to give "greater weight to global civil society perspectives," efforts that, by curbing hegemonic geo-political and market forces, would make room for greater participation "both by countries in the South and by transnational social forces" committed to human rights and democratization. In the field of political and moral initiatives, Falk stresses especially the need to reign in global market operations and to accord higher priority to ecological concerns than is currently granted. To be sure, all such efforts are liable to encounter charges of "unrealism" or moral utopianism—charges, however, that cannot be given much weight: "The challenge is certainly formidable, but the opportunity is present to a historically unprecedented degree."[17]

Falk's proposals are seconded and amplified by defenders of cosmopolitan democracy. Thus, Held envisages a series of possible transformations in the field of global governance, some of which aim at the formation of a "global parliament" (perhaps bicameral and with limited revenue-raising capacity), enhanced political regionalization, and compulsory jurisdiction before the International Court of Justice. Suggestions of this kind are further detailed and expanded by Archibugi, with a main focus on structural reform of global institutions. Patterned on the "Campaign for a More Democratic United Nations" (the so-called CAMDUN conferences), one of Archibugi's central recommendations concerns the creation of a United Nations second assembly, a chamber that would represent peoples rather than their governments. Such a creation, he writes, would put in place an institutional forum that would allow "world citizens to have a voice in international affairs to complement [and sometimes contest] the actions of their own governments." The significance of the second chamber would be further advanced if it made room for the representation not only of majority parties but also of oppositional groups, national minorities, and new social movements. Proposals for structural reform also involve the current composition and functions of the Security Council, with Archibugi listing such possible innovations as removal of the veto power, expansion of council membership, and inclusion of nonstate or civil society institutions. The challenge of cosmopolitan democracy, he concludes, is not that of "substituting one power with another," but

of "reducing the role of [top-down] power in the political process while increasing the influence" of democratic participation.[18]

Needless to say, cosmopolitanism and the stakes of global civil society
cannot be advanced merely by institutional tinkering and structural reform
(important though the latter may be). The chances of global democracy, one
can plausibly argue, can be genuinely increased only by sustained cross-cultural interactions and by reciprocal learning processes involving many dimensions of people's concrete or ordinary lives. Examples of such learning
processes are interfaith dialogues (exemplified by the Parliament of the
World's Religions and numerous interfaith groups and associations), cross-
cultural exchange programs involving teachers, students, and workers, and
interactive social movements concerned with ecology, the lot of women, and
indigenous peoples. These concerns are the central theme of Elise Boulding's
pioneering book titled *Building a Global Civic Culture: Education for an Interdependent World*. As Boulding writes, the term civic culture—though multi-
vocal—signifies basically a pattern of "how we share a common space, common resources, and common opportunities and manage interdependence in
that 'company of strangers' which constitutes 'the public.'" The ingredients
of civic culture have been explored and catalogued in a number of nation-
states; however, today we have to enlarge our horizon, for there is also "a
larger company of strangers—the five [or six] billion residents of the planet."
In the course of the past century, Boulding notes, citizens' or people's associations have dramatically exploded, spanning nearly the entire globe. These
transnational or cross-cultural associations "cover the whole range of human
interests," including (for example) chambers of commerce, service clubs,
churches, associations of farmers, teachers, athletes—any type of group seeking relationships with like-minded people across local and national confines.
Again, all these initiatives can be derided as utopian and "unrealistic"—but
only if we are ready to declare education and learning itself utopian. For, education always involves a kind a venture and transformation. In Boulding's
words, reflective education is key to the "crafting of human beings" or the
unfolding of "personhood," which, in turn, is key to the unfolding of a
broader potential—that of a global civic culture.[19]

Boulding's comments bring us back, by way of conclusion, to Kant's conception of human history with a "cosmopolitan intent." As previously indicated, Kant was by no means unaware of the serious roadblocks obstructing the path toward cosmopolis, obstacles having to do mainly with the
"crookedness" of the human timber; but this was not a counsel of despair.
His views on the topic were further elaborated in his famous "philosophical sketch" for "perpetual peace" (composed some ten years after the earlier

essay). There, although noting the unwillingness of national governments to form a *civitas gentium* or global polis, Kant also stressed some counter-vailing tendencies pursuing the global "intent" by different means. "The peoples of the earth," he wrote, "have entered in varying degrees into a universal community, and it has developed to the point where a violation of rights in *one* part of the world is felt *everywhere*." Hence, the idea of a cosmopolitan civic code (*Weltbürgerrecht*) is "not fantastic or overstrained," but is rather a "necessary complement to the unwritten code of domestic and international law, transforming it into a publicly sanctioned code of humanity (*öffentliches Menschenrecht*)." Under the pressure of this global or cosmopolitan code the traditional anarchy of states is subtly being trans-formed, in the sense that "states find themselves compelled to promote the noble cause of peace, though not exactly from motives of morality." And Kant adds: "While the likelihood of its being attained is not sufficient to enable us to *prophesy* the future theoretically, it is enough for practical pur-poses. It makes it our duty to work our way towards this goal, which is more than an empty chimera."[20]

More than two centuries have passed since Kant wrote these famous lines. Although we may still be stirred by, and drawn to, his eloquent plea for global peace, we can hardly ignore the distance separating us from his time. This distance is not only temporal, but also political, cultural, and lin-guistic. Contemporary advocates of "cosmopolitan democracy" tend to favor a more lively and vibrant type of democracy than seems compatible with Kant's somewhat pale, law-focused republicanism. Thus, Anthony Gid-dens's call for a "democratization of democracy" and even for a "democracy of the emotions" does not resonate too well with Kant's more reticent sen-sibilities. Closely connected with this aspect is the commitment of today's cosmopolitan democrats to a strong version of cultural pluralism, a commit-ment straining against and probably transgressing the confines of Kantian proceduralism. In our age of globalization, such democrats have to welcome a much greater range and depth of cultural diversity than would have been accessible (or congenial) to the philosopher of Königsberg. Cultural diver-sity carries over into the domain of language—where Kant's philosophical discourse can no longer be taken as universal standard but has to compete with a great variety of philosophical idioms and languages. A case in point is the very notion of "cosmopolis" or "cosmopolitanism." Can we be sure that members of different cultures share similar or compatible meanings of "cosmos"? We are reasonably certain that they hold sharply divergent views regarding "polis" and politics. In one of his recent writings devoted precisely to the issue of (Kantian or post-Kantian) cosmopolitanism, Jacques Derrida has ably pinpointed the dilemmas of language in a globalizing world. In conclusion, here are some of his comments:

> If the extension—most often hegemonic—of such and such a language operating in nearly all-powerful fashion (say English) can serve as the vehicle of philosophical universalism and of general philosophical communication, then philosophy demands at the same time and by the same token that one liberates oneself from aspects of dogmatism and authoritarianism which that language can produce. The point is not to exempt philosophy from language and a particular idiom. The goal is not to promote an abstractly universal philosophy devoid of idiomatic embodiment, but *on the contrary*: to put philosophy to work in an infinite multiplicity of idioms, thereby promoting modes of philosophizing which are neither particularistic and untranslatable nor abstractly transparent and univocal with an aura of bland universality.[21]

Notes

1. Immanuel Kant, "Idee zu einer allgemeinen Geschichte in weltbürgerlicher Absicht," in *Ausgewählte kleine Schriften* (Leipzig: Meiner, 1914), 23–38. For an English translation see Hans Reiss, ed., *Kant's Political Writings*, trans. H. B. Nisbet (Cambridge: Cambridge University Press, 1970), 41–53 (in the above, that translation is slightly altered).

2. For Kant's awareness of this fact see "Idee," 29–38; and *Kant's Political Writings*, 46–48.

3. Although politically understandable, the retreat into cultural "relativism" or ethnocentrism is self-defeating, as it robs oppressed and marginalized people of their claim to justice and equity.

4. An example here is the work of Martin Wight who distinguished between "realists" and "rationalists" (or abstract idealists), adding the further category of bottom-up "revolutionists." See Martin Wight, in *International Theory: The Three Traditions*, ed. Gabriele Wight and Brian Porter (New York: Holmes & Meier, 1992), especially: "The Realists are those who emphasize and concentrate upon the element of international anarchy, the Rationalists those who emphasize and concentrate on the element of international [legal] intercourse, and the Revolutionists are those who emphasize and concentrate upon the element of the society of states or international society" (7). Regarding the history of global or cosmopolitan projects compare S. J. Hemleben, *Plans for World Peace through Six Centuries* (Chicago: University of Chicago Press, 1943); and F. H. Hinsley, *Power and the Pursuit of Peace* (Cambridge: Cambridge University Press, 1963).

5. Stephen Toulmin, *Cosmopolis: The Hidden Agenda of Modernity* (New York: Free Press, 1992), 1, 3, 203, 206. Compare also Timothy Brennan, *At Home in the World: Cosmopolitanism Now* (Cambridge, Mass.: Harvard University Press, 1997); Pheng Cheah and Bruce Robbins, eds., *Cosmopolitics: Thinking and Feeling Beyond the Nation* (Minneapolis, Minn.: University of Minnesota Press, 1998).

6. Francis Fukuyama, *The End of History and the Last Man* (New York: Free Press, 1992), ix–x.

7. See Kenichi Ohmae, *The Borderless World: Power and Strategy in the Interlinked Economy* (New York: Harper, 1990); and Lowell Bryan and Diana Farrell, *Market Unbound: Unleashing Global Capitalism* (New York: John Wiley, 1996).

8. See "Editors' Introduction," in Daniele Archibugi and David Held, eds., *Cosmopolitan Democracy: An Agenda for a New World Order* (Cambridge, UK: Polity Press, 1995), 13; and David Held, "Democracy and the New International Order," in the same volume, 106. In his essay, Held explicitly criticizes Fukuyama for his triumphalism and his notion that "contemporary [liberal] democracy is the final and good political order" (97). Compare also Held, *Democracy and the Global Order: From the Modern State to Cosmopolitan Governance* (Cambridge, UK: Polity Press, 1995), and Held, ed., *Prospects for Democracy: North, South, East, West* (Cambridge, UK: Polity Press, 1993). For critiques of the shortcomings of Western liberal democracy see Michael J. Sandel, *Democracy's Discontent* (Cambridge, Mass.: Harvard University Press, 1996); C. B. Macpherson, *The Life and Times of Liberal Democracy* (Oxford: Oxford University Press, 1977); Peter Bachrach, *The Theory of Democratic Elitism: A Critique* (Boston: Little, Brown, 1967).

9. Samuel Huntington, "The Clash of Civilizations?" *Foreign Affairs*, vol. 72 (Summer 1993), 26, 35, 39. See also Huntington, *The Clash of Civilizations and the Remaking of World Order* (New York: Simon & Schuster, 1996).

10. Edward W. Said, *Culture and Imperialism* (New York: Knopf, 1993), 282, 291, 311, 319. Critiquing the temptation of "nativism" or cultural essentialism, he adds, "The Muslims or Africans or Indians or Japanese, in their idioms and from within their own threatened localities, attack the West, or Americanization, or imperialism, with little more attention to detail, critical differentiation, discrimination, and distinction than has been lavished on them by the West. . . . This is an ultimately senseless dynamic" (311). Compare also Anthony Smith, *The Geopolitics of Information: How Western Culture Dominates the World* (New York: Oxford University Press, 1980); and John Tomlinson, *Cultural Imperialism: A Critical Introduction* (Baltimore, Md.: John Hopkins University Press, 1991).

11. Immanuel Wallerstein, *Geopolitics and Geoculture: Essays on the Changing World-System* (Cambridge: Cambridge University Press, 1991), 158, 189, 193–94, 216–30. See also Giovanni Arrighi, Terence K. Hopkins, and Immanuel Wallerstein, *Antisystemic Movements* (London and New York: Verso, 1989); and Clifford Geertz, *The Interpretation of Cultures: Selected Essays* (New York: Basic Books, 1973).

12. Chandra Muzaffer, *Human Rights and the World Order* (Penang: Just World Trust, 1993), 15, 23–24. Compare also Muzaffer, ed., *Human Wrongs: Reflections on Western Global Dominance and Its Impact upon Human Rights* (Penang: Just World Trust, 1996); and Mike Featherstone, ed., *Global Culture: Nationalism, Globalization and Modernity* (Newbury Park, Calif.: Sage, 1990).

13. See his "Introduction" to Tu Weiming, ed., *Confucian Traditions in East Asian Modernity* (Cambridge, Mass: Harvard University Press, 1996), 7, 9; also his "Epilogue" to Wm. Theodore de Bary and Tu Weiming, eds., *Confucianism and Human Rights* (New York: Columbia University Press, 1998), 300, 303.

14. See Held, "Democracy and the New International Order," in *Cosmopolitan Democracy*, ed. Archibugi and Held, 115–16; and Archibugi, "From the United Nations to Cosmopolitan Democracy," in the same volume, 133. For Archibugi, a further reason for the undesirability of a world state is the "massive concentration of force" likely to accompany such a state.

15. Richard Falk, "The World Order between Inter-State Law and the Law of Humanity: The Role of Civil Society Institutions," in Archibugi and Held, eds., *Cosmopolitan Democracy*, 170–71. As Falk adds candidly, "The law of humanity is associated with the future; it is more a matter of potentiality than of history or experience. . . . Its formal reality has been established through the primary agency of states and qualifies as a domain of inter-state law. But the historical potency of the international law of human rights is predominantly a consequence of its implementation through the agency of civil society" (163). Compare also Falk, *Predatory Globalization: A Critique* (Cambridge, UK: Polity Press, 1999); *On Humane Governance: Towards a New Global Politics* (Cambridge, UK: Polity Press, 1995); and his "Cultural Foundations for the International Protection of Human Rights," in Abdullahi Ahmed An-Na'im, ed., *Human Rights in Cross-Cultural Perspectives: A Quest for Consensus* (Philadelphia: University of Pennsylvania Press, 1992), 59, where he writes, "Human rights, cultural renewal, and participatory democracy are implicated, for better or worse, in a common destiny."

16. Falk, "The World Order," 164, 168–69.

17. Falk, "The World Order," 175–79. See also Falk, S. Kim, and Saul Mendlovitz, eds., *The United Nations and a Just World Order* (Boulder, Colo.: Westview, 1991); J. W. Müller, ed., *The Reform of the United Nations*, 2 vols. (New York: Oceania, 1992); Boutros Boutros-Ghali, *An Agenda for Peace* (New York: United Nations, 1992).

18. Archibugi, "From the United Nations to Cosmopolitan Democracy," 137–58; Held, "Democracy and the New International Order," 111–12.

19. Elise Boulding, *Building a Global Civic Culture: Education for an Interdependent World* (Syracuse, N.Y.: Syracuse University Press, 1990), xix–xx, 35, 163–64. Compare also Boulding, *The Underside of History: A View of Women through Time* (Boulder, Colo.: Westview, 1976); and *Women: The Fifth World* (New York: Foreign Policy Association, 1980). Boulding's plea for a global civic culture has in the meantime been endorsed by many other writers, including prominently Anthony Giddens in his *Runaway World: How Globilization is Reshaping Our Lives* (New York: Routledge, 2000), 95–96.

20. See Kant, "Perpetual Peace: A Philosophical Sketch," in Reiss, ed., *Kant's Political Writings*, 107–8, 114 (translation slightly altered).

21. Jacques Derrida, *Le droit à la philosophie du point de vue cosmopolitique* (Paris: Editions UNESCO, 1997), 37–38. The task for Derrida is not to forget but to rethink Kant's teaching in a manner moving beyond the "old and tiresome opposition between Eurocentrism and anti-Eurocentrism" (31). See also his *Cosmopolites de tous les pays, encore un effort!* (Paris: Galilée, 1997).

CHAPTER THREE

~

"Asian Values" and Global Human Rights: Tensions and Convergences

"Human rights" today is a global agenda. While previously functioning as part of broader political ideologies (say, progressive liberalism), human rights in our time operate as an autonomous ideology or global program— equipped with its advocates and missionaries, and also its detractors. As history teaches, the status of missionaries is always ambivalent, because one can distinguish between the quality of the message and the role of the messenger. While the message may be intrinsically sound, the *modus operandi* of the messenger may be suspect or obnoxious. Thus, to take a very egregious example, the Christian gospel may announce "good news" to the world, but the manner in which Christianity was extended into the New World, by Spanish missionaries and soldiers, was surely bad news for the Indians. It is estimated that, in the course of less than a century, the European excursion into the Americas resulted in the deaths of some 70 million native inhabitants, victims of killing, starvation, and disease.[1] A later historical example is the spreading of French revolutionary ideas throughout Europe by Napoleon's armies. If nothing else, historical examples of this kind are a summons to caution. In our time, advocates of human rights are typically (though not always) citizens and emissaries of the "West"; and one does not have to be a student of Noam Chomsky to realize that the West has amassed the most formidable arsenal of military, economic, and technological power—a fact that buttresses talk of global hegemony. In this situation, the distinction between message and messenger becomes relevant again. On the whole, one would hope for fewer messengers who are zealots and for more self-critical, reflectively engaged individuals; differently phrased, one would wish for fewer Sepúlvedas, and more of the likes of Las Casas.[2]

The name of Las Casas evokes again the message of "good news." Basically, human rights are meant to be good news for the underprivileged, the downtrodden, and the dispossessed. As one can show, this has historically been the function of human rights—from the assertion of baronial rights against kings in *Magna Carta* to the proclamation of citizen rights against feudal absolutism in the French Revolution to the demand for social and economic rights in the era of industrial capitalism. Thus, rights were always meant to be a protective shield of the weak against the mighty. However, detached from their historical and social contexts, rights (taken abstractly) have a double-edged status; they can also serve as weapons of aggression and domination in the hands of the powerful. The baronial rights against the king can turn into privileges asserted against peasants and serfs; the revolutionary rights of citizenship can deteriorate into weapons of exclusion wielded against foreigners and strangers. In our own time, the property rights claimed by a few, immensely wealthy individuals or corporations can serve as instruments to keep the vast masses of humankind in misery and in (economic as well as political) subjugation. Here is an illustration of the complex and deeply conflictual relation between West and non-West, North and South in our current world.[3] Generally speaking, rights-claims should always give rise to questions like these: Whose rights (or liberties) are asserted, against whom, and in what concrete context? Do rights-claims advance the cause of justice, equity, and human well-being, or are they obstacles on this road? Basically, all these questions boil down to the simple query: Are rights rightly claimed, or what is the "rightness" of rights (a query that is etymologically inscribed in the connection between *ius* and *iustitia* and in the subjective and objective senses of the German *Recht*)?

What these considerations indicate is that rights are in a certain sense contextual—which does not necessarily vitiate their universality. To ward off governmental manipulation, rights are often claimed to be universal and absolute—which, though correct in this usage, is otherwise equivocal. Property rights, for instance, may very well be universal claims, but this leaves untouched questions of the amount of property and the rightness of its exercise. In Hegelian language, rights may well be rational "ideas," but their enactment "stands in the world" and, as such, calls for situated judgment regarding justice and equity. To counter claims of universality—most often advanced by Western intellectuals indebted to the Enlightenment legacy—critics frequently assert the purely ethnocentric character of "rights-talk" and hence its function as a mere tool of Western global hegemony.

Most prominent among the critics of Western-style universality today are the proponents of so-called Asian values and Islamic values. Sometimes, under conditions of extreme provocation, such proponents allow themselves to be lured into the counterposition of "cultural relativism"—which is a bad bargain. For, on the assumption of radical relativism, what moral grounds would the critics have to challenge the sway of Western hegemony? How could they challenge the infliction of "wrongness" if "wrong" is merely a contingent choice? This chapter focuses on the issue of universality in reference specifically to the challenge or contestation coming from the side of Asian values:

1. The first section will examine the status of rights and their presumed universality in general terms.
2. The second part probes more particularly the issue of the universality or nonuniversality of Asian values.
3. In conclusion, an effort will be made to draw some lessons from this inquiry both for contemporary rights-discourse and global politics.

Universalism versus Relativism

Given its status as a global agenda, human-rights talk surely merits and calls for philosophical scrutiny. Are human rights permanent or "transcendental" endowments or are they revocable gifts? In fashionable contemporary language: do rights have "foundational" status or are they merely arbitrary fictions (perhaps comforting illusions)? Such questions, to be sure, are not novel discoveries but have exercised human ingenuity for many centuries. To anchor rights more securely, many prominent thinkers (especially in the West) have attempted to ground them alternatively in human "nature," in human "reason," or in a divinely sanctioned "spirit" or spirituality. Despite their captivating universal zeal, all these attempts are unfortunately marred by drawbacks. If the first option is chosen, one can legitimately ask how "nature," as a causal nexus, can function as the source of moral or legal titles. (In the philosophy of Thomas Hobbes, nature was depicted as granting to human beings a "right to everything"—which in the end turned out to be a right to nothing). If the accent is placed on unaided human "reason," rights can quickly deteriorate into discriminatory weapons of exclusion—against the unrational, the barbarians (not to speak of "brute" nature). If, finally, the focus is shifted to a divinely created spirit or spirituality, the question can hardly be suppressed whether God as omnipotent creator cannot also omnipotently withdraw or cancel the benefit of rights (for example, on account of guilt or evil-doing). No doubt, all these drawbacks can be subject to further cross-questioning, and much philosophical labor has been devoted to these issues—but without resulting in the secure establishment of a justificatory solution.

In our time, the search for foundations is continued by "natural law" philosophers, but also—and perhaps more incisively—by some proponents of analytical philosophy. Thus, Alan Gewirth has attempted to provide a strictly conceptual-deductive grounding by deducing human rights from the very concept of human "action" or "agency." As he writes, human rights are entitlements to "the necessary conditions of human action," that is, to those conditions that "must be fulfilled if human action is to be possible either at all or with general chances of success in achieving the purposes for which humans act"—these purposes being chiefly freedom and well-being. For Gewirth, action or agency supplies the "metaphysical and moral basis" of human dignity and personhood—thus providing human rights with a kind of self-grounding; as a corollary, the latter might also be termed "natural rights" in that they pertain to human beings simply in their capacity as actors or agents.[4] Despite its apparent logical tightness, however, several quandaries beset this conceptual scheme.

One qualm concerns the move from logic to morality, from internal consistency to obligation (what has been termed the "naturalistic fallacy"). More important is another point: Because (as Gewirth recognizes) the exercise of rights always involves claims against others, their grounding would have to be sought not in singular action as such but in human interactions (which are always concretely situated and not logically deducible). Aware of the difficulties involved in "foundational" arguments, many contemporary proponents of human rights modestly "fudge" or circumvent the task of ultimate justification—while continuing to uphold the requirement of an absolute-universal grounding. Thus, Jack Donnelly, a leading expert in this field, bluntly disclaims that human rights can be derived from "God, nature, or the physical facts of life"; instead, they are said to be grounded in "man's *moral* nature," in the need for "human dignity," and hence to reflect the choice of "a particular vision of human potentiality." Although admitting the role of social-historical contexts, Donnelly insists (with Gewirth) that rights are anchored in "the person and his or her inherent dignity" and thus establish "the social conditions necessary for the effective enjoyment of moral personality." Social context in this view appears basically as an external constraint arising from "the limitations, peculiarities and advances" of prevailing anthropologies—while "the universality of claims of human rights reflects their source in human nature."[5]

As indicated before, attempts at a "natural grounding" of rights have always been met with skepsis, if not outright denial. Apart from other iconoclastic pronouncements, Jeremy Bentham is remembered for having famously denounced the idea of natural rights as "nonsense on stilts." In our contemporary setting, grounding efforts are most prominently debunked by deconstructionists and deconstructive pragmatists; among the latter, no one has been more eloquent and stinging in his rebuke than Richard Rorty. For Rorty, attempts at ultimate justification are basically misguided and possibly obnoxious. In their theoretical structure, attempts of this kind are anchored in knowledge claims that can be traced to Plato and his successors. "Foundationalist philosophers, such as Plato, Aquinas, and Kant," he writes, "have hoped to provide independent support for such summarizing generalizations" as the notion of human endowments, and they tried to infer these generalizations from further premises—all of which can be summed up under the label "claims to knowledge about the nature of human beings." In the wake of Nietzsche's and Dewey's writings, however, the latter claims have become implausible.

In Rorty's view, there is today "a growing willingness to neglect the question 'What is our nature?' and to substitute the question 'What can we make of ourselves?'" Basically, what recent (especially pragmatist) philosophy has disclosed is "our extraordinary malleability," the fact that we are a "flexible, protean, self-shaping animal" rather than the rational animal dear to traditional thought. With this insight, "human rights foundationalism" is simply "*outmoded*," making room instead for cultural constructivism. In line with the Argentinian jurist Eduardo Rabossi, Rorty agrees that Western culture has recently adopted the shape of a "human rights culture," made possible by economic and technological progress. One should note that Rorty is quite willing to defend this culture, and even its superiority over other alternatives—but he does so on purely ethnocentric or culture-specific, and not foundationalist grounds:

> I quite agree that ours [Western culture] is morally superior, but I do not think this superiority counts in favor of the existence of a universal human nature. . . . We see our task as a matter of making our own culture—the human rights culture—more self-conscious and more powerful, rather than of demonstrating its superiority to other cultures by an appeal to something transcultural.[6]

As matters stand, the debate about the universality of human rights is impaled on the sketched dilemma, and is likely to remain so for some time to come. What both foundationalists and antifoundationalists (both proponents of universal grounding and of contextual relativism) ignore or bypass is the question of "rightness," that is, the question (alluded to earlier) of whether and how rights-claims advance or thwart the cause of justice—which intrinsically involves social relationships. For foundationalists, rights are anchored in an invariant human "nature," "reason," or spiritual "dignity," with social relationships (and their justice/injustice) being irrelevant or at best marginal to their conceptual definition. For antifoundationalists, on the other hand, rights are historically and contextually contingent or else willfully constructed or fabricated—an approach leaving the justice of social relations unaccounted for or suspended in mid-air. Taking seriously the social character of human rights—the fact that human beings are basically social or "political" creatures (in Aristotle's sense)—rescues rights from the grip of abstractly universal fictions, while also redeeming them from contingent willfulness.

As one should note, the privileging of social rightness (or ethical "goodness") does not by itself cancel universal aspirations. On the contrary, precisely because of their social embeddedness, justice and the proper (right) exercise of rights are perennial issues in all human societies. To be sure, with this shift of focus, the meaning of universality is subtly transformed from a necessary precondition to a goal or horizon (*entelechy*), or from a premise to a promise. What this transformation entails is that, far from being rooted in a pre-given human nature, rightness and rights are corollaries of a laborious practice: the ongoing practice of "humanization," that is, the steady cultivation of the sense of justice and fair-mindedness (traditionally called "virtues"). Seen as a social practice, humanization cannot be a purely individual or monological achievement, but requires interaction, collaboration and appropriate institutional arrangements; depending on the character of these arrangements, rightness may be furthered and strengthened or else obstructed and derailed.[7]

The shift of focus affects human rights also in another sense by transforming their globally universal scope or the global character of universality. From the perspective of humanization, globalism cannot be taken as a ready-made premise or *fait accompli*, but again only as part of a difficult practice—more precisely, an ongoing learning experience involving the participation and collaboration of diverse cultures around the world. In turn, such a learning experience presupposes attentiveness to different, possibly alien teachings and a willingness to review and possibly revise one's own predilections—a disposition that cannot be a one-way street but demands multilateral engagement. On this score again, both foundationalism and antifoundationalism are glaringly deficient. By assuming a uniform human nature—the sameness of human identity—prior to and outside all social interactions, foundationalists see no need to enter into the travail of a learning process; since everything is already presupposed or known, nothing further needs to be looked for. On the other hand, by regarding cultures as self-enclosed systems or language games, deconstructive contextualists are bound to treat learning across borders either as impossible or else as (disguised) strategies of colonization.

Thus, in celebrating "our human rights culture," Rorty is willing to affirm its "superiority" and its qualification as a possible article of export—but without any readiness to face "otherness" or the risk of a possibly transforming and disorienting learning experience. Still, Rorty's candor may yet be preferable to the haughty disdain for otherness (meaning non-Western cultures) often displayed by foundationalists and quasifoundationalists. A case in point is the attitude of Donnelly toward "Asian values." Although willing to acknowledge something valuable in Chinese traditions, Donnelly basically stresses the need for a one-way learning process—namely, by contemporary China from "our human rights culture." As he writes, despite its ancient standing, the Chinese system of values and social relations is "incompatible with the vision of equal and autonomous individuals that underlies international human rights norms. In fact, the 'Western' emphasis on individual rights is likely to seem little short of moral inversion." Adopting the authoritative tone of an emissary, he adds, "Sovereignty, development, and traditional conceptions of social order do not absolve Asian governments from the requirements to implement internationally recognized human rights."[8]

The Question of "Asian Values"

When moving from human rights to the theme of "Asian values," it seems advisable to proceed with caution. First of all, considered geographically, "Asia" is a vast continent comprising a multitude of different cultural strands. Conventionally, it is true, the term *Asian values* has been linked chiefly with Confucian teachings, with Buddhist and Taoist legacies being treated more like variations on, or internal reactions to, the former; still, to avoid oversimplification, same awareness of diversity should be maintained. More important, the term is sometimes invoked in a starkly provocative manner, with the result that "Asian values" and human rights are pitted against each other as antithetical or incommensurable spheres. As previously indicated, however, this battle of relativisms—"Asian" versus "Western" types of ethnocentrism—is ultimately self-defeating; on the assumption of radical antithesis, mutual critique becomes pointless (or else a means of strategic harassment).

Yet, caution is required on this point as well. The rejection of antithesis does not necessarily vindicate the doctrine of a smooth synthesis or harmony, predicated on the notion that "Asian" values and "Western" human rights are simply slight modifications of a common theme or different stages on the same evolutionary trajectory. Thus, Louis Henkin's assertion that "Asian values" (meaning Confucian values) "are universal values too" can probably be accepted only with many provisos and caveats. On the whole, it seems preferable as well as prudent to accept Henry Rosemont's argument in favor of the need to distinguish between different (though non-antithetical) moral paradigms or language games, which he terms "concept clusters," and the further need to juxtapose such moral clusters to the domain of "ethics" understood as a mode of preconceptual lived experience (or a mode of "goodness" antedating "rights"). As he observes, the term *ethics* refers basically to human praxis and the "evaluation of human conduct" on a practical level, while "morals" or "morality" denotes a theory of principles and axioms—characteristic chiefly of modern Western philosophy.[9]

Based on these distinctions, Rosemont perceives modern human-rights discourse as a distinctive "concept cluster"—a cluster attractive and meritorious in many ways, but also subject to severe limitations. Moving on to the Asian context, a curious dilemma emerges; classical Chinese language (used by early Confucians) lacked most of the terms constitutive of modern rights-talk. In Rosemont's presentation, that language not only had no lexical item for *moral*; it also had no equivalents for such terms as *freedom, liberty, autonomy, individual, utility, principles, rationality, rational agent, action, objective, subjective, choice, dilemma, duty,* or *rights.* Now, if these items are viewed as key terms in moral theorizing, one might conclude that classical Confucianism offered no relevant moral or ethical teachings at all—a conclusion that seems preposterous and an obstacle to cross-cultural learning. Actually, all one can legitimately infer is that classical Confucians were not "moral philosophers in our sense," and correspondingly, that modern Western rights-talk is one among several ways or options of moral theorizing—an option eminently appropriate for modern liberal individualism but inappropriate and debilitating in many other respects:

> I maintain that the concept cluster of early Confucian ethics is very different indeed from the concept cluster of contemporary Western moral philosophy. . . . The most fundamental challenge raised by early Confucian ethics is that contemporary moral philosophy has become increasingly irrelevant to concrete ethical concerns, utilizing an impoverished—and largely bureaucratic—technical vocabulary emphasizing law, abstract logic, and the formation of policy statements. Contemporary moral philosophy, the Confucian texts suggest, is no longer grounded in the real hopes, fears, joys, sorrows, ideas, and attitudes of flesh-and-blood human beings.[10]

In Rosemont's account, early Confucianism offers precisely an antidote to modern rational abstractions by focusing attention on concrete human experiences in the ordinary life-world. In contrast to the "unencumbered" individualism celebrated in Western modernity, classical Confucians were concerned with the "qualities of persons" and with "the kinds of persons who have or do not have these qualities"; where modern morality invokes "abstract principles," they invoked "concrete roles and attitudes toward these roles." Most important, classical texts had a different view of what it means to be human; shunning the fiction of isolated monads inhabiting a presocial "state of nature," they depicted human beings as necessarily (and not just accidentally) engaged in social contexts and as exhibiting their "nature" not in singular desires or volitions but in "human interactions" and patterns of shared responsiveness. Rosemont's comments on this point are thoroughly grounded in the Confucian notion of "humaneness" (jen) according to which individuals acquire their properly human status only through a difficult process of "humanization" involving the cultivation of qualities required for "rightful" interactions (or interactions guided by "rightness," li).

This linkage between humaneness and humanization has been most eloquently stressed by Tu Weiming in several of his writings. As he notes in his book *Humanity and Self-Cultivation*, humaneness or "being human" is not simply a static essence or fixed premise, but rather denotes a practical performance or achievement, a process of "learning to be human" that is a life-long undertaking. As part of this process, "self-cultivation" does not refer to private self-indulgence or egocentrism, but rather to a nurturing of self in relationships, particularly in the relations of family, society, state, and global community. As Tu emphasizes, moreover, humanization for Confucians was not limited to "mundane" settings, but had a self-transcending or transgressive quality, extending ultimately (in the classical formula) to "Heaven, Earth, and the myriad things." This transgressive aspect is stressed also in one of Tu's more recent writings where we read that "the move toward the unity of Heaven and humanity" challenges every self-enclosure, and especially the "blatant form of anthropocentrism characteristic of the intellectual ethos of the modern West." In lieu of this ethos, Confucianism sponsors an "anthropocosmic" outlook anchored in "communication between self and community, harmony between human species and nature, and mutuality between humanity and Heaven."[11]

By accentuating human embeddedness in multiple relationships, Confucianism—in the eyes of its critics—runs the risk of fostering conventionalism, if not abject conformism; by asserting the constitutive character of contexts, its teachings are accused of denying selfhood, or else of reducing selves to so-cial functionaries and pliant tools. Responding to these charges, Roger Ames has introduced a number of important pointers and clarifications—pointers having to do ultimately with the issue of paradigm shifts or the move between different "concept clusters." As Ames emphasizes, the relation between West-ern modernity and Confucianism should not be construed in a binary or anti-thetical fashion, with the result that the former would celebrate "unencum-bered" individuals and the latter social or societal "encumbrances," thus pitting autonomy versus heteronomy. What is required, instead, for an under-standing of Confucianism is a rupture of these binary schemes and a willing-ness to contemplate a different self–other relation. In Ames's words, many commentaries on classical Chinese texts have privileged social duties over selfhood or "humaneness," to the point of affirming a kind of self-erasure or total self-submission, which is nothing but an "echo of Hegel's 'hollow men' interpretation of Chinese culture." However, attributing such self-erasure to the Chinese tradition simply "sneaks both the public/private and individual/society distinction in by the back door," vitiating the Chinese notion of self-hood or personhood, which is neither a monadic ego nor a mere social func-tion or construct. What Western critics of Confucianism often have in mind is the "contest between state and individual that has separated liberal demo-cratic and collectivist thinkers" in our century but has "only limited applica-bility" to the Chinese model. For, in the latter, self-realization requires "nei-ther a high degree of individual autonomy nor capitulation to the general will"; rather, it involves "benefiting and being benefited by membership in a world of reciprocal loyalties and obligations."[12]

These considerations—with their emphasis on different "concept clus-ters"—have clear implications for the relation between "Asian values" and human rights, and especially for the issue of moral "universality" or univer-salism. Reacting against charges of parochialism or ethnocentrism, defenders of Confucian ethics often are led to assert the universal sweep of classical teachings—a sweep congruent and on a par with the universality claimed by Western human-rights discourse. Louis Henkin's phrase (previously quoted) that Asian or Confucian values "are universal values, too" points in this di-rection. Yet, clearly, there are different types of universality and different modes of universalizing experience. Here again, Roger Ames offers some helpful guidance by differentiating between "top-down" and "bottom-up" forms of moral discourse.

As he writes, modern moral philosophy (in the West) starts basically from universal axioms or principles and then proceeds to subsume particular situ-ations under the former. By contrast, classical Confucianism focuses first of all on immediate life-contexts and then expands its concerns outward in steadily widening concentric circles. Ethics in the classical tradition is "a cultural product that derives from the ethos or character of the society and is embodied in its ritual patterns of conduct" (that is, in rightness or *li*). This approach is evident in the Confucian doctrine of "graduated love" centered on the family, a doctrine predicated on "the priority of the immediate and concrete over universal principles and ideals." The same approach also is manifest in the traditional Chinese distrust of formal legal procedures in favor of face-to-face interactions. Contrary to Western allegations of social conformism, the "bottom-up emergent order" sanctioned by Confucianism actually provides "an internal check on totalitarianism." As Ames adds,

> Given that order is defined from the bottom up, and concrete conditions temper generalizations to yield varying degrees of appropriateness, the notion of universalizability is certainly problematic. In fact, the Chinese have approached doctrines of *universals* with the caution of a culture fundamentally reluctant to leave the security of immediate experience for the more tentative reaches of transcendent principles.[13]

Ames's comments probably should not be read as a simple rejection of universality, equaling a retreat into parochialism. Congruent with his critique of binary (self-versus-society) schemes, his observations should more plausibly be taken as a salutary reminder cautioning against univocal construals of universality, a reminder making room for diverse configurations of the universal/ particular nexus. Ultimately, what this reminder brings into view is not some radical incommensurability, but rather the hazards and dilemmas involved in the assumption of a smooth synthesis or fusion of cultural perspectives. Against this background, struggling against relativism and ethnocentrism can only mean entering into a sustained, perhaps agonal dialogue in which differences of "clusters" are acknowledged from the start and where all participants are willing to undergo a mutual learning experience without necessarily expecting a final synthesis.

The importance of mutual learning is strongly underscored by Tu Weiming when he exhorts both human-rights proponents and defenders of Confucianism to accept reciprocal challenges. As it happens, he writes, the Confucian personality ideals may perhaps "be realized more fully in the liberal-democratic society than either in the traditional imperial dictatorship or a modern authoritarian regime." On the other hand, beneficiaries of Western individual rights might do well to recognize how "our human-rights culture" has been corrupted by "excessive individualism," "vicious litigiousness," and related ills. Only this willingness to learn can provide the space for a

genuine global moral discourse, that is, for a rights-discourse fitting our globalizing age. Although of a more skeptical temper, Henry Rosemont likewise
sees the only chance for contemporary rights-talk in a genuinely global discussion and contestation. If we do not wish to abandon our responsibilities,
he states, if instead we wish

> to seek new perspectives that might enable [philosophy] to become as truly all-
> encompassing in the future as it has mistakenly been assumed to have been in the
> past, we must begin to develop a more international philosophical language which
> incorporates the insights of all of the worldwide historical traditions of thinkers
> who addressed the questions of who and what we are, and why and how we should
> lead our all-too-human lives.[14]

Rights: An Entangled Web

The discussion of "Asian values" and their universal/particular status throws
into relief the broader question of the universality of rights in general. As one
should note, Western liberal rights-discourse is challenged today not only
from the Asian-Confucian side but also from the side of Islamic values and,
more broadly, from the angle of traditional and indigenous cultures around
the world. The situation is further complicated by claims advanced on the
part of socially and economically disadvantaged or exploited groups sidelined
by the advances of global capitalism and technology. In the literature on human rights, it is customary to distinguish among three "generations" of rights:
first, civil and political rights (anchored in modern Western individualism);
next, social and economic rights (sponsored chiefly by socialist movements);
and finally, cultural and collective rights (championed mainly by non-
Western and indigenous peoples). A basic question here concerns the interrelation of these different rights-claims. Paralleling the equation of Asian
and universal rights, some commentators perceive an easy synthesis or sym-
biosis of the three generations patterned on familial harmony. Thus, commenting on the issue, Sumner Twiss remarks somewhat placidly that the "international human rights community" recognizes and accepts "all three
generations or types of human rights as important and interrelated and need-
ing to be pursued in a constructive balance or harmony." Although in a given
situation "one or another generation may merit special emphasis," there is no
possible dilemma because the three generations are "indivisible."[15]

Despite its emotive appeal or attractiveness, this vision of harmony stands
in need of corrective criticism. As in the confrontation between "Asian values" and Western universality, the three generations of rights are not simply

variations on one common denominator ("human rights") but should be seen again as distinct "concept clusters," which, although partially overlapping, are embroiled in critical dialogue and mutual contestation. Thus, the cluster of civil and political rights is not simply continuous or smoothly compatible with the cluster of social and economic rights—as is demonstrated by the hegemonic position of the former in Western human-rights discourse (especially after the so-called defeat of socialism/communism and the marginalization of the labor movement). In a similar, and even aggravated way, individual civil rights are often in conflict with the preservation of cultural and collective claims—as is evident in the havoc frequently wrought by individual and corporate property rights in non-Western "developing" societies and especially among indigenous peoples. On this score, the clusters of socioeconomic and of collective-cultural rights tendentially merge or coalesce in that both share the brunt of hegemonic global agendas.

The conflictual character of modern rights-discourse is eloquently highlighted by Rosemont when he calls that discourse a "bill of worries." In Rosemont's account, there is no smooth way of simply "extending" individual rights into the social and economic domain, because the realization of "second generation" rights (such as adequate housing and health care) typically requires a curtailment of "first generation" rights (chiefly private property). Hence, belief in a ready-made synthesis of rights-claims is "more an article of faith" than based on plausible arguments. Worries further intensify once attention is shifted to "third generation" rights, that is, to the defense of cultures, indigenous peoples, and ecological resources (where the very concept of "rights" becomes dubious or problematical). In light of the troubles afflicting Western society (and its hegemonic discourse), Rosemont recommends caution and critical contestation. Given prevailing social and existential dilemmas, he writes,

> how can Americans justify insisting—by diplomatic, military, economic, or other means—that every other society adopt the moral and political vocabulary of rights? . . . The questions become painful to contemplate when we face the reality that the United States is the wealthiest society in the world, yet after over two hundred years of human-rights talk, many of its human citizens have no shelter, a fifth of them have no access to health care, a fourth of its children are growing up in poverty, and the richest two percent of its peoples own and control over fifty percent of its wealth.[16]

At this juncture, it seems advisable to recall some points made at the beginning of this chapter: namely, that rights traditionally have been protective shields of the underprivileged and oppressed, and that the concrete enactment of rights needs to be assessed in terms of their justice or rightness. Regarding the diversity of rights-claims, what these points suggest is that social context matters crucially and that, in the contemporary global context, greater attention needs to be given to second and third generation rights than is customary in hegemonic global-rights discourse. One may also usefully recall here Roger Ames's distinction between "top-down" and "bottom-up" modes of universalization and cross-cultural moral argument. This distinction concurs roughly with Richard Falk's opposition (previously invoked) of different types of global governance and citizenship: namely, "globalization from above" and "globalization from below." In Falk's presentation, "globalization from above" denotes basically a strategy of global control carried forward under the auspices of "unleashed" marked forces, international finance capital, and Western-based media and technology; by contrast, "globalization from below" involves reliance on the momentum generated by peoples' movements and aspirations, especially movements in Third and "Fourth" World societies. Paralleling this opposition is a shift of accent in the global human-rights discourse from the near-exclusive concern with "first-generation" rights (focused on individual interests and property claims) to a stronger preoccupation with "second and third generation" rights seen as protective shields of underprivileged social and cultural groups and populations. For Falk, the latter groups include prominently unskilled laborers, women, ethnic minorities, and indigenous peoples. As he writes at one point, "The example of the fate of indigenous peoples as a subordinate culture victimized by a dominant culture suggests the relevance of exclusion and inclusion in evaluating the normative adequacy of human rights as a protective framework at a given time and place."[17]

Falk's views are echoed and corroborated by a number of intellectuals writing from diverse cultural and ethnic perspectives. Thus, in their book *Rethinking Human Rights*, Smitu Kothari and Harsh Sethi criticize the preeminence accorded to legalistic and individualistic conceptions of rights, a preeminence that hides from view the plight and suffering of the vast majority of humankind, including the majority of people in their native India. Against the predominant rights-discourse mired in proceduralism, Kothari and Sethi seek to marshal a human-rights praxis or a "politics of human rights," that is, "a social praxis, rooted in the need of the most oppressed communities, that aims to create shared norms of civilized existence." In attacking hegemonic abuses, both writers extend their critique to oppressive features in Indian culture—*not* with the purpose of negating or erasing Indian cultural traditions, but of recovering in these very traditions resources fostering the advancement of human liberation and social justice (with Gandhi serving as their chief mentor).[18]

In a similar vein, speaking mainly from an Islamic perspective, Chandra Muzaffer challenges both the dominant human-rights discourse allied with Western hegemony *and* unjust or oppressive practices perpetrated by Islamic governments (in violation of the deeper spirit of Islam). As he writes, pointedly, "Though formal colonial rule has ended, Western domination and control continues to impact upon the human rights of the vast majority of the people of the non-Western world in ways which are more subtle and sophisticated but no less destructive and devastating." Faced with the confluence of hegemonic strategies and moral rhetoric, many people in the non-Western world "have become skeptical and critical of the West's posturing on human rights." At the same time, skepsis regarding Western aims cannot serve as an alibi for abusive domestic policies. In Muzaffer's words,

> Some Asian governments . . . have chosen to focus solely upon the adverse consequences of crass individualism upon the moral fabric of Western societies. . . . [But] it is not just the moral crisis of Western society that we lament; we are no less sensitive to the moral decadence within our own societies—especially within our elite strata. If we adhere to a universal spiritual and moral ethic that applies to all human beings, we should not hesitate to condemn the suppression of human rights and the oppression of dissident groups that occur from time to time in a number of our countries. Our commitment to spiritual and moral values, drawn from our religions, should never serve as a camouflage for authoritarian elites who seek to shield their sins from scrutiny.[19]

What the preceding discussion points to, it is important to keep in mind, is not a simple negation of universality or moral universalism, but rather a rethinking of human rights in a direction that gives primacy to considerations of global justice, which in turns sustains rights as a protective shield. Such a rethinking or re-figuration treats universality not as a *fait accompli*, but rather as a hope or yearning; above all, it deprives any given culture—especially Western culture—of pretensions to monopolize universal "truth," placing its trust instead in the difficult process of interactive dialogue potentially enlisting participants around the globe. Given the diversity of cultural perspectives or "clusters," this dialogue is often going to be agonal or conflictual: both domestically and globally threats to the just exercise of rights need to be challenged—though preferably not "from above" (the lectern of an intellectual elite) but "from below" by enlisting the empowering resources of local cultures and practices.

The importance of critical dialogue in the latter sense is vividly underscored by Abdullahi An-Na'im when he insists on the needed concurrence of both "internal" and "cross-cultural" contestation, adding that proponents of critical views are more likely to achieve acceptance of their position "by showing the authenticity and legitimacy of their interpretation within the framework of their own culture." The basic point for An-Na'im is that contemporary human-rights discourse cannot possibly achieve genuine universality unless it is conducted and articulated "within the widest range of cultural traditions"; only by enlisting both intracultural and cross-cultural sensibilities for justice and rightness can a way be found for "enhancing the universal legitimacy of human rights." In this respect, An-Na'im is in agreement with Charles Taylor's reflections on the prospect of a "world consensus on human rights." Pointing to the vast distance between Gewirth's stress on self-actualization and the Buddhist notion of "no-self-nature," Taylor ponders the diversity of views and "concept clusters" that a global human-rights discourse has to mediate or negotiate:

> This perhaps gives us an idea of what an unforced world consensus on human rights might look like. Agreement on [some] norms, yes; but a profound sense of difference, of unfamiliarity, in the ideals, the notions of human excellence, the rhetorical tropes and reference points by which these norms become objects of deep agreement for us. To the extent that we can only acknowledge agreement with people who share the whole package, and are moved by the same heroes, the consensus will never come or must be forced.[20]

Notes

1. See Tzvetan Todorov, *The Conquest of America: The Question of the Other*, trans. Richard Howard (New York: Harper & Row, 1984), 133–37. As Todorov notes, "If the word genocide has ever been applied to a situation with some accuracy, this is here the case" (133).

2. For the confrontation between Gines de Sepúlveda and Bartolomé de las Casas see my *Alternative Visions: Paths in the Global Village* (Lanham, Md.: Rowman & Littlefield, 1998), 71–73. More than two centuries later, when Christianity extended itself into China, a controversy arose over whether Christian dogma should adjust itself to "Asian values," that is, to Chinese language and worldviews. As in the earlier case, the defenders of absolute universalism (Christ's message is the same everywhere and at all times) triumphed. See George Minamiki, *The Chinese Rites Controversy* (Chicago: Loyala University Press, 1985).

3. According to the 1999 UN Report on Human Development, the combined wealth of the world's three richest families is greater than the annual income of 600 million people in the least developed countries. During the last four years, the world's 200 richest people have doubled their wealth to more than $1 trillion; in the same period, the number of people living on less than one dollar a day has remained steady a 1.3 billion. See *South Bend Tribune* (July 12, 1999), A6, and *Human Development Report 1999* (Oxford: Oxford University Press, 1999).

4. Alan Gewirth, *Human Rights: Essays on Justification and Application* (Chicago: University of Chicago Press, 1982), 3–7. Given the status of human rights as necessary conditions of action, their denial in Gewirth's view amounts to self-contradiction.

5. Jack Donnelly, *The Concept of Human Rights* (New York: St. Martin's Press, 1985), 31–32, 35. Donnelly describes his own theory as "constructivist" and "dialectical," which may be terms hiding ambivalence. While holding that "human nature" is in a sense "conventional," he also maintains that his theory is "fundamentally consistent with . . . the classic natural rights tradition," while also being compatible with the approach of Gewirth, *Human Rights* (32, 36). In a more recent study, Donnelly writes more forthrightly (and more foundationally), "The term *human rights* indicates both their nature and their source: they are the rights that one has simply because one is human. They are held by all human beings, irrespective of any rights or duties individuals may (or may not) have as citizens, members of families, workers, or parts of any public or private organization or association. They are universal rights." See Donnelly, *International Human Rights* (Boulder, Colo.: Westview Press, 1998), 18.

6. Richard Rorty, "Human Rights, Rationality, and Sentimentality," in *On Human Rights*, ed. Stephen Shute and Susan Hurley (New York: Basic Books, 1993), 115–17. As Rorty adds, the "best explanation" of Darwin's and Dewey's "relatively easy triumph" over foundationalism is "that the nineteenth and twentieth centuries saw, among Europeans and Americans, an extraordinary increase in wealth, literacy, and leisure. This increase made possible an unprecedented acceleration in the rate of moral progress" (121).

7. In this respect, Rorty is not far off the mark when he points to the importance of "sentimental education" in the cultivation of rights; see *On Human Rights*, 122. Regarding the goal of humanization, one might also wish to confer with Gewirth's formula of "freedom and well-being."

8. Jack Donnelly, "Human Rights and Asian Values: A Defense of 'Western' Universalism," in *The East Asian Challenge for Human Rights*, ed. Joanne R. Bauer and Daniel A. Bell (Cambridge: Cambridge University Press, 1999), 80, 83. Softening his stance somewhat, he adds, "But this does not mean that Asian societies ought to follow 'Western' models blindly. Quite the contrary, internationally recognized human rights leave considerable space for distinctively Asian implementations of these rights. . . . Human rights are treated as essentially universal, but substantial space is allowed (sic!) for variations in implementing these universal norms" (83).

9. See Henry Rosemont Jr., "Why Take Rights Seriously? A Confucian Critique," in *Human Rights and the World's Religions*, ed. Leroy S. Rouner, (Notre Dame, Ind.: University of Notre Dame Press, 1988), 168, 173–74; and Louis Henkin, "Epilogue: Confucianism, Human Rights, and 'Cultural Relativism,'" in *Confucianism and Human Rights*, ed. William Theodore de Bary and Tu Weiming (New York: Columbia University Press, 1998), 314.

10. Rosemont, "Why Take Rights Seriously?" 169, 173–75. Without in any way endorsing cultural relativism, Rosemont insists that the move from one "concept cluster" to another requires much more cultural sensitivity and attention to problems of translation than is customary among foundationalists. Universality, from this perspective, is an ongoing agonistic achievement rather than a fixed premise.

11. Tu Weiming, "Epilogue: Human Rights as a Confucian Moral Discourse," in *Confucianism and Human Rights*, ed. de Bary and Tu Weiming, 302. In the same essay, Tu speaks of Confucian "core values," namely, "the perception of the person as a center of relationships rather than simply as an isolated individual, the idea of society as a community of trust rather than merely a system of adversarial relationships, and the belief that human beings are duty-bound to respect their family, society, and nation" (and global community) (299). See also his *Humanity and Self-Cultivation: Essays on Confucian Thought* (Berkeley, Calif.: Asian Humanities Press, 1979); and *Confucian Thought: Selfhood as Creative Transformation* (Albany, N.Y.: State University of New York Press, 1985). Compare my "Humanity and Humanization: Comments on Confucianism," in *Alternative Visions*, 123–44.

12. Roger T. Ames, "Rites as Rights: The Confucian Alternative," in *Human Rights and the World's Religions*, ed. Rouner, 205–6; Rosemont, "Why Take Rights Seriously?" 177.

13. Ames, "Rites as Rights," 206–7. Ames illustrates the different approaches to universality by pointing to contrasting conceptions of human equality, where Western human-rights discourse stresses numerical or quantitative equality (read: sameness) of individuals, while Confucianism cultivates "qualitative parity": "Where rights-based order strives to guarantee a minimum and yet vital sameness, ritual-based order seeks to guarantee tolerance. For it is the basic nature of harmony, the aspiration of ritual practice, that is enhanced by a coordinated diversity among its elements" (208). See also Tu Weiming, "Epilogue," 299; and the exchange between Ames and Jack Donnelly: Ames, "Continuing the Conversation on Chinese Human Rights," and Donnelly, "Conversing with Straw Men While Ignoring Dictators: A Reply to Roger Ames," *Ethics and International Affairs* 11 (1997): 177–206, 207–13.

14. Rosemont, "Why Take Rights Seriously?" 180. If this goal is to be accomplished, he adds, "the Western philosophical tradition will have to incorporate more non-Western philosophy than it has in the past" (168). See also Tu Weiming, "Epilogue," 305.

15. Sumner B. Twiss, "A Constructive Framework for Discussing Confucianism and Human Rights," in de Bary and Tu Weiming, eds., *Confucianism and Human Rights*, 32, 34.

16. Henry Rosemont Jr., "Human Rights: A Bill of Worries," in de Bary and Tu Weiming, eds., *Confucianism and Human Rights*, 57, 60. As he adds, "I would also argue that industrial capitalism can never become the norm for most of the world's peoples, which should make rights talk even more suspect" (62). Compare also these comments, adding to his bill of worries: "Isn't there a hint of desperation in having to claim that trees have rights? . . . I believe we fundamentally misunderstand our human relations to trees, animals, our great-great grandchildren, and the natural world that sustains us by seeing them all as rival rights claimants. This view must see us as essentially distinct from the entire nonhuman world, in the same way that free, autonomous individuals are already cut off from each other in the 'original position'" (of Rawls) (62). According to a recent report of the Center on Budget and Policy Priorities in Washington, D.C., the wealthiest 2.7 million Americans have as much to spend today as the poorest 100 million Americans; the top one-fifth of U.S. households now earns half of all the income in the United States.

See "Gap Between Rich and Poor Found Substantially Wider," *New York Times* (5 September 1999), 14Y. Still greater disparities prevail on a global scale; see n. 3.

17. Richard Falk, "Cultural Foundations for the International Protection of Human Rights," in *Human Rights in Cross-Cultural Perspectives: A Quest for Consensus*, Abdullahi Ahmed An-Na'im, ed. (Philadelphia: University of Pennsylvania Press, 1992), 48. See also Falk, "The Making of Global Citizenship," in *Global Visions: Beyond the New World Order*, ed. Jeremy Brecher et al. (Boston: South End Press, 1993), 39–50; "Human Rights and the Dominance Pattern in the West: Deforming Outlook, Deformed Practices," in *Human Wrongs*, ed. Chandra Muzaffer (Penang: Just World Trust, 1996), 234–42; and his *On Humane Governance: Towards a New Global Politics* (Cambridge: Polity Press, 1995).

18. Smitu Kothari and Harsh Sethi, eds., *Rethinking Human Rights* (Delhi: Lokayan, 1989), 9.

19. Chandra Muzaffer, "From Human Rights to Human Dignity," in *Debating Human Rights: Critical Essays from the United States and Asia*, ed. Peter Van Ness (London and New York: Routledge, 1999), 26, 28, 30. See also Muzaffer, *Human Rights and the World Order* (Penang: Just World Trust, 1993) where, commenting on the "generations" of rights, he states, "By equating human rights with civil and political rights, the rich and powerful in the North hope to avoid coming to grips with those economic, social and cultural challenges which could well threaten their privileged position in the existing world order. What the rich and powerful do not want is a struggle for economic transformation presented as a human rights struggle, a struggle for human dignity" (39).

20. See Charles Taylor, "A World Consensus on Human Rights," *Dissent* (Summer 1996): 20; also his "Conditions of an Unforced Consensus on Human Rights," in *The East Asian Challenge for Human Rights*, ed. Bauer and Bell, 124–44. See also Nadullahi Ahmed An-Na'im, "Introduction," in *Human Rights in Cross-Cultural Perspectives*, ed. An-Na'im, 2–4; also his "Toward a Cross-Cultural Approach to Defining International Standards of Human Rights," in the same volume, 19–43. Compare also An-Na'im, "The Cultural Mediation of Rights," in *The East Asian Challenge for Human Rights*, ed. Bauer and Bell, 147–68; his "Islamic Foundations for Religious Human Rights," in *Religious Human Rights in Global Perspectives*, ed. John Witte Jr. and Johan van der Vyver (Dordrecht: Martinus Nijhoff, 1966), 337–60; and Alison D. Renteln, *International Human Rights: Universalism Versus Relativism* (Newbury Park, Calif.: Sage, 1990).

~

CHAPTER FOUR

Beyond Fugitive Democracy: Some Modern and Postmodern Reflections

Democracy is a great word whose history remains unwritten, because that history has yet to be enacted.
                                                                —Walt Whitman

There is a mystification in liberalism.
                                                                —Maurice Merleau-Ponty

As a political concept, "democracy" shares a prominent feature with other political concepts: contestability. Throughout Western history, intense dispute has raged over the virtues and defects of democracy understood as popular rule. Still, during past centuries, such dispute has tended to be limited to a comparison of regimes, that is, to the relative merits and demerits of democracy when compared with monarchy and aristocracy. According to a tradition reaching back to antiquity, democracy was assumed to be suffering from numerous inherent blemishes—including fickleness and demagoguery—rendering it less appealing than competing regimes. In more recent times, these reservations have almost completely vanished, making room instead for near-universal endorsement in societies around the globe. Yet, endorsement has by no means removed contestation; on the contrary, the more widely democracy is hailed, the more fiercely its meaning and constitutive features are embroiled in controversy. For a while, the chief contenders for capturing its essence were "liberal democracy" and "people's democracy," the former center-staging individual rights of citizens, the latter absolute popular rule and sovereignty. With the dismantling of the Soviet Union, the terms of the debate have again shifted, though without diminishing its intensity;

bracketing Marxist revolutionary ideas, liberal democrats and "civic republicans" were left to wrestle with each other over the spoils—read: the intrinsic meaning—of democracy. Of late, the complexity of the contest has been further heightened by the arrival of "postmodern" champions of radical democracy bent on debunking (or deconstructing) both the individualist and the collectivist premises of their older rivals.

In the following pages I want to complicate matters still further, namely, by injecting contestation into the camp of postmodern voices, and more generally the camp of those seeking an alternative to both liberal-individualist and republican (or communitarian) models. As articulated by some of its proponents, the path beyond traditional models seems to lead into a kind of no-man's land, a democratic space without people (*demos*), that is, in the direction of a complete "virtualization" of politics. In the case of other proponents, the people's role is nearly smothered in a profuse welter of social structures, in layers upon layers of "subsystems" and public or semipublic arenas of social life. In these and related conceptions, the people or popular rule seems to be literally "on the run," a fugitive from politics in the sense described by Sheldon Wolin in his important essay, "Fugitive Democracy." As Wolin asks in that text, with his usual poignancy, "Why is it that democracy [in our time] is reduced, even devitalized by form? Why is its presence occasional and fugitive?"[1] Taking seriously Wolin's query, this chapter seeks to disentangle some of the quandaries afflicting modern and contemporary democracy. The discussion proceeds in three stages:

1. In the first section, an attempt is made to sketch (in broad strokes) the development of modern democracy, with particular attention to its republican and liberal-individualist varieties.
2. The second part shifts the focus to more recent, that is, late modern or else "postmodern" formulations that in some form or other seek to transcend or escape from the conundrums besetting modernist conceptions.
3. After sorting out and critiquing some of these recent initiatives, the concluding section argues in favor of a distinct kind of late modern or postmodern approach that may tentatively be labeled transgressive or "transformational" and that in many ways is indebted to some of Wolin's teachings.

The Story of Democracy

In textbooks of political philosophy, democracy is customarily presented as one type of political regime juxtaposed with other regime types. Seen from this typological angle, democracy appears as a universal category or transtemporal idea, as one particular mode of what Claude Lefort calls the "*mise en scène*" (or staging) of politics. What this view neglects is the experiential dimension of democracy, its inherence in concrete-temporal struggles and agonies. Contrary to what textbooks may suggest, democracy is not just one regime option among others equally available at all times and places, but rather constitutes a response to historical challenges and aspirations. This aspect is clearly evident both in antiquity and in modern times. As Aristotle recognized, democracy—or what he termed "polity"—was not an invariant feature of Athenian life but rather followed on the heels of long periods of monarchical and aristocratic rule. The same can be said of the protracted development of democracy in modern times, a development that had to move through the watersheds of the Glorious Revolution in England, the American and French Revolutions in the late eighteenth century, and the many revolutionary and semirevolutionary upheavals punctuating the rise of Western industrial society during the last two hundred years. In large measure, democracy thus appears unintelligible apart from its history and ongoing actualization; instead of functioning as a "noumenal" idea, popular self-rule is part of a narrative, which can be recited in the form of a "story" or "tale" of democracy.[2]

In this context, given the need for brevity, only a rough sketch of that story can be offered. Moreover, the sketch will bypass democracy in antiquity for a number of reasons having to do mainly with important restrictions imposed on popular self-government at that time. What is important is that we refrain from reducing the story to a simple linear sequence of regimes. Looked at from the angle of modernity, the development of democracy involves more than the mere replacement of one type of government by another, of monarchy or royal absolutism by popular rule; judged in terms of Michel Foucault's words, more than such a linear transition seems to be at stake in the "cutting off of the king's head" and the final enthronement of the people. As it appears, the tale of modern democracy is embroiled in, and even forms part and parcel of, a larger story, one carrying philosophical-metaphysical or else existential implications. Differently put, the story of the transfer of power—from king and aristocracy to people—is inserted in the modern age in a story of changing worldviews, of epochs of human self-understanding (or in Heideggerian terms, of epochs of the "disclosure of being"). As we know, the Glorious Revolution in England was preceded by the Renaissance and by dramatic changes in the conceptualization of the world—changes linked with such names as Bacon, Descartes, and Hobbes. Assisted by a vast supporting cast, these thinkers dealt a mortal blow to the premodern (Platonic-Aristotelian) worldview, which in modified form had persisted throughout the Middle Ages: Descartes by anchoring human knowledge and action in the thinking subject (or *cogito*), Bacon by construing the relation between the subject and nature (extended matter) as a project of mastery through science, and Hobbes by conceptualizing social and political life as a relentless struggle among egos culminating in the establishment of an absolute, sovereign power (*Leviathan*).[3]

Viewed in retrospect—as part of an unfolding civilizational story—the change of worldview inaugurated by the onset of modernity was at least as dramatic as, and probably more dramatic than, the parallel or subsequent shift from royal power to popular rule. In many ways, one might say, the former change overshadowed and structured the latter. As many historians of political thought have shown, the Platonic-Aristotelian worldview of antiquity and the Middle Ages was not structured in the same manner as that of the modern age; above all, it was not grounded or "centered" in the human subject, certainly not the willing subject, and hence was not basically egocentric or anthropocentric. Perhaps one should say that the older (premodern) framework was centered or stabilized in a different way by foregrounding a divinely ordered cosmos, at least partially accessible to human insight, and by the assumption of a divine-natural teleology or purposiveness pervading and guiding all living beings. In terms of political philosophy, public power—including royal, aristocratic, and democratic power—was circumscribed or tamed in earlier times not just by contracts or procedural rules but by a substantive "*telos*" or goal animating all political life—a goal that Aristotle formulated as the "good life." To be sure, the traditional framework was challenged or contested already in antiquity by sophists and skeptics, and it was partially undermined in the late Middle Ages by the rise of nominalism and voluntarism—a rise which deeply affected also conceptions of the divine by shifting the accent from God's wisdom to God's infinite power.[4] However, the real shattering of the older framework occurred during early modernity with the replacement of a transhuman *telos* by human rationality and will.

Seen against this background, Hobbes inevitably emerges as the paradigmatic and, in many ways, the most consistent political thinker of modernity. In a curious fashion, Hobbes's theory combined or straddled the dominant political models of modernity: the liberal-individualist and the republican-collectivist models. In bold argumentative strokes, Hobbes dismantled or dissolved the Aristotelian cosmos into an array of self-interested and self-seeking (that is, power-seeking) subjects, while insisting at the same time that these egos can find public safety only through the (contractual) establishment of an all-powerful "superego" representing society at large. Although frequently interpreted in a royalist sense, Hobbes's *Leviathan* can in fact be shown to be indifferent to regime types. Undercutting the royalist-antiroyalist struggles of his time, his postulated superego can with equal plausibility be lodged in a king and in the collective body of citizens in a democracy. In the latter instance, the supreme power can be said to be vested in the combined will (or "general will") of the collectivity in a manner that aggregates and synthesizes the partial wills or strivings of individual citizens—thus correlating the will-power of "microsubjects" with that of the "macrosubject" of the state. In the words of Mark Roelofs, the innovative radicality of Hobbes resided in his "consistent anthropocentrism," manifest in the emphasis on "individual willfulness, nominalist epistemology, and political theory as ideology." As he adds, "For Hobbes—and for all modernists after him—the individual is will, pure and simple," while reason is "simply the will's problem-solving capacity." Uninhibited by any "sense of natural station" or a "preordained essence seeking fulfillment," the Hobbesian subject "burst across modern Europe and surged around the globe, planting urbanism, industrialism, and finance capitalism everywhere."[5]

As we know, the Hobbesian linkage of "microsubjects" and "macrosubject" subsequently broke apart, making room instead for the competing paradigms of individualist liberalism (or liberal individualism) and republican populism (despite occasional minglings of the two models). The most eloquent early spokesman of liberal individualism was Locke, who, although sharing Hobbes's reliance on self-seeking individuals (in the "state of nature"), sought to eliminate the need for a Hobbesian superego or sovereign power. Differently put: While accepting by and large Hobbes's modernist premises, Locke aimed to avoid his conclusions by placing his trust in parliamentary government and the "rule of law" (often identified with the rule of reason). As seems evident, however, the modern rule of reason, also called modern "natural law," was basically dislodged from traditional moorings. Unhinged from an overarching teleology, the Lockean rule of law was ultimately anchored—just like the Hobbesian state—in a contractual arrangement, that is, in human will and calculating rationality. Small wonder then that the modern liberal "law state" (*Rechtsstaat*) has always been marked by a precarious ambivalence manifest in the conflicting tendencies of either investing the "law" with a Hobbesian superpower or else allowing society to drift back into anomie (or the state of nature). On this point Roelofs offers again some insightful comments:

Hobbes' successors did not share his confidence that a determinant, absolute sovereign could be routinely trusted to find it in his self-interest to protect those of his subjects. They chose rather to put that kind of trust in the law as interpreted and enforced by an independent judiciary, thereby investing in the law precisely, albeit covertly, the same awesome, arbitrary, and absolute sovereignty that Hobbes granted his sovereign. This is a distinctively modern constitutionalism, the belief that men can, through a self-inflicted terror, peacefully engage themselves in a framework of positive law.[6]

The other strand of modern politics, emphasizing collective popular rule in a strong republican sense, was articulated chiefly by Jean-Jacques Rousseau, who transferred the absolute power of the Hobbesian sovereign to the people, more specifically to the "general will" of the people. In this manner, the supreme superego of the *Leviathan* now emerged as a generalized or collective superego, as the unified "macrosubject" anchoring and stabilizing democratic rule (although Rousseau curiously managed to combine collective will with the liberal notion of the "law state"). In the words of Jürgen Habermas, "The concept of *popular sovereignty* stems from the republican appropriation and reevaluation of the early-modern notion of sovereignty initially coupled with the absolute ruler." The latter motif, which goes back to Jean Bodin and Hobbes, was carried over by Rousseau "to the will of the united people," which (in Habermas's terms) he "fused with the classical idea of the self-rule of free and equal persons and incorporated in the modern concept of autonomy." In its effects, popular sovereignty was just as awesome or fear-inspiring as the Hobbesian *Leviathan*—as became palpably evident during the French Revolution. Identifying itself with the people's general will, the Jacobin Committee of Public Safety declared bluntly, "Whereas the French people has manifested its will, everyone who is opposed to it is outside its sovereignty; everyone outside the sovereignty is an enemy. . . . Between the people and its enemies, there is nothing in common but the sword." As Jean Elshtain comments soberly on this statement, "There is no appeal to any higher court than the sovereign, and if this sovereign is identified with 'the people', and certain persons or groups are declared no longer part of the people, then they, too, become foreigners—even worse, enemies."[7]

The story of modern popular democracy (or people's democracy) did not come to an end, of course, with Rousseau and the French Revolution. The ensuing two centuries offer many variations on the theme of people's democracy—variations that often appear as a mere gloss on the Jacobin committee's formula. In the middle of the last century, Karl Marx transferred Rousseau's "general will" or popular sovereignty to the proletariat, thus installing the latter as the new superego or collective identity and as the decisive engine of revolutionary social change.[8] On the opposite side of the political spectrum, collective identity was increasingly linked or identified with the "nation" (*la Nation*) or the "nation-state," a strategic move that encouraged or fueled steadily more virulent forms of nationalism or chauvinism. All these developments came to a head in the twentieth century with the rise of dramatically opposed types of collective identity or sovereign superego: fascism and communism (mass movements that both came to be subsumed, perhaps hastily, under the common label of "totalitarianism"). Fascism and Stalinist Communism, Auschwitz and the Gulag, thus emerged as the distinctive shorthand labels for the agonies of our age, as glaring reminders of "man's inhumanity to man" in an ostensibly civilized world. All along, one needs to add, democratic-populist sovereignty was tempered, and perhaps sidetracked, by liberal constitutionalism, by the Lockean legacy of proceduralism and the "law state" (*Rechtsstaat*)—a legacy that, precisely in response to totalitarianism, increasingly yielded to its inherent tendency toward individualist self-seeking and anomie. The latter tendency was powerfully supported by the expansion of corporate capitalism and market liberalism around the world, an expansion bent on reducing politics and public life to an adjunct of private enterprise. Not much insight is required, however, to see that these liberal countermechanisms, though containing the totalitarian danger, were themselves the outgrowth of the modernist paradigm governed by individual self-interest and contractual reason.

Postmodernism and Democracy

So far the story of modern democracy (with due apologies for the brevity of the narrative). The time has come to move from storytelling to a more constructive assessment of the preceding tale, to an appraisal of what has been called "democracy's discontent" in our time.[9] It seems to me that the task for democratic theory today is to rethink or reconceptualize popular rule in a manner steering clear of the lure of sovereignty or collective identity (on the right and on the left)—and to do so *without* sidetracking or nullifying popular rule through the privileging of the market and corporate liberalism or neoliberalism. The latter caveat is particularly important in a time when corporate liberalism reigns almost uncontested as the dominant ideology on a global scale. As experience in both Western and non-Western societies teaches, the unlimited sway of global market forces can have deleterious effects on working class and subaltern populations throughout the world, effects which may undercut aspirations to any form of democratic self-rule.[10] To put the issue in more sharply theoretical terms, the task of democratic theorizing (in my view) is to move beyond the modern fascination with self-seeking "micro-" and "macrosubjects," and to do so without exacerbating or deepening "democracy's discontent." As it happens, recent decades have witnessed a number of promising initiatives in that direction, especially initiatives undertaken by a group of thinkers often labeled late or postmodern. Particularly from the postmodern camp, a massive attack has been launched on modern subject-centered metaphysics, and above all on the conception of a "macrosubject" claiming to encompass or "totalize" entire populations (in violation of intrinsic modes of "otherness"). The question that can be raised, however—and that permeates the following pages—is whether postmodern initiatives have an enabling or disabling potential for public life—whether the stress on radical noncommunality pushes democracy into aporia or an abyss.

Among leading political thinkers attuned to postmodern arguments, the attack on a populist "macrosubject" was spearheaded by Ernesto Laclau and Chantal Mouffe in their important study *Hegemony and Socialist Strategy: Towards a Radical Democratic Politics* (1985). Aiming their critique at totalizing agendas on the political left, Laclau and Mouffe challenged in that text the role of a collective identity or stable "essence" of the people as it functioned in traditional or orthodox Marxism. Following a modernist (left-Hegelian) trajectory, orthodox Marxism—they claimed—was still addicted to a grand narrative or metanarrative (in Lyotard's sense), namely, to the "monist(ic) aspiration" to capture "the essence and underlying meaning of History." In the thought of Marx, this aspiration surfaced in the installation of the "proletariat" as the collective superego totalizing the society's future, and in the celebration of "revolution" as the eschatological dénouement of social struggles. In their book, Laclau and Mouffe offered a historical overview of the development of these conceptions from the time of Marx through later stages of revisionism to our time. The first real break with orthodoxy, in their view, occurred in the work of Antonio Gramsci, especially with his elaboration of the notion of cultural and political hegemony. Yet, despite these advances, Gramsci's perspective remained circumscribed in crucial ways, particularly by his tendency to ascribe the ultimately unifying power to an "ontologically" construed class identity. For Laclau and Mouffe, the challenge of our time was to face up more resolutely to the "crisis" of both democracy and traditional socialism. In their words:

> What is now in crisis is a whole conception of socialism which rests upon the ontological centrality of the working class, upon the role of the Revolution (with a capital "r"), as the founding moment in the transition from one type of society to another, and upon the illusory prospect of a perfectly unitary and homogeneous

collective will that will render pointless the moment of politics. The plural and multifarious character of contemporary social struggles has finally dissolved the last foundation of that political imaginary.[11]

From a somewhat different angle (and with closer attention to both left-wing and right-wing forms of collectivism), Claude Lefort has attempted to develop a conception of democracy beyond the modernist bounds of sovereignty and collective identity. In his study *Democracy and Political Theory* (1988), Lefort introduced the important distinction between "polity" or "the political" and "politics"—where politics refers to overt, empirical political strategies while polity (or the political) denotes the constitutive, quasitranscendental matrix of political life, that is, the public space that allows the *mise en scène* (or staging) of politics. According to Lefort, political theorists in the past have often reduced polity to politics, that is, to empirical agents and events, while neglecting the constitutive staging of political life. His strongest invectives are addressed at past construals which tended to substantialize or essentialize the political by postulating a concrete embodiment of public space, particularly its embodiment in such representative figures as kings, emperors or princes. Thus, he notes, during the *ancien régime*, monarchical rule functioned as the holistic (totalizing) representation of the political as such, with ultimate sovereignty being directly inscribed in the king's body (seen as collective superego). The French Revolution meant to signal a sharp break with this kind of direct embodiment; however, it did so only partially or potentially. In fact, postrevolutionary developments during the nineteenth century led to the emergence of new, so-called democratic regimes in which "the people, the nation and the state take on the status of universal categories." Conceptions of this kind, Lefort asserts, are the outgrowth of a nostalgic regression, an effort to recapture and resubstantialize the public space. In its virulent form, this regression takes the shape of political fundamentalism and totalitarianism. Under totalitarian auspices, he writes, the idea of popular sovereignty has repeatedly given rise to the fantasy of a "substantial [collective] identity," the fantasy of "a homogeneous and self-transparent society, of a People-as-One."[12]

In contrast to this collectivist fantasy, Lefort espouses a notion of democracy that is much more elusive and in a way "disembodied." In his view, genuine or radical democracy testifies to a "highly specific" kind of public staging (*mise en scène*) such that "we would in vain try to find models for it in the past, even though it is not without its heritage." The specificity of democracy for Lefort resides in its radical relocation of sovereign power from a site of overt rule to an absent site or a site of empty presence.

"Of all regimes we know," he writes, modern democracy is "the only one to have represented power in such a way as to show that power is an empty place and to have maintained a gap between the symbolic and the real." Without encouraging anarchy, emptiness of the democratic space means "that [ultimate] power belongs to no one; that those who exercise power do not possess it; that they do not, indeed, embody it." Seen from this angle, radical democracy appears marked by a kind of disembodiment or disincorporation, by the institution of a "society without a body" that resists or undercuts any "organic totality." Democracy signals a society "without any positive determination" and unrepresentable by "the figure of a community." While thus terminating or transgressing traditional forms of public identity, democracy for Lefort also involves a decentering of modern metaphysics, a shift away from epistemic security and the foundational warrants of beliefs and actions. As he states in a bold passage that reverberates in much contemporary or postmodern literature,

> In my view, the important point is that democracy is instituted and sustained by the dissolution of the markers of certainty. It inaugurates a history in which people experience a fundamental indeterminacy as to the basis of power, law, and knowledge, and as to the basis of relations between self and other, at every level of social life.[13]

Among contemporary Continental thinkers often labeled "postmodern," no one is more closely associated with the decentering of subjectivity (on both the micro and macro levels) than Jacques Derrida. In a way, the theme runs like a connecting thread throughout his evolving opus. In an early essay, dating from 1968, Derrida raised the issue of the status and possibility of philosophical anthropology, and thereby of the status and possibility of "man" (human being) as a subject. Pondering the climactic events of that year, the essay distanced itself sharply from the vogue of existentialist (subject-centered) humanism permeating France during the postwar years, a vogue leaving its imprint on all stripes of thought. "Humanism or anthropologism during that period," Derrida noted, "was the common ground of Christian or atheist existentialisms, of the philosophy of values (spiritualist or not), of personalisms of the right and left, and [even] of Marxism in the classical style"; this humanist subject-focus was "the unperceived and uncontested common ground of Marxism and of Social-Democratic or Christian-Democratic discourse." Although protesting against narrowly "anthropologistic" (or existentialist) readings of the philosophies of Hegel, Edmund Husserl, and Martin Heidegger, the essay perceived prominent humanist features in their respective works. Thus, in the case of Husserl, despite certain transgressive and trans-subjective leanings, it was still "humanity"—in the sense of a "transcendental humanism"—that functioned as the governing *telos* of his phenomenology. The case of Heidegger was slightly more complicated because of his resolute effort to "overcome" traditional metaphysics and any kind of humanist teleology. Nevertheless, despite these "deconstructive" moves, it was possible to detect a "subtle, hidden, stubborn privilege which, as in the case of Hegel and Husserl, leads us back to the position of the *we* [plural subjectivity] in discourse." Derrida at this point turns to Nietzsche as the thinker offering a more radical new departure, pointing toward a genuine "end of man." Nietzsche's overman, we read, "burns his texts and erases the traces of his steps. His laughter then will burst out, directed toward a return which will no longer have the form of the metaphysical repetition of humanism."[14]

In his later writings, Derrida resolutely transferred the critique of humanism to the political domain or the arena of public "staging"; almost invariably, the target of deconstructive efforts was the notion of a macrosubject or collective subjectivity, that is, the assumption of a commonality inhabiting somehow a collective "we." Thus, although seemingly paying tribute to the Marxist legacy, his *Specters of Marx* in many ways gave pride of place to Max Stirner's radical anti-collectivism, his insistence on the absolute "uniqueness" and singularity of particular human lives. In this manner, Marx's emphasis on the working class and on the need for class struggle was sidelined or decentered, making room instead for a postmodern "virtualization" of political struggle and social emancipation (what Derrida also calls a "spectropolitics").[15] A similar trajectory was pursued a few years later in *Politics of Friendship*—as will be shown in chapter 8. Distancing itself from traditional portrayals accentuating a mutual "bonding" establishing an "us" or "we," the study presented friendship as a remote relation (or better, nonrelation) between incommensurable agents starkly differentiated both from each other and themselves. Relying on such late modern (or postmodern) thinkers as Nietzsche and Maurice Blanchot, Derrida's book sketched the horizon of what he called "another politics," a politics and a democracy "to come" which completely excises the notion of a shared "we." In his words, the new "politics of friendship" emerging in the wake of humanism inaugurates a "community of solitary friends," that is, a "community without community, friendship without the community of the friends of solitude," or else an "anchoritic community."[16]

Curiously, the critique of humanism (in the sense of micro- and macrosubjects) has of late also infected the position of Jürgen Habermas, a thinker not suspected of any postmodern sympathies. In developing his model of a "deliberative democracy"—supposedly correcting the defects of both liberal and republican variants—Habermas takes issue with the humanist (or subject-centered) premises operative in these two conceptions. As he writes, the deliberative model "drops all those motifs employed in the philosophy of consciousness" (read: philosophy of the subject) that would lead one either to ascribe popular self-government to a "macrosocial subject" or else to rely on rule mechanisms among "competing individual subjects." While the former (republican) approach views the citizenry as "a collective actor that reflects the whole," as a "goal-oriented subject-writ-large," the latter (liberal) approach presents individual actors as "dependent variables in power processes." By contrast, deliberative (or discursive) democracy corresponds to the "image of a decentered society," one that has given up the "philosophy of the subject." Reflecting the high complexity characterizing modern social life, the "self" of citizens in this version "disappears in the subjectless forms of communication that regulate the flow of discursive opinion and will-formation." Instead of invoking the prerogatives of a sovereign *demos* (seen as collective superego), the model puts its trust in the institutionalization of appropriate "procedures and conditions of communication."[17]

Toward a Transformative Democracy

Although invigorating by pointing beyond modernist dilemmas, the sketched late modern and postmodern initiatives are fraught with quandaries of their own, especially the tendency to radically disaggregate and thereby disempower the "people" and hence to "virtualize" democratic politics. This (potentially) disabling effect has recently been the target of a sharp critique by Richard Rorty. As will be shown in greater detail in the following chapter, Rorty's *Achieving Our Country* denounces the shift among progressive intellectuals from practical humanist engagement to a spectatorial stance of detached weariness. Instead of helping to reconstruct society, he complains, such intellectuals often retreat into despair or utopian whim. Thus, people "who find Foucault and Heidegger convincing" often view society in eschatological terms "as something we must hope will be replaced, as soon as possible, by something utterly different," by a completely new politics. Prominent catchwords in this outlook are abyss, radical otherness, and ineffability. Thus, "we are told over and over again" that Jacques Lacan has shown human desire to be "inherently unsatisfiable," that Derrida has demonstrated meaning to be "undecidable," and that Jean-François Lyotard has proven "commensuration between oppressed and oppressors to be impossible." As it happens, Rorty shares with postmodern thinkers the distaste for modernist metaphysics and Enlightenment rationalism; however, he finds this dislike entirely compatible with a humanist pragmatism (along John Dewey's lines)—something postmodernists are unable to grasp.[18]

It seems to me that democrats may well sympathize with Rorty's indict-ment, while finding his own remedy—recourse to an unreconstructed pragmatism—contestible (and perhaps callous). As previously indicated, the accent on distance and noncommunity is problematic at any time, but espe-cially in an age governed globally by corporate liberalism—an ideology in-trinsically bent on disaggregating people. Exposed to the vagaries of the global market, common or "subaltern" people cannot fairly be denied the right to act as *demos* to resist exploitation. The latter point is actually ac-knowledged by most postmodern writers. Although vigorously denouncing the dangers of collectivism, Lefort is by no means ready to embrace the coun-terpanacea of liberal individualism. To treat popular rule or "the people" merely as a fiction or a "pure illusion, as liberal thought encourages us to do," he writes, "is to deny the very notion of [political] society, to erase both the question of sovereignty and that of the meaning of the institution, which are always bound up with the ultimate question of the legitimacy of what exists." For Lefort, the difficulty of grasping democracy as a regime resides in its both actual and hidden status (that is, in the people's absent presence). Once pop-ular rule is entirely effaced, the enabling potency of the democratic "staging" vanishes, making room instead for supposedly empirical self-interests. At this point, a "de facto conflict" begins to pervade society in a quasi-Hobbesian vein, and the metaphorical reference to an "empty place" gives way to "the unbearable image of a real vacuum." In Lefort's view, little is gained (and much lost) by the move of replacing the fiction of "unity-in-itself" with that of "diversity-in-itself"; in both cases, practical engagement on the public stage succumbs to a static metaphysics.[19]

Similar considerations can be found in *Hegemony and Socialist Strategy*. Al-though critical of "totalizing" forms of closure, Laclau and Mouffe there do not simply opt for fragmentation or an absolute antagonism of self-interests. While chiding universalism for its complicity with collectivist designs, the remedy for them is not particularism with its bent to "essentialize" separate units. As they write, there is no benefit in moving "from an essentialism of the totality to an essentialism of the elements"—despite the seeming attrac-tiveness of this move in our age. Instead of following this bent, the study sees a need to reformulate "bourgeois individualism," that is, to rethink the no-tion of the individual agent along lines no longer subservient to "the matrix of possessive individualism." In a more recent work, Chantal Mouffe protests even more resolutely against the (mistaken) identification of postmodern theoretical initiatives with a retreat from political engagement or a lapse into private whim. Responding in part to Rorty, she interprets her own collaboration with Laclau not as an apolitical exercise but precisely as a move toward a "radical democratic politics." In her own reading, *Hegemony and Socialist Strategy* was meant to inaugurate a new political "imaginary," one that speaks to "the tradition of the great emancipatory struggles" of modern times. The sketched trajectory could be defined as "both modern and postmodern," in that it actively and politically pursued the "unfulfilled project of modernity" while ceasing to cling to the metaphysical premises of that project (as Habermas still tends to do). Critique of these premises does not mean an abandonment of modern humanist aspirations, especially the "achievement of equality and freedom for all"; but it does imply a rethinking of subjectivity (on both the micro and macro levels).[20]

Together with Mouffe, I find the merit of postmodernism in its critique of modern "subjectivity," that is, in its insistence on decentering or deconstructing the modern (Cartesian) ego, including the collective superego. Such deconstruction, however, must not be equated with a simple erasure of human agency, especially the agency of "the people"—an erasure that would surrender democracy to the vagaries of the market, or else to extreme "libertarian" ideologues for whom any conception of a "we" is anathema. Much (and perhaps everything) depends then on the kind of decentering envisaged by defenders of radical democracy along modern/postmodern lines. In my own view, genuine decentering can only happen when the self or human agent is exposed to an "other" or to "others" upon whom it calls and by whom it is in turn called into question. Although the theme of otherness or alterity is prominent in postmodern literature, its import is undercut when the "other" is stylized as a purely abstract cipher or an empty foil. As soon as the encounter with otherness is concretized and perceived as a mode of "concrete negation," decentering of the self or ego identity cannot remain a rhetorical ploy but assumes the contours of self-transformation, that is, of the arduous labor of self-overcoming or self-transcendence. Seen in this light, one might say about radical or modern/postmodern democracy the following: the "people" invoked in popular self-government—in Lincoln's phrase, "government of the people, by the people, for the people"—is not a fixed or static identity but rather the emblem of human self-transformation and maturation, of the striving for self-rule which always remains a task and a challenge.

This view of democracy as ongoing self-transformation has important implications chiefly in two respects: first, with regard to ethics or the relation of ethics and politics; and secondly, regarding the role and significance of multiculturalism. Like the notion of democracy sketched above, ethics is closely connected with the decentering of the ego and the overcoming of narrow self-interest. All the great ethical teachers of the past—from Confucius and Aristotle to Hegel—have stressed the need of self-transcendence and transformation, that is, the need to undergo the sustained labor of formative maturation or "*paideia*" leading to a kind of "turning" (or *periagoge*). All or most of the great religions of the world emphasize a similar type of transformative process. In his own idiom, Gandhi spoke of the desire to "reduce himself to zero" to be properly of service to others—where "reduction to zero" surely does not mean self-erasure or self-annihilation but rather a rechanneling of human energies in the direction of the public good, a rechanneling requiring the cultivation of moral dispositions (or virtues). Seen against this background, the accent placed by recent (postmodern) thinkers on decentering properly calls into question modern anthropocentric and egocentric assumptions, which reverberate widely in dominant strands of liberal ideology. To this extent, recent formulations of democracy as a decentering and formative process reveal a deeper ethical and metaphysical significance, reconnecting these formulations—perhaps surprisingly—with older traditions of political thought.[21]

The second implication—relating to multiculturalism—is of equal importance and even bound to increase in significance over time. As we know, many democratic societies today are already multicultural; but the steady momentum of globalization is liable to deepen and multiply cultural, ethnic, and religious interactions, both on the domestic and the global level. If, construed along modern/postmodern lines, democracy means a transformative learning process, then multiculturalism constitutes a popular pedagogy or *paideia par excellence*. As stated before, democratic learning involves the ongoing transformation of people's self-definition, their self-decentering in response to the demands of "otherness." In this respect, recent political theory—again partially under the influence of postmodernism—has advanced the innovative notion of a "politics of difference," where difference signifies neither random fragmentation nor an assortment of fixed "natures" or collective identities. Among others, Iris Marion Young has eloquently articulated this conception, especially in her book *Justice and the Politics of Difference*. As Young emphasizes, recognition of group or cultural differences must not be confused with a return to social hierarchies or else with a lapse into invidious cultural prejudices. From the vantage of radical democracy, multicultural politics completely rejects the lure of "essentializing" cultural or ethnic groups or endowing them with invariant traits, while at the same time acknowledging their legitimate difference and refusing to steamroll them into bland uniformity in an aggressively appropriating gesture. A similar conception has been advanced by Charles Taylor in his reflections on the tension between globalism and a multicultural "politics of recognition."[22]

As Taylor rightly insists, multicultural politics requires a willingness to undergo a learning experience, that is, a readiness to shoulder the travail of self-transformation and transcendence. Seen from this vantage, radical and plural democracy demands both the affirmation and the denial of democratic agency without self-contradiction (along the lines of Sartre's famous motto that "the for-itself is not what it is and is what it is not"). In counteracting exploitation or domination, the people (*demos*) rightfully exercises political agency in an enabling or empowering mode, while succumbing to deconstructive criticism when claiming to "be" or "embody" public power and hence being entitled to "lord it" over others (dissident individuals or groups). Such a view presents democracy as a difficult and tensional regime, but it also saves it from being "fugitive" or an empty chimera. These comments lead me back to the starting point of this chapter: Sheldon Wolin's complaint about the fugitive character of contemporary democracy, its plight of being under siege or "on the run" from all kinds of disaggregating and disempowering forces.

In his effort to chart an alternative, more promising path for democracy, Wolin also emphasizes the transformative quality of the democratic venture, its rootedness in concrete experiences of suffering, exploitation, and domination. What is crucial about democracy, he writes, is not its governmental structure but "how it is experienced"; for history teaches that "revolutions activate the *demos* and destroy boundaries that bar access to political experience." In contrast to the modern fascination with "state" and state control, democracy in Wolin's account needs to be "reconceived as something other than a form of government: as a mode of being that is conditioned by bitter experience, doomed to succeed only temporarily, but is a recurrent possibility as long as the memory of the political survives." Viewed in this light, popular self-rule is fragile, but no mere illusion. The possibility of democratic renewal, Wolin asserts, is not fictional but draws on a "simple fact"—namely, "that ordinary individuals are capable of creating new cultural patterns of communality at any moment." By reclaiming their democratic potential of agency, ordinary people are enabled to "renew the political" by contesting "the forms of unequal power that democratic liberty and equality have made possible." In focusing on the experience of common people, Wolin's argument (in my judgment) resonates with Maurice Merleau-Ponty's insistence on the need to view politics, especially democratic politics, "from the ground up" or from a grassroots perspective. As Merleau-Ponty stated, reflecting particularly on the practices of liberal democracy,

> Whatever one's philosophical or even theological position, a society is not the temple of value-idols that figure on the front of its monuments or in is constitutional scrolls; the value of a society is the value it places on human relations. . . . To un-

derstand and judge a society, one has to penetrate its basic structure to the human bond upon which it is built; this undoubtedly depends upon legal relations, but also upon forms of labor, ways of loving, living, and dying.[23]

Notes

1. Sheldon S. Wolin, "Fugitive Democracy," in *Democracy and Difference: Contesting the Boundaries of the Political*, ed. Seyla Benhabib (Princeton: Princeton University Press, 1996), 39.

2. Iris Marion Young has recently reminded us of the importance of "storytelling" in political discourse; see her essay "Communication and the Other: Beyond Deliberative Democracy," in *Democracy and Difference*, ed. Benhabib, 131–32. Her perspective is fleshed out in her more recent book *Inclusion and Democracy* (New York: Oxford University Press, 2000). Regarding Claude Lefort, see his *Democracy and Political Theory*, trans. David Macey (Minneapolis: University of Minnesota Press, 1988), 11, 219.

3. Regarding Michel Foucault, see his "Truth and Power," in *Power/Knowledge: Selected Interviews and Other Writings 1972–1977*, ed. Colin Gordon (New York: Pantheon Books, 1980), 121.

4. As Jean Elshtain writes,: "In post-Occam theology . . . God is less and less represented as the fullness of reason and goodness in His relational complexity and more and more embodied as the site of sovereign will. God's volitionality trumps other features of the *imago Dei* . . . . God's power in this vision is not only absolute but even somewhat arbitrary. God's right is coterminous with His sovereign power." See Jean Bethke Elshtain, *New Wine and Old Bottles: International Politics and Ethical Discourse* (Notre Dame, Ind.: University of Notre Dame Press, 1998), 12.

5. H. Mark Roelofs, "Democratic Dialectics," *Review of Politics*, 60 (Winter 1998), 9. Accentuating the break with the past, Roelofs states, "God (prescient, creative, ordering, loving) has vanished, replaced by 'nature' (blind, dumb, plain, only ultimately mysterious). Likewise vanished is all trace of any cosmologically sustained hierarchy, any 'Great Chain of Being'. . . . Hobbes's purpose clearly was to wipe the slate clean of all that" (8).

6. Roelofs, "Democratic Dialectics," 14.

7. See Elshtain, *New Wine and Old Bottles*, 15–16. The statement of the Jacobin Committee is taken from Elshtain. Regarding Habermas see his "Deliberative Politics: A Procedural Concept of Democracy," in *Between Facts and Norms: Contributions to a Discourse Theory of Law and Democracy*, trans. William Rehg (Cambridge, Mass.: MIT Press, 1996), 300.

8. Concentrating on Lenin as paradigmatic figure, Roelofs describes the gist of "social revolutionary" democracy in these terms, "Social revolutionary democracy is a one-party nation in which a morally committed people (*demos*), congregated by a charismatic hero, share a single sovereign historical enthusiasm for overcoming great evils and beginning the march upward toward distant goals of social justice." See "Democratic Dialectics," 18.

9. See Michael J. Sandel, *Democracy's Discontent: America in Search of a Public Philosophy* (Cambridge, Mass.: Belknap Press, 1996).

10. Above all, unrestricted financial speculation and rapid transfers of portfolio capital can today throw entire societies into disarray and near chaos, plunging millions of ordinary people into unemployment and misery. See on this point Kalinga Seneviratne, "The Currency Crisis, Human Rights and the Media," *Just Commentary*, no. 11 (April 1998), 1–3.

11. Ernesto Laclau and Chantal Mouffe, *Hegemony and Socialist Strategy: Towards a Radical Democratic Politics*, trans. Winston Moore and Paul Cammack (London: Verso, 1985), 1–4. Elaborating on the traditional "imaginary" they add, "Peopled with 'universal' subjects and conceptually built around History in the singular, it has postulated 'society' as an intelligible structure that could be intellectually mastered on the basis of certain class positions and reconstituted, as a rational, transparent order, through a founding act of a political character. Today, the Left is witnessing the final act of the dissolution of that Jacobin imaginary" (2). For a detailed critical review of the book see my "Hegemony and Democracy" in *Margins of Political Discourse* (Albany, N.Y.: State University of New York Press, 1989), 116–36.

12. Lefort, *Democracy and Political Theory*, 11–13, 16–20.

13. Lefort, *Democracy and Political Theory*, 17–19, 223–26. For a detailed review and exegesis of Lefort's study see my "Post-Metaphysical Politics" in *The Other Heidegger* (Ithaca, N.Y.: Cornell University Press, 1993), 87–96.

14. Jacques Derrida, "The Ends of Man," in *Margins of Philosophy*, trans. Alan Bass (Chicago: University of Chicago Press, 1982), 114–18, 122–24, 127, 136.

15. As Derrida writes in a chapter titled "In the Name of the Revolution," "The century of 'Marxism' will have been that of the techno-scientific and effective decentering of the earth, of geopolitics, of the *anthropos* in its onto-theological identity or its genetic properties, of the *ego cogito*—and of the very concept of narcissism whose aporias are . . . the explicit theme of deconstruction." Later in the same chapter, after having introduced the notions of "spectropolitics" and "virtualization," Derrida turns to Max Stirner saying: "We take seriously the originality, audacity, and precisely the philosophico-political seriousness of Stirner who also should be read without Marx or against him." See Derrida, *Specters of Marx: The State of the Debt, the Work of Mourning, and the New International*, trans. Peggy Kamuf (New York: Routledge, 1994), 98, 107, 117, 121.

16. Derrida, *Politics of Friendship*, trans. George Collins (London: Verso, 1997), 10, 35–37, 42–43, 62; also "The Politics of Friendship," *Journal of Philosophy* 85 (1988), 643–44.

17. Habermas, "Deliberative Politics," in *Between Facts and Norms*, 298–99, 301. The complexity of Habermas's model is further heightened by his differentiation of public deliberation from the "systemic" demands of the economy and the state—governed by efficiency standards—and by the pre-deliberative welter of interests inhabiting the social lifeworld. As Carol Gould writes, Habermas's model "sees the state and the economy as falling outside it and hence as themselves not amenable to democratization. Thus it tends to reduce the sphere of the political—as state—to administration and of the economy to the private domain of pure means-ends relations. Further, it is incomplete in construing the public too exclusively in terms of discourse or argumentation and not also in terms of

common practical activities oriented to shared goals." See Carol C. Gould, "Diversity and Democracy: Representing Differences," in *Democracy and Difference*, ed. Benhabib, 174.

18. Richard Rorty, *Achieving Our Country: Leftist Thought in Twentieth-Century America* (Cambridge, Mass: Harvard University Press, 1998), 7, 36, 96–97.

19. Lefort, *Democracy and Political Theory*, 232–33. Similar sentiments can be found in the study's Introduction, where Lefort wonders about the benefits of anti-Marxism (or anti-collectivism) "when it results in a restoration of rationalism combined with liberal humanism, in the willful ignorance of the latter's inability between the wars to understand the drama that was unfolding in the world, and in particular its inability to understand the depths from which the collective identifications and death wishes sprang" (4).

20. See Laclau and Mouffe, *Hegemony and Socialist Strategy*, 103–4, 142, 182–84; also Mouffe, "Radical Democracy: Modern or Postmodern," in *The Return of the Political* (London: Verso, 1993), 10, 12–13. In her essay, Mouffe criticizes Rorty for his pragmatic "bourgeois liberalism," while simultaneously distancing herself from an extreme or "apocalyptic postmodernism" (10, 15). For a detailed critical review of *The Return of the Political*, see my "The Return of the Political: On Chantal Mouffe," *Constellations* 3 (1996), 115–20.

21. This aspect deserves emphasis especially in view of the widespread tendency to equate postmodernism blandly with ethical relativism and even nihilism. For an explicit linkage of radical (postmodern) democracy with strands in "conservative thought" see Mouffe, "Radical Democracy," 15–18. To be sure, as Mouffe realizes, care must be taken to screen traditional teachings of their frequent association with authoritarianism and autocratic elitism.

22. See Iris Marion Young, *Justice and the Politics of Difference* (Princeton: Princeton University Press, 1990), 11, 156–63, 169–71; Charles Taylor, "The Politics of Recognition," in Amy Gutmann, ed., *Multiculturalism and "The Politics of Recognition"* (Princeton: Princeton University Press, 1992), 58–61. For a more detailed discussion of both works see my "Democracy and Multiculturalism," in *Democracy and Difference*, ed. Benhabib, 278–94. For a trenchant recent discussion of the issues of multiculturalism see Bhikhu Parekh, *Rethinking Multiculturalism: Cultural Diversity and Political Theory* (London: Macmillan, 2000).

23. Maurice Merleau-Ponty, *Humanism and Terror*, trans. John O'Neill (Boston: Beacon Press, 1969), xiv; Wolin, "Fugitive Democracy," in *Democracy and Difference*, ed. Benhabib, 38, 43–44. In supporting democratic renewal, Wolin explicitly draws attention to the pitfalls of an extreme postmodernism dwelling exclusively on heterogeneity, singularity, and the absence of demos. He writes, "A range of problems and atrocities exists that a locally confined democracy cannot resolve. Like pluralism, interest group politics, and multicultural politics, localism cannot surmount its limitations except by seeking out the evanescent homogeneity of a broader political. . . . Clearly homogeneity . . . need not now be equated with dreary uniformity, any more than equality need be mere leveling. What it does require is understanding what is truly at stake politically: heterogeneity, diversity, and multiple selves are no match for modern forms of power" (44). Compare also Wolin, "What Revolutionary Action Means Today," in *Dimensions of Radical Democracy: Pluralism, Citizenship, Community*, ed. Chantal Mouffe (London: Verso, 1992), 240–53.

~

CHAPTER FIVE

Achieving Our World
Democratically: A Response to
Richard Rorty

James Baldwin ends his famous book *The Fire Next Time* with these moving lines: "If we—and now I mean the relatively conscious whites and the relatively conscious blacks, who must, like lovers, insist on, or create, the consciousness of the others—do not falter in our duty now, we may be able, handful that we are, to end the racial nightmare, and achieve our country, and change the history of the world."[1]

When they were first penned in 1963, in the midst of the civil rights struggle in the United States, these lines stirred the conscience of a nation and awakened many people previously on the sidelines to a full awareness of the infamy of racial hatred and injustice. There can be no doubt that, partly under the inspiration of Baldwin and Martin Luther King, Americans were able—at least for a time—to "achieve" their country in a better, nobler way than before, thus living up more seriously to the promise contained in their history. In the meantime, nearly half a century has passed and, despite many ennobling ventures, much "nightmare" still remains—both in the United States and in the rest of the world. With sickening repetitiveness, the conscience of humankind is affronted by large-scale atrocities, from genocide and ethnic cleansing to random outbursts of violence; almost invariably, the root causes of these calamities can be traced to racial, cultural, and/or economic factors. In our time of rapid globalization or intensified global interdependence, is it still possible to heed Baldwin's challenge to shoulder "our duty now"? Is there a chance—in the opening of the new millennium—to "achieve" our global humanity by drawing on the promise contained in the histories of multiple countries?

Shouldering Baldwin's challenge both at home and abroad requires courage, perseverance, and some forward-looking hope—untainted by mere wishful thinking. Such courage is hard to come by at a time when many (if not most) intellectuals in the West take pride in cultivating a morose pessimism and debilitating forms of hopelessness. Fortunately, the intellectual landscape is not entirely bleak; its dark hues are alleviated every so often by bright bursts of innovative energy. In the American setting, the pragmatist philosopher Richard Rorty not long ago came forward with a stirring plea for practical-political reorientation. Based on his Massey lectures delivered at Harvard University (1997), his book *Achieving Our Country* deliberately invoked Baldwin's challenge as a guidepost for Americans in the new millennium. Pointing to recent intellectual trends or fashions, Rorty chided his fellow intellectuals for having largely abandoned the democratic potential of the "American dream"; more specifically, he bemoaned their tendency to replace practical engagement with convoluted and often esoteric theoretical speculations. The following presentation takes Rorty's exhortation to heart—but by transforming and expanding his vision. As it stands, *Achieving Our Country* makes for both exhilarating and frustrating reading. Its message is captivating in its forward-looking and energizing élan; it is also frustrating, however, in its nostalgia (chiefly for American Progressivism) and its often narrow-hearted appeal to "American national pride." This presentation proceeds in three steps:

1. The first section highlights Rorty's important and innovative contributions to a renewal of the democratic agenda in contemporary America.
2. In the next section, attention is shifted to drawbacks or limitations of this agenda, especially to a certain lingering "binary" metaphysics infesting Rorty's arguments.
3. To conclude, an effort is made to expand the significance of Baldwin's challenge, by reflecting on the possibility of "achieving" our diversified humanity along democratic lines.

Achieving Our Country

Rorty's text opens with the portrayal of a bleak scenario: the widespread loss of faith in the future, especially faith in the future of U.S. democracy. To foster such faith, Rorty reminds his readers, requires cultivation of a sense of national pride—and to generate and sustain such pride, responsible artists and intellectuals have to be willing to tell uplifting narratives about their country. The problem in the United States at the turn of the millennium is that few (if any) inspiring images and stories are being proffered. Apart from a simple-minded chauvinism which surfaces in moments of crisis, the very notion of national pride has atrophied; in fact, most descriptions of America's future are written "in tones either of self-mockery or of self-disgust." To illustrate this point, Rorty refers to novels by Neal Stephenson, Richard Condon, Thomas Pynchon and others, whose combined effect is to debunk democratic hopes. In Stephenson's *Snow Crash*, the United States in the coming century is entirely in the grip of giant corporations whose managers have crushed dreams of a free, egalitarian society; at this juncture, pride in being a U.S. citizen has been replaced by a ruthless status division between "haves" and "have-nots," between elite and rabble on a worldwide scale. Similar dystopias are projected by Condon, Pynchon, and Leslie Silko, whose novels exude a spirit not of social protest or reform but of "rueful acquiescence in the end of American hopes."[2]

Sounding a theme that will be developed later in greater detail, Rorty at this point detects an affinity between these dystopian novels and the teachings of various European philosophers who have gained a hearing in American academia in recent decades. Prominent among the latter are thinkers like Martin Heidegger, Michel Foucault, Jacques Derrida, and others. In Rorty's view, there is an (overt or covert) complicity between recent American literature and the down-beat quality of much of European or "Continental" philosophy. "One does not need to know," he writes, "whether Silko has read Foucault or Heidegger to see her novels as offering a vision of recent history similar to the one which readers of those two philosophers often acquire." In this vision, the history of the United States—and indeed the entire history of the West since the Enlightenment—is marked by deep-seated "hypocrisy and self-deception." Thus, readers of Foucault often are infected by a melancholy fatalism accepting the eternal "return of the same"; they tend to believe that emancipation as a whole has been a sham and that "no shackles have been broken in the past two hundred years." In a similar vein, Heidegger's ruminations on technology (*Gestell*) tend to have a demoralizing and disempowering effect; above all, the U.S. role in "blanketing the world with modern technology" is equated with the "spread of a wasteland." Reading at the same time works like *Snow Crash* and Continental philosophical texts, Rorty states, young American intellectuals are liable to be convinced that theirs is a "violent, inhuman, corrupt country." But far from stirring them into action, this insight reinforces their lethargy: it does not move them "to formulate a legislative program, to join a political movement, or to share in a national hope."[3]

In *Achieving Our Country*, this contemporary mood of dejection is sharply contrasted with the upbeat élan pervading intellectual life during the first part of the twentieth century, an élan exemplified by early American pragmatism and the Progressive Movement. For left-leaning intellectuals of that period, the United States was not a quagmire but destined to become "the first cooperative commonwealth, the first classless society," a country in which income and status would be equitably distributed and in which individual liberty would be matched with equal life chances. For Rorty, the leading exemplars of this upbeat spirit were Walt Whitman and John Dewey—ably supplemented and supported by such writings as Herbert Croly's *The Promise of American Life* (1909). Both Whitman and Dewey upheld the vision of an improved, more democratic America—not for the sake of mere entertainment but in the hope of "mobilizing Americans as political agents." Imbued with a thoroughly secular sense of civic culture (or civic religion), both writers aimed to rid their country of ancient phobias and prejudices; basically they wanted to generate among their compatriots a sense of pride in "what America might, all by itself and by its own lights, make of itself." Averse to other-worldly speculations, Dewey and Whitman both perceived the United States as a grand-scale experiment that places "ultimate significance in a finite, human historical project, rather than in something eternal and nonhuman."[4]

A major part of *Achieving Our Country* is taken up with an account of the decline of American progressivism since mid-century with what the text calls the "eclipse of the reformist Left." In Rorty's view, a proper assessment of American progressivism is clouded by its frequent confusion or contamination with "socialist" or "Marxist" programs—ideologies that have been thoroughly discredited by events in our time (especially Stalinism and Maoism). To mark the distance from discredited ideologies, Rorty proposes to drop the term "Old (or socialist) Left" and to substitute instead "reformist Left" as a label covering all those Americans who, between 1900 and the onset of the Vietnam War, struggled for greater social justice within the bounds of constitutional democracy. Although including some self-defined "socialists" and "Marxists," the group was made up predominantly of social democrats and reformers. The text returns at this point to Herbert Croly's progressivist restyling of American liberalism or liberal democracy, especially his critique of the cult of rugged individualism as responsible for "a morally and socially undesirable distribution of wealth." Like Dewey, Croly urged Americans to set aside a self-centered (or libertarian) individualism and to substitute a "more highly socialized democracy" for an "excessively individualized" one. Ever since the time of Croly, Rorty comments, the proposition that the na-

tion (or the state) should take responsibility for social justice and redistribution has marked "the dividing line between the American Left and the
American Right."[5]

In Rorty's account, several events during the 1960s signaled a watershed in
the development of progressive thought in the United States; foremost among
these events were the civil rights struggle and the onset of the Vietnam War
(highlighted by the Tonkin Gulf Resolution in 1964). He writes, the mid-
sixties saw "the beginning of the end of a tradition of Leftist reformism" which
dated back to the Progressive Era; while prior to this period the emphasis was
on consensus and constructive engagement, Leftist discourse subsequently took
a mostly "antisystemic" turn by either intoning "full-throated calls for revolution" or else retreating from the political domain (into what Rorty subsequently calls the stance of "cultural" Leftism). Major intellectual guideposts for
the turn were the writings of C. Wright Mills, Christopher Lasch, and others,
writings that abandoned hope in domestic reform and insisted on the need for
radical antisystemic change. For Lasch, American progressivism (that is, the
tradition of the "reformist Left") was basically wedded to an illusion. As he
wrote retrospectively (to Rorty's dismay) in *The Agony of the American Left*,
"Even when they originated in humanitarian impulses, progressive ideas led
not to a philosophy of liberation but to a blueprint for control"; the reason for
this was that "the structure of American society makes it almost impossible for
criticism of existing policies to become part of political discourse."[6]

According to *Achieving Our Country*, a major outcome of the shift in the
1960s was the emergence of a new movement on the Left whose primary
concern was cultural and existential rather than economic in character and
whose basic political stance tended to be antisystemic if not apocalyptic (in
a purely speculative or rhetorical way). Under the pressure of the Vietnam
War and other events, Rorty notes, the older reformist Left gave way, especially in academia, to a "cultural Left" whose members came to specialize in
what they call the "politics of difference" or of "identity" or "recognition,"
and to worry more "about stigma than about money," more "about deep and
hidden psychosexual motivations than about shallow and evident greed."
Intellectually, the turn to culture was aided and abetted by the steady inroad
of Continental philosophy—"mostly apocalyptic French and German
philosophy"—whose study replaced political economy as "an essential preparation in Leftist politics." In contrast to the older reformist Left, the newer
cultural variety abandoned faith in reformism and propagated instead a
wholesale exodus from the ills of modern society, ills that are variously identified as "patriarchy," "technocratic rationality" or else "phallogocentrism."
Apart from the proliferation of Continental philosophy courses, a prominent

result of the changed outlook in academia was the rise of so-called culture studies, a rise predicated on the notion that students need to learn about and to "recognize otherness" (or the identity of others). Culture studies in this context should be taken in a broad sense as comprising such topics as gender studies, black history, gay studies, Hispanic-American studies, and the like, with the focus always resting on groups of people hitherto unrecognized or not fully recognized and hence on "victims" of existing society. Whereas the older reformist Left tried to help people humiliated by poverty or unemployment, the newer cultural initiatives are basically directed toward people marginalized and humiliated "for reasons other than economic status."[7]

In Rorty's presentation, one of the central trademarks of cultural Leftism—and one of its chief defects—is its privileging of theory over practice and hence its adoption of a purely "spectatorial" stance in preference to concrete engagement. As he writes, the contemporary Left, especially in academia, seems to think that "the higher your level of abstraction, the more subversive of the established order you are" and "the more sweeping and novel your conceptual apparatus, the more radical your critique." Here is a somewhat longer quote, which vividly captures Rorty's indictment:

> When one of today's academic Leftists says that some topic has been "inadequately theorized," you can be pretty certain that he or she is going to drag in either philosophy of language, or Lacanian psychoanalysis, or some neo-Marxist version of economic determinism. Theorists of the Left think that dissolving political agents into plays of differential subjectivity, or political initiatives into pursuits of Lacan's impossible object of desire, helps to subvert the established order. Such subversion, they say, is accomplished by "problematizing familiar concepts." Recent attempts to subvert social institutions by problematizing concepts have produced a few very good books. They have also produced many thousands of books which represent scholastic philosophizing at its worst.

He adds, "These futile attempts to philosophize one's way into political relevance" are symptomatic of what happens "when a Left retreats from activism and adopts a spectatorial approach to the problems of its country." Predictably, disengagement from practice produces "theoretical hallucinations" which often take on "Gothic" dimensions.[8]

To illustrate the perils of excessive theorizing, Rorty comments briefly on some of the leading and most frequently invoked figures in Continental philosophy since Nietzsche's time. An example of the Gothic strain in contemporary theorizing is Michel Foucault's treatment of "power" as a haunting and ubiquitous specter. In its Foucauldian usage, Rorty notes, power is everywhere and nowhere, an uncanny agency that has left "an indelible stain on every word in our language and on every institution in our society." The ubiquity of this agency, he adds, is "reminiscent of the ubiquity of Satan, and thus of the ubiquity of original sin—the diabolical stain on every human soul." Following in Foucault's footsteps, many cultural Leftists have come to dwell morbidly on power and domination as pervasive ghostly presences—thereby abandoning the arena of practical politics where citizens "can join forces to resist sadism and selfishness" in favor of "a Gothic world in which democratic politics has become a farce." The detrimental effect of Foucauldian theorizing is matched by that of other Continental thinkers dear to cultural Leftists, including Heidegger, Derrida, and Emmanuel Levinas. Although applauding the critical stance taken by these thinkers vis-à-vis a self-confident (or "foundational") Enlightenment rationalism, Rorty firmly dismisses their relevance in practical-political terms. Invoking a traditional liberal bifurcation of private and public domains, he insists that their teachings should basically be "relegated to private life and not taken as guides to political deliberation."[9]

These comments lead Rorty back to the legacy of political reformism, rashly and prematurely sidelined (in his view) by culturalism and Continental thought. By way of conclusion, he offers two basic suggestions designed to lead American Leftism back onto its proper course. The first is that the Left should "put a moratorium on theory" and "try to kick its philosophy habit." According to the second, the Left should "try to mobilize what remains of our pride in being Americans" and shed its overt or semiconscious "anti-Americanism" carried over from the late sixties. To accomplish both goals, Americans can still find vital resources in the writings of Whitman and Dewey who, apart from being eminently practical, also provided all the theory and "spiritual uplift" required for public business. The older reformist Left, Rorty reminds his readers, was wedded to a "melting-pot" image of the United States, and it did so by proclaiming "that all of us—black, white, and brown—are Americans" and that we should respect each other precisely and only as such. By contrast, recent cultural Leftists have abandoned assimilation (equated with sameness), insisting instead that we should "preserve otherness rather than ignore it" and hence "respect one another in our differences." Reversing this trend, Rorty proposes that, rather than respecting differences, Americans should "cease noticing those differences" to create again a "sense of commonality" for the purpose of reinvigorating national politics.[10]

Critical Rejoinders

In many respects, *Achieving Our Country* is a bravura performance—"vintage Rortyan," as some people might say. No one (certainly no one on the American Left) can be sanguine about the malaise pervading contemporary U.S. democracy: a malaise manifest in widespread political apathy and in the placid acceptance of social and economic inequality under the aegis of a refurbished "frontier individualism." No one can also be sanguine about certain tendencies in American academia fostering the sequestering of intellectual life in ever more elusive and esoteric language games inaccessible (and irrelevant) to the public at large. Here, Rorty's call for renewed intellectual courage and a return to political practice has a stirring and extremely timely significance. To remain vigilant and responsibly alert, intellectuals have to pay close attention to social context and hence to switch from "spectatorship" to engaged "agency," with the aim of removing social ills and preventing their country from dividing "into a nation of rich and a nation of poor." As it happens, American Leftists do not have to start from scratch but can rely on valuable precedents; by aligning themselves with Whitman and Dewey they will be able to see the struggle for social justice as "central to their country's moral identity."[11]

One of the central and in many ways most illuminating aspects of the text is the distinction between the older reformist Left and the newer cultural Left, with the dividing line located somewhere in the decade of the Sixties. With this distinction, Rorty has no doubt captured an important intellectual shift in the twentieth century. Within this broad epochal scenario, Rorty's own credentials as an old-style reformer are beyond question. To be sure, one may quarrel about his particular brand of reformism, especially his self-styled "militant anti-Communism" during the Cold War—a stance he found curiously compatible with opposition to the Vietnam War (despite the vaunted "domino theory" much propagated at the time).[12] Leaving this point aside, one cannot fail to be impressed by the bold contours of his account, nor by a certain fair-mindedness surfacing in his text. Despite his own clear preference for reformism, he is not unaware of the limits of the older Left, nor of the contributions of its more recent successor. Regarding the older reformist Left, *Achieving Our Country* contains a longish recital of its failings, having to do mostly with a certain racial and cultural obtuseness (a point to which it will be necessary to return later). On the other hand, the newer cultural Left is credited at one point with "extraordinary success." As Rorty admits, in addition to being centers of "genuinely original scholarship," recent "cultural studies" programs have in large part achieved what they were designed to do: they have "decreased the amount of sadism in our society." Partly as a result of these programs, "casual infliction of humiliation" is much less socially acceptable than it was in the first part of the century.[13]

Apart from such occasional admissions, fair-mindedness also surfaces in repeated calls for reconciliation, that is, for a constructive dialogue or bridge-building between the generations of older and newer Leftism. Here is a re-markable passage eloquently expressing this plea:

> The heirs of the student Left and the heirs of the older, reformist Left are still un-reconciled with one another. I want to suggest that such a reconciliation could be started by agreeing that the New Left accomplished something enormously im-portant, something of which the reformist Left would probably have been inca-pable. It ended the Vietnam War. It may have saved our country from becoming a garrison state. Without the widespread and continued civil disobedience con-ducted by the New Left, we might still be sending our young people off to kill Viet-namese . . . in the name of anti-Communism.

If the latter accomplishment is joined with the domestic reduction of sadism and humiliation, Rorty's account surely goes a good stretch of the way to-ward a rapprochement between generations otherwise at odds with each other. Sorting out the "pluses" and "minuses" on both sides of the ledger, Rorty in the end settles for a kind of stand-off, in the sense that "the hon-ors should be evenly divided between the older, reformist Left and the New Left of the Sixties."[14]

Unfortunately, conciliatory gestures of this kind do not reflect the text's basic tenor. Despite encouraging concessions, readers can hardly forget the persistent disparagement of cultural Leftism and the relentless invectives ad-dressed at a "spectatorial, disgusted, mocking Left" incapable of agency and national pride. As indicated before, Rorty's receptivity and sympathies for newer cultural initiatives are narrowly circumscribed—including his recep-tivity for Continental philosophy. To be sure, Rorty is on record as a prag-matic "antifoundationalist" opposed to traditional metaphysics of every kind. Hence, in *Achieving Our Country* (and elsewhere), he applauds Continental thinkers for their critique of Enlightenment rationalism—with the proviso or on condition that this critique fully concurs with "traditional liberalism" or the stance of "old-fashioned reformist liberals."[15] Although pleasantly ac-commodating, this combination of antifoundationalism and nostalgic liber-alism inevitably comes at a price: above all, it brings back into play a num-ber of (supposedly banished) metaphysical binaries or dichotomies. Prominent among these binaries are the oppositions between theory and practice, inside and outside, private and public—and also between nation-state and global community.

In *Achieving Our Country*, the distinction between the reformist Left and the cultural Left basically coincides with the distinction between practice

and theory, between agency and spectatorship. In its main thrust, the indictment of cultural Leftism focuses on its concern with "theorizing" the world
and offering "redefinitions" of our contemporary situation. In stark contrast
to this concern, Rorty upholds the "primacy of the practical over the theoretical"—what he also calls (following Hilary Putnam) the "primacy of the
agent point of view."[16] Here, the reader may wish to pause and raise questions. Clearly, this primacy is not just a fact of life but an argumentative preference (hiding a theory). Even John Dewey—invoked as the authoritative
mentor of American pragmatism—did not just engage in random activism,
but rather articulated (not untheoretically) a new vision or framework of
U.S. politics; and the same can be said of Achieving Our Country. On a general level, one may have more principled qualms about Rortyan pragmatism—to the extent that it reduces "truth" and "goodness" to "what works"
or practical efficacy. Surely, there are many things in this world which
"work"—even work with ghastly efficiency—without having any trace of
truth or goodness about them (for example, Nazi concentration camps).

In general terms, complaints about "theorizing" probably should not be
overdone. Partly under the influence of "postmodern" and postfoundational
writings, a veritable vendetta has been launched in some quarters against
theorizing or philosophizing of all kinds—a vendetta that also affects practical or political reasoning. Some of the results of this vendetta can hardly be
pleasing to social reformers, Rortyan or otherwise: results like the unleashing
of senseless double-talk or the upsurge of anti-intellectual fundamentalism.
As indicated before, Rorty himself is appreciative of the works of some Continental "theorizers"—but restricts their relevance to the private domain, far
removed from public-political affairs. At this point, another traditional dualism emerges between inside and outside, private and public. Curiously, despite his remonstrations against Descartes and Kant, Rorty's arguments regarding privacy—especially the privacy of the "liberal ironist"—reinstate the
category of subjectivity (now a "linguistified" subjectivity) in its traditional
place of honor. Seemingly, in this perspective, individual human life can be
"privatized" or internalized without repercussions on the public domain, just
as the latter can be "externalized" or extricated from existential concerns
without shriveling into an empty husk. What this view neglects is the interpenetration of inside and outside, the fact that the relation between "private"
and "public" does not have "foundational" status but needs to be continuously renegotiated through the exercise of prudential judgment.

Reflections of this kind are prone to lead to a reevaluation of the role of
cultural Leftism, beyond Rorty's mostly critical remarks. In light of the public-
private nexus, the intensive theorizing of the cultural Left also discloses a

public-political significance which deserves to be retrieved. Contrary to Rorty's dismissal, one can plausibly find in culturalism potentially fruitful public initiatives, steps prone to invigorate public-political thinking by moving it beyond the confines to old-style reformism (as well as old-style socialism). In *Achieving Our Country*, Rorty discloses his fondness for welfare legislation and ever new "bureaucratic" ventures; he also avows his attachment to constructivism or social engineering.[17] In this respect, recent experiences have surely shown the flaws of massive bureaucratic interventions; they have also demonstrated the dangers of technocracy and managerial elitism—dangers precisely for democratic agency. From this angle, Continental theorizing can have, and has had, a beneficial effect by recovering the important difference between technology and praxis, between instrumental and practical-political rationality. At the same time, culturalist concerns with "otherness" have brought to the fore the intrinsic limits of political control and domination—above and beyond the traditional liberal focus on individual privacy. Another innovative move is the transgression of the "reform-versus-revolution" dichotomy, which is a mainstay of *Achieving Our Country*.[18]

The public-political significance of cultural Leftism, however, extends even further. Precisely in comparison with the older (Rortyan) Left, there are two crucial features meriting attention: the respect for cultural difference and the incipient rise of cosmopolitanism. As indicated before, Rorty is highly uncomfortable with identity questions and the culturalist focus on difference; in line with the older reformism, he prefers a "melting-pot" image where Americans, rather than respecting differences, would simply "cease noticing" them. However, viewed in historical context, this image was basically a sham, disguising the hegemonic predominance of one culture—white, male, Anglo-Saxon—over women and all sorts of minorities. Disarmingly, Rorty acknowledges the shortcomings of American reformism in this regard—but without any effect on his anticulturalist stance. As he writes, most of the direct beneficiaries of he older reformist Left were "white males." Although women received the right to vote in 1920, male reformers afterward "pretty much forgot about them for forty years." Right up to the early sixties, he candidly confesses, male Leftists in faculty lounges and hiring halls "often spoke of women with the same jocular contempt, and of homosexuals with the same brutal contempt," as did Right-wing males in the country clubs. At the same time, the situation of African Americans was dismal; it was "deplored, but not changed," by a predominantly white, Anglo-Saxon Left.[19]

The other feature deserving attention is an incipient cosmopolitanism noticeable among segments of the newer Left. Here the recognition of difference joins hands with a broader inter-culturalism or cross-culturalism (which is sharply distinguished from old-style imperialism as well as from Marxist internationalism). One of the more jarring aspects of Rorty's text is his repeated insistence on American "national pride." Surely, one need not quarrel with a restrained patriotism, with a distinct sympathy for and loyalty to one's country's values and traditions. However, in Rorty's account, national pride often takes on connotations of ethnocentric pridefulness, disdainful of other countries or nations. Thus, when his text states that "America does not need to place itself within a [common] frame of reference" and that "America will create the taste by which it will be judged," such phrases cannot be good news to developing countries currently under the sway of U.S. hegemony.[20] More importantly, quite apart from intended or unintended consequences, national pride in Rorty's sense is increasingly unsettled—for good or ill—by the relentless process of globalization gripping our world today. *Achieving Our Country* offers a dramatic account of this process. "What industrialization was to America at the end of the nineteenth century," we read, "globalization is at the end of the twentieth." As Rorty adds, in a passage which hardly can be contested: "Globalization is producing a world economy in which an attempt by any one country to prevent the immiseration of its workers may result only in depriving them of employment." Echoing numerous critical analyses of economic globalization, his text perceives on the horizon a dark dystopia: the emergence of an international class division between "haves" and "have-nots," between rich and poor nations, North and South.[21]

Yet, Rorty seems less concerned about the "world economy" as such than its effects on social and economic conditions in America. His dystopian vision of the future is particularly tailored to domestic repercussions. As a result of economic globalization, he notes, the large majority of Americans will find their standard of living steadily shrinking; in due course, we are likely to "wind up with an America divided into hereditary social castes." To counteract this trend, Rorty takes recourse to the standard reformist (and socialist) remedy: centralized government intervention at the level of the nation-state. At the same time, he derides cultural Leftists for their cross-cultural or cosmopolitan leanings, stating that their habit of "taking the long view and looking beyond nationhood to a global polity is as useless as was faith in Marx's philosophy of history, for which it became a substitute." Here a final dichotomy emerges, now on a purely political level: that between nation-state and global community. Surely, one of the truisms about globalization is that nation and world are increasingly entwined. Accordingly, a proper Leftist policy would need to involve a combination of local, national, and global initiatives. Against this background, the formula "achieving our country" needs to be revised, in the sense that Americans today can achieve their country only if other societies and nations are able to achieve theirs. By the same token, Americans will be able to regain their national pride only on the condition of fostering and promoting pride in humanity at large.[22]

Recognition and Redistribution

By way of conclusion, some more general comments seem in order. *Achieving Our Country* is largely correct in its diagnosis of contemporary ills, though not in its recommended remedy. Under the combined impact of liberal triumphalism and intellectual forms of "Gothicism," democratic agency has indeed been in retreat in the United States (and other Western countries) for some time. In this situation, Rorty's call for greater political engagement and his denunication of growing social and economic disparities seem to be on the mark. Equally valuable is his attempt at bridge-building, at fostering a conciliatory dialogue between the older reformist and the newer, more culturally oriented Left. One of the critical reservations voiced above was that Rorty's bridge-building appears lopsided: with recent culturalists basically being downgraded in favor of old-style reformers. Here a more balanced or even-handed approach seems called for. For clearly, old-style reformism was not without its flaws—cultural-ethnic and gender insensitivity being one of it main defects. In this regard, recent accents on otherness and difference have provided a corrective, clearing the way for more genuinely democratic—and more ethically appealing—policies.

Today, at the dawn of the new millennium, the task of "democratizing democracy" can no longer be restricted to American Leftism, but has global or cosmopolitan significance. Given the double complexity of the global community—its cultural diversity and its social and economic cleavages—cosmopolitan democracy can be advanced only by a carefully nuanced approach heeding equally both dimensions of difference (in Rorty's terms: the effects of both social sadism and economic exploitation). In some of her recent writings, Nancy Fraser has ably and succinctly pinpointed the two dimensions under the rubrics of "recognition" and "redistribution." In her work, Fraser prefers the term *recognition* to the notion of "difference politics," mainly because *recognition* underscores the socially constituted, status-related character of group differences, while also counteracting the tendency, occasionally present in culturalism, to reify (or "essentialize") existing cultural, ethnic, or religious distinctions. "Redistribution," on the other hand, takes seriously existing economic or class disparities, especially disparities fostered by the accelerating process of economic globalization. In Fraser's account, the major ills prevailing both domestically and globally are "misrecognition" and "maldistribution."[23]

In a similar vein, David Held—in pleading for a "cosmopolitan democracy"—is keenly aware of the formidable obstacles obstructing this goal, obstacles having to do mainly with economic North–South divisions and with entrenched cultural, ethnic, and religious antagonisms (that is, with problems of maldistribution and misrecognition). To overcome these obstacles, contemporary democratic politics has to promote both greater economic equality, mainly through redistribution of resources, and greater cultural sensitivity, chiefly through dialogue and reduction of reciprocal prejudices. In his recent book *Predatory Globalization*, Richard Falk equally supports the vision of a cosmopolitan community seen as an alternative to economic and technological hegemony—that is, the vision of a genuinely "humane governance on behalf of the peoples of the world." As he realizes, the disparity of material conditions, cultural orientations, and resources makes it difficult to "universalize aspirations" without appearing naïve or disingenuous. In this situation, the appropriate posture is to remain "tentative" and to engage in critical dialogue "across civilizational and class boundaries as to the nature of humane governance." Through such a "bottom-up process," he adds, areas of "overlapping consensus" may begin to emerge and a start can then be made on "negotiating differences in values and priorities." Seriously pursued, such an interactive dynamic could in time yield a coherent democratic politics sustaining "humane governance" around the globe.[24]

Returning to Rorty, there are indications that this vision of human governance might not be entirely unacceptable to him. As he writes at the close of *Achieving Our Country*, if his proposed reforms were accepted in the United States, and if many other countries and societies were to adopt similar reforms, then one might begin to envisage a global community, perhaps along the lines of an "international federation." Still, to make this outcome even half-way feasible, important accents of his text would need to be revised. Most importantly, the repeatedly invoked Whitmanesque celebration of brotherhood/sisterhood would have to be more generously enlarged to allow celebration of the kinship of humanity.

Citing from *Leaves of Grass*, Rorty at one point quotes Whitman as saying that he "who would be the greatest poet" must "attract his own land body and soul to himself and hang on its neck with incomparable love." Today, in the midst of globalization, Whitman's love or sympathy needs to be transformed in the direction of a more global love: a democratic friendship among peoples. To protect our world from spoliation and destruction, people around the globe should follow Whitman's dictum by attracting our earth "body and soul" to themselves. In her book *The Work of Friendship*, Dianne Rothleder comments on the one-sidedness of Rortyan "solidarity"—limited as it is to national solidarity—and a certain underdevelopment of the notion of friendship in his thought. Such a notion of friendship, she argues (persuasively), would go a long way toward correcting the excesses both of an overly private individualism and an overly robust publicity (manifest in the stress on national pride).[25] Embracing such a notion also would enable Rorty to link up with the Aristotelian tradition—perhaps prematurely sidelined. In that tradition, genuine friendship combines respect for otherness (recognition) with emphasis on a measure of social and economic equality (redistribution). Although limited by Aristotle to the realm of the *polis*, his praise of *philia* may still provide inspiration for the emerging *cosmopolis* in the new millennium.

Notes

1. James Baldwin, *The Fire Next Time* (New York: Dell, 1988), 116.

2. Richard Rorty, *Achieving Our Country: Leftist Thought in Twentieth-Century America* (Cambridge, Mass.: Harvard University Press, 1998), 4–7.

3. *Achieving Our Country*, 6–8.

4. *Achieving Our Country*, 8, 5–17, 19–21.

5. *Achieving Our Country*, 41–43, 46–50. The citations are from Herbert Croly, *The Promise of American Life* (New York: Capricorn Books, 1964), 22, 25. Originally published in 1909.

6. *Achieving Our Country*, 55, 57–60, 65–66, 69. The reference is to Christopher Lasch, *The Agony of the American Left* (New York: Vintage, 1969), 10, 29. Rorty inserts into his account here some autobiographical notes, disclosing both his own and his forebears' strong involvement in progressive politics. Curiously, he presents himself both as a "teenage Cold War liberal" and as an opponent of the Vietnam War; see *Achieving Our Country*, 58–61.

7. *Achieving Our Country*, 76–80.

8. *Achieving Our Country*, 92–94. Rorty adds, "I now wish to say that, in committing itself to what it calls 'theory', this Left has gotten something which is entirely too much like a religion. For the cultural Left has come to believe that we must place our country within a theoretical frame of reference, situate it within a vast quasi-cosmological perspective" (95). The meaning of *Gothic* is taken from Mark Edmundson's book *Nightmare on Main Street: Angels, Sadomasochism, and the Culture of the Gothic* (Cambridge, Mass.: Harvard University Press, 1997).

9. *Achieving Our Country*, 94–97. For some of Rorty's more detailed writings on recent Continental philosophy see, for example, his *Objectivity, Relativism, and Truth: Philosophical Papers*, 2 vols. (Cambridge: Cambridge University Press, 1991–1993) and *Consequences of Pragmatism* (Minneapolis: University of Minnesota Press, 1982). For his distinction between private and public domains (under the rubrics of private "irony" and

public "solidarity") see his *Contingency, Irony and Solidarity* (Cambridge: Cambridge University Press, 1989). In addition to the above examples, the Gothic character of contemporary cultural Leftism is also manifest in Jacques Derrida's *Specters of Marx: The State of the Debt, the Work of Mourning, and the New International*, trans. Peggy Kamof (New York: Routledge, 1994).

10. *Achieving Our Country*, 91–92, 97–98, 100–101, 106.

11. *Achieving Our Country*, 50–51, 82.

12. As one may recall, Maurice Merleau-Ponty sketched a different, more nuanced approach when he wrote: "We find ourselves in an inextricable situation. . . . It is impossible to be an anti-Communist and it is not possible to be a Communist." See his *Humanism and Terror: An Essay on the Communist Problem*, trans. John O'Neill (Boston: Beacon Press, 1969), xxi.

13. *Achieving Our Country*, 75–76, 80–82.

14. *Achieving Our Country*, 67–68, 71.

15. *Achieving Our Country*, 35, 96.

16. *Achieving Our Country*, 27, 29–30. As he writes, "To those who want a demonstration that less suffering and greater diversity should be the overriding aims of political endeavor, Dewey and Whitman have nothing to say. They know of no more certain premises from which such a belief might be deduced" (30). Compare also Hilary Putnam, *Pragmatism: An Open Question* (Oxford: Blackwell, 1995).

17. *Achieving Our Country*, 60, 96.

18. Rorty occasionally pays tribute to the role of civil disobedience, but without drawing any conclusions for his reformist argument; see *Achieving Our Country*, 54, 56. Apart from the binaries mentioned above, there is another important dualism meandering through his text: that between immanence and transcendence, between secular humanism and religion—with a tendency to collapse the latter into the former. According to Rorty, both Whitman and Dewey espoused a "thoroughgoing secularism," which would enable a "utopian America to replace God as the unconditional object of desire"; he paraphrases Whitman to the effect that "we are the greatest poem because we put ourselves in the place of God: . . . We define God as our future selves." *Achieving Our Country*, 15, 18, 22.

19. *Achieving Our Country*, 75. Rorty may be correct in saying that "during the same period in which socially accepted sadism has steadily diminished, economic inequality and economic insecurity have steadily increased" (83). But this is no reason to devalue the former.

20. *Achieving Our Country*, 29. In fairness, one should note that Rorty adds these lines: "The sort of pride Whitman and Dewey urged Americans to feel is compatible with remembering that we expanded our boundaries by massacring the tribes which blocked our way, that we broke the word we had pledged in the Treaty of Guadalupe Hidalgo, and that we caused the death of a million Vietnamese out of sheer macho arrogance" (32).

21. *Achieving Our Country*, 84–85. Compare in this context also Saskia Sassen, *Globalization and Its Discontents: Essays on the New Mobility of People and Money* (New York: New Press, 1998). Sassen writes in that book that the "global city" is increasingly divided into cities of the rich and the poor, "Global cities concentrate a disproportionate share of

global corporate power and are one of the key sites for its valorization. But they also con-centrate a disproportionate share of the disadvantaged and are one of the key sites for their devalorization. . . . This joint presence is further brought into focus by the increasing disparities between the two" (xxxiv).

22. *Achieving Our Country*, 85–86, 98. Actually, Rorty himself does not seem strictly opposed to cosmopolitanism. As he notes at one point, the need for national engagement remains "even for those who, like myself, hope that the United States of America will someday yield up sovereignty to what Tennyson called 'The Parliament of Man, the Federation of the World'" (3).

23. Nancy Fraser, "Social Justice in the Age of Identity Politics: Redistribution, Recognition and Participation," in *Redistribution or Recognition? A Political-Philosophical Exchange*, ed. Nancy Fraser and Axel Honneth (London: Verso, 2000); also Kevin Olson, ed., *Adding Insult to Injury: Social Justice and the Politics of Recognition* (London: Verso, 2000), and Fraser, *Justice Interruptus: Critical Reflections on the "Postsocialist" Condition* (New York: Routledge, 1997).

24. Richard Falk, *Predatory Globalization: A Critique* (Cambridge, UK: Polity Press, 1999), 168. See also David Held, "Democracy and the New International Order," in *Cosmopolitan Democracy: An Agenda for a New World Order*, ed. Daniele Archibugi and Held (Cambridge, UK: Polity Press, 1995), 116.

25. Dianne Rothleder, *The Work of Friendship: Rorty, His Critics, and the Project of Solidarity* (Albany, N.Y.: State University of New York Press, 1999), 124–25. Regarding the distinction between private and public domains compare Eric M. Gander, *The Last Conceptual Revolution: A Critique of Richard Rorty's Political Philosophy* (Albany, N.Y.: State University of New York Press, 1999). See also Rorty, *Achieving Our Country*, 26, 105.

PART TWO

Pluralism: Variations on Self–Other Relations

CHAPTER SIX

~

Transversal Encounters:
Calvin Schrag and Postmodernity

In our age of consumerism and proliferating technical gadgetry, basic existential questions are prone to be sidelined or repressed—though perhaps never completed erased. Despite the pervasive amnesia or absent-mindedness cultivated by the media, a certain mindfulness stubbornly persists, giving rise to such anxious questions as: What are these gadgets all about, and how are we to live our lives properly in their midst? As can readily be seen, such worries harken back mindfully to older, nearly perennial themes of human self-search and discovery, epitomized in such classical mottoes as "Know thyself" and "The unexamined life is not worth living." In a long string of publications, the philosopher Calvin Schrag has persistently endeavored to "examine" human life—the very point or meaning of being human—in the midst of our turbulent and fast-paced era. Not long ago, Schrag has offered his readers a relatively slender treatise that elegantly and concisely summarizes the fruit of his lifelong examination: *The Self after Postmodernity* (a revised version of his Gilbert Ryle Lectures of 1995). The title of the book refers to a certain debunking or dismissal of selfhood often associated with postmodernity, evident in such popular phrases as the "death of man," the "death of the author" or the "deconstruction of the subject." As Schrag comments wryly and acerbically, "the postmodern announcement of the death of the subject, like the news release of the death of Mark Twain, was a bit of an exaggeration."[1]

In a way, *The Self after Postmodernity* seeks to clear a path through contemporary philosophical thickets: above all, beyond or between the conundrums of modernity versus postmodernity, foundationalism versus antifoundationalism, reason (*logos*) versus storytelling (*mythos*), self and/versus other.

111

In large measure, the path favored by Schrag endeavors to recapture or re-energize individual agency or the role of the human subject—though now a subject concretely situated in finite social, cultural, and religious contexts. To be sure, it might be possible to find a different sense in the cited post-modern announcements, by reading them not as parallels to the news release about Mark Twain but as code words signaling a profound decentering or problematization of the modern subject, triggered not by consumerist amnesia but precisely by a deepening of self-reflection. Questions like these may be seen as a kind of background noise to Schrag's text—though they can initially be held in abeyance to permit an attentive scrutiny of his perspective. The following chapter proceeds in three steps:

1. The first section offers a condensed synopsis of the book's main lines of argument, focused on the status of the self in a postmodern setting.
2. The second part raises a number of afterthoughts or reservations having to do mainly with the issue of a situated and revitalized subject.
3. In conclusion, an effort will be made to indicate the relevance of Schrag's approach to contemporary social and political developments, especially to the emergence of a global civil society or community.

The Self after Postmodernity

In modern Western philosophy, selfhood in the sense of individual subjectivity has traditionally functioned as a crucial cornerstone or linchpin, but this cornerstone has come under increasing pressure in the course of the twentieth century. Appropriately for the occasion, Schrag's text pays tribute to Gilbert Ryle as a pioneer who early on punctured the Cartesian conception of the "thinking substance" (*ego cogitans*) by caricaturing the latter as a "ghost in the machine." The lasting contribution of Ryle's work, Schrag notes, was "a dismantling of the Cartesian portrait of the human subject as an interiorized mental substance"; to this extent, his work may "indeed find a place in the history of twentieth-century philosophy as one of the early illustrations of deconstructionist thought."[2]

Partly in response to Ryle (as well as to Wittgenstein), the puncturing of the subject was carried forward under the auspices of the "linguistic turn," which became a prominent *leitmotif* in Anglo-American analytical philosophy. Concurrently and largely independently of Ryle, a similar movement arose in Continental European philosophy, prominently triggered by Martin Heidegger's path-breaking *Being and Time* and subsequently deepened and expanded by a host of existentialist and structuralist writers from Gabriel Marcel to Maurice Merleau-Ponty and beyond. In the wake of structuralism, the puncturing or deconstructive project was pursued with single-minded vigor by a group of thinkers variously labeled "post-structuralists" or "post-modernists" whose agenda culminated in the postmodern announcements mentioned before. In this postmodern ambiance, Schrag observes, "questions about the self, and particularly questions about the self as *subject*, are deemed anathema." To the extent that the older vocabulary is retained, the self is associated with "multiplicity, heterogeneity, difference, and ceaseless becoming, bereft of origin and purpose. Such is the manifesto of postmodernity on matters of the human subject as self and mind."[3]

It is chiefly the single-mindedness of this manifesto that triggers Schrag's objections. Although concurring with Ryle and his successors in their assault on the Cartesian thinking subject and the entire traditional "substance-theory" of self, he insists that a debunking of this foundationalist model does not and should not entail "a jettisoning of every sense of self." In Schrag's view, the valuable lesson to be learned from anti-Cartesian moves in our era is that modernity's portrayal of the mind as a "transparent mental mirror" and epistemological bedrock has little to contribute to a proper understanding of the human self "in its manifest concretion as speaking and narrating subject." The basic deficiency of the modern portrayal resided indeed in the construal of "an abstracted, insular knowing subject" severed from "the context and contingencies out of which knowledge of self and knowledge of the world arise." Once this abstract model is put aside, however, we are by no means left empty-handed or at the mercy of chaotic multiplicity. According to Schrag's text, precisely the debunking of the erroneous traditional view clears the way to a more genuine grasp of selfhood. In the aftermath of deconstruction, he notes, what happens surprisingly is that "a new self emerges, like the phoenix arising from its ashes"; this self is no longer abstract but concrete, a "praxis-oriented self, defined by its communicative practices."[4]

In focusing on a concretely situated selfhood, defined by its "communicative practices," Schrag also seeks to make a contribution to the modernity/ postmodernity conundrum in another sense by situating himself vis-à-vis the "differentiation of culture-spheres." In the wake of Kant's three Critiques, modern social and sociological theorists—led prominently by Max Weber— had argued that the gist of modernity and modernization consists in the progressive separation and indeed "stubborn differentiation" of the value-spheres of science, morality, and art. Reacting to this proliferation of spheres, modern dialectical thinkers—from Hegel to Marx and beyond—sought to overcome the divisiveness of the modernizing process by emphasizing either the unifying role of universal reason or the unifying potential of a political movement. In a modified vein, Jürgen Habermas in recent times has sought to reconnect the value-spheres under the rubric of a "communicative rationality," a conception that—by stressing the respective integrity of science, morality, and art—also aims to salvage the "project of modernity" seen as a commitment to reason and rationalization. On the other side of the spectrum, postmodern thinkers have shown pronounced lack of interest in the problem of value-spheres and their interconnections, delighting instead in the prospect of infinite dispersal, dissemination, and multiplication. Here again, Schrag takes exception to postmodernism's excess. As indicated before, his text relies on the integrative role of "communicative practices"—practices that, in contrast to Habermas's approach, are anchored not in abstractly rational claims but rather in modes of concrete engagement in the life-world. In Schrag's account, situated selfhood inserts itself into the unfolding trajectories of science, morality, and art—amplified by the sphere of religion—while simultaneously articulating itself in the modalities of discourse, action, social community, and transcendence.[5]

The successive chapters of the book move step by step through the different modalities of self-understanding, always paying due attention to the historical context of value- or culture-spheres. Paying tribute to the linguistic turn, the opening chapter, "Self in Discourse," seeks to uncover the self or "who" involved in discursive practices—where the question of "who" is sharply distinguished from the "what" question of Cartesian metaphysics and the substance-theory of self. As Schrag notes, inquiry into the "who" is not of an "abstract universal nature" but rather aims at a "concrete and historically specific questioner." Seen from this angle, the notion of discourse or discursive practice challenges or disrupts prevalent dichotomies in contemporary linguistic philosophy, especially the dualisms of speech and language, of *parole* and *langue*, and also of linguistic behavior and the semantics of meaning. Functioning in a discourse or discursively, selfhood is not fixed or static but rather dynamically "emergent" or becoming, its unfolding and recognition signal an "adventure of hermeneutical self-implicature," an implication of self in a broader historical narrative.[6] The text at this point celebrates the figure of a narrating self, a "*homo narrans*" or a storyteller "who both finds herself in stories already told and strives for a self-constitution by emplotting herself in stories in the making." In Schrag's account, this narrative perspective provides a sheet anchor both against the Cartesian *cogito* and also—still more importantly—against the disassembling and disaggregating tendencies fostered by postmodernism (as evident in some writings of Jean-François Lyotard). Returning to the notion of *homo narrans*, Schrag insists that narrative allows for a certain unification of selfhood amidst diversity—although the latter should not be misconstrued in terms of a rigid "sameness."[7]

Narrative, in Schrag's presentation, involves not only storytelling in the sense of reciting a tale but also story-enactment through concrete engagement in an unfolding life-praxis. Taken in the latter, "stronger" sense, narrative points to the "dynamics of the self as life-experiencing subject," to the "emplotment of a personal history"—which not merely is a mental exercise but a concretely embodied enterprise. Drawing on the lessons of phenomenology, the chapter "Self in Action" underscores the importance of "embodiment" for a proper understanding of the active life—where embodiment serves again as an antidote to Cartesian metaphysics and especially to the "mind–body" conundrum (where a "ghostly interior" resides in a causal mechanism). Due attention is given at this point to Merleau-Ponty's notion of the "lived body" (*le corps vécu*), to Gabriel Marcel's celebration of "incarnate" existence, and to Jean-Paul Sartre's definition of the body as a "synthetic totality of *life* and *action*." As Schrag elaborates, formulations of this kind do not at all coincide with a merely accidental conjunction according to which the self would just happen to "have" or be located in a body seen as a disposable garment (or, in Plato's terms, as "prison house" of the soul). In fact, the notions of incarnate existence or embodied being require a radical rethinking or reconfiguration of modern conceptions of space or spatiality that present "space" simply as an outer container or as a serialized juxtaposition of spatial points. The focus on bodily praxis or enactment, by contrast, brings into view a different mode of in-dwelling, a mode where the body does not occupy space, but rather "*inhabits* space," moving freely in a realm of "embodied spatiality."[8]

Having portrayed narrative from the (embodied) actor's perspective, the text quickly adds some caveats designed to shield selfhood from a simple relapse into traditional subjectivity. Faithful to his contextual starting point, Schrag reminds readers of the complex interlacing of action and reaction in every concrete "interactive" situation. Seen from the angle of interaction, narrative involves a "dialectic of acting and suffering" that discloses the who of action as "at once agent and patient," as *both* "an active or originating force and a reactive or responding force." In more strictly philosophical terms, human selfhood coincides neither with "a sovereign and autonomous self" completely impervious to forces of "alterity," nor with a self caught in "the constraints of heteronomy" and fully governed or determined from outside. Rather, the self in action lives "*between* autonomy and heteronomy, active and reactive force, pure activity and pure passivity"; it articulates itself grammatically in the "middle voice." Support for his mediating or mid-point position, in Schrag's view, can be found in Gilles Deleuze's portrait of the "rhizomatic self" energized in its self-formation by the play of active and reactive forces, and also in some of Michel Foucault's comments on the role of "bio-power" in human life. As he insists, however, none of these interactive models can or should detract from the importance of active self-initiative, and above all from the vital function of choice or decision seen as the catalyst constituting human selfhood. It is at this point that Søren Kierkegaard enters prominently into the discussion, especially with his accent on the "either/or" quality of self-formation. In Schrag's words: "It is this accentuation of choice that provides the peculiar hallmark of Kierkegaard's existential reflections on the experience of self"—a hallmark that enables him to transform the Cartesian motto into "I choose, therefore I am."[9]

Returning to the aspect of interaction—and bracketing Kierkegaard for the time being—the next chapter shifts the focus to political praxis and specifically to the "Self in Community." The notion of "communicative praxis" or "communicative practices," mentioned before, surfaces here again disclosing human selfhood as "discovering and constituting itself in relation to other selves." Compounding its other flaws, postmodernity is found to be particularly deficient in this domain. Seconding Richard Rorty, Schrag considers it difficult "to situate any positive role for community within the parameters of postmodern discourse." To be sure, the point for him is not to privilege community or the "we-experience" over individual selfhood or "I-experience," since both can be shown to be intricately "entwined"; to this extent, both "sociologism" and "egologism" are equally unacceptable alternatives. As he acknowledges, moreover, community seems to be particularly elusive in the modern context where it has been (and continues to be) so often overshadowed by domination, alienation, and oppression, that is, by attempts to appropriate the "other" and assimilate it to the self. In Schrag's view, "egology" must resolutely be left behind, meaning that "the otherness of the other needs to be granted its intrinsic integrity, so that in seeing the face of the other and hearing the voice of the other I am *responding* to an exterior gaze and an exterior voice rather than carrying on a conversation with my alter ego." Not unexpectedly, the testimony of Emmanuel Levinas is invoked at this point, and especially his notion of the "face" of the other as the inaugural event of moral awareness.[10]

Although endorsing the accent on alterity, Schrag finds it important to caution against a narrow reading of that term. As he notes, self in community should not be restricted to "face-to-face" encounters or close interpersonal relationships, since being-with others acquires its full meaning only "against the backdrop of wider historico-cultural forces." Above all, self-formation implies also an understanding of oneself in larger contexts: "as a citizen of a polis, a player in an ongoing tradition of beliefs and commitments, a participant in an expanding range of institutions and traditions." To be sure, community cannot or should not be reduced to the rule of customs and conventions, heralding a lapse into mere conventionalism. Hence, it is important to define community as "principally a creative and self-affirming modality of being-with-others in society." The basic task of the self in community is to be both responsive and responsible in social interactions, that is, to cultivate the virtue of responding "in a fitting manner." In pursuing this task, crucial guidance is provided by the voice of "conscience," defined by Heidegger as a liberating call to "authentic" self-being. Amplifying Heidegger's account, Schrag turns to the eighteenth-century philosopher Joseph Butler, whose theory of the "moral sense" presented conscience as a "superior principle of reflection" able to guide individual and social life with practical discernment.[11]

The notion of practical discernment or critique implies a distantiation of the self from prevailing conventions, which opens the path to a consideration of the "Self in Transcendence," the theme of the final chapter. As Schrag notes right away, there are different modes of transcendence that need to be carefully distinguished. In a sense, language transcends speech performance, just as action—in Sartre's sense—implies a self-projection transcending present conditions. In these and similar instances, transcendence is still narrowly circumscribed, lacking (so to speak) a vertical dimension. There is, however, also a stronger sense pointing to an alterity exceeding "the economy of intramundane forms." Steps in this direction can be found in Plato's "ideas," in the Kantian "noumenal" realm, and in the metaphysical notion of God as an infinite and supremely perfect being. More recent and still more poignant examples are provided by Rudolph Otto's notion of the "holy" (*das Heilige*) and by Karl Jaspers's doctrine of the "Encompassing" functioning as the ultimate limit of rational comprehension. Particularly in these latter instances, the term *transcendence* signals an encounter with what Emmanuel Levinas has named a "radical exteriority," a phrase motioning toward a transcendent realm "residing on the other side of the economics of human experience." At this point, the voice of Kierkegaard reenters the discussion and, in fact, begins to modulate the book's remaining argument. Basically, Schrag locates the Danish thinker's significance both in his religiosity and in his transformation of modernity, in the sense that the "inclusion of religion" should be seen as "one of the more urgent requirements" for updating the doctrine of modern culture-spheres. In terms of the issue of transcendence, Kierkegaard's importance resides in his distinction between "religiousness A" and "religiousness B"—where the former designates a mundane "religion of immanence" while the latter points to a radical leap beyond or rupture of immanence, a leap "fracturing all efforts by the self to find the God-relationship within itself" and thus clearing the way to the encounter with "a radically transcendent Other."[12]

With regard to the culture-spheres of modernity, Kierkegaard's religiosity (religiousness B) provides, in Schrag's view, several important lessons. First of all, as a mode of distantiation, radical transcendence or alerity furnishes a "critical principle," permitting the critical assessment of conditions in the "intramundane" spheres of science, morality, art, and (organized) religion. By relativizing all situational contexts, religiousness B supplies "the requisite safeguards against ideological hegemony, irrespective of whether such hegemony has staked its claims in the spheres of science, morality, art, or institutionalized religion." The second major lesson of Kierkegaard's work resides in its contribution to the "unification" of modern culture-spheres, an issue that, in Schrag's view, constitutes the "storm center" of the modernity-postmodernity dispute. While many modern philosophers saw reason as the gateway to synthesis, most postmodernists revel in the unleashing of difference and incommensurability. Here, Kierkegaard comes to the rescue by offering a unity grounded not in reason but in radical alterity and faith, while simultaneously banishing the specter of chaotic dispersal.

Schrag invokes at this juncture the metaphor of "transversality" suggesting a process that achieves "convergence without coincidence," "conjuncture without concordance," or "union without absorption." By allowing for a coordination without assimilation, he writes, transversality can be helpful "in elucidating the unifying function of [Kierkegaardian] transcendence." The third major lesson operates on the level of the culture-spheres themselves, where religiousness B shows its transformative quality by contributing to the "transfiguration and transvaluation of the life of self and society." In our time, this Kierkegaard-effect is amplified by Levinas's accent on transformative ethics (the latter seen as response to "the Other as absolute exteriority"). In Schrag's view, a prime example of alterity's incursion is the paradox of gift-giving in the sense that such giving escapes the "economy of production and consumption," transcending radically the "requirements of reciprocity." In this respect, giving is closely related to *caritas* or the Kierkegaardian "works of love" where love—even if unrequited—is freely offered and thereby exceeds the bounds of Aristotelian friendship.[13]

Some Afterthoughts

Although condensed, the preceding synopsis should convey both the broad sweep and the intellectual subtlety of Schrag's text. Having moved through the different modalities of selfhood, the reader is prone to come away with a sense of exhilaration, a sense of having participated in a rich adventure journeying through the multiple dimensions of the human condition. A small *chef d'oeuvre*, the text elicits praise both in terms of style and content. Like few professional academics today, Schrag is able to express his thoughts in language free of jargon, manifesting his desire to engage his readers reflectively rather than impress them with obscure rhetoric. In terms of content, praise is due especially to the impressive scope of intellectual horizons, ranging from Plato and Aristotle to Kant and Hegel and to the leading figures of twentieth-century philosophy. Although cognizant of the latest intellectual developments, his writings—and this text in particular—exude the aura of mature seasoning, of a perspective wedded to the *longue durée* disinclined to trendiness and any desire to please the *idola fori*.

It is precisely on the latter score, however, that qualms may arise regarding the very title of the text: the suggestion that postmodernity somehow denotes a distinct historical phase that we have now survived or left behind. This suggestion is awkward and disorienting in several ways. First of all, the title may give aid and comfort to all those "survivors"—quite large in number—who have habitually bemoaned postmodern initiatives as a stark assault on the finer qualities of Western civilizations. To critics of this kind, the announcement of postmodernity's demise may be welcome news—but news that, again, may be premature. In Schrag's presentation, the term *postmodernity* designates an array of diverse features—an array that is disorienting in its own way. On the one hand, and perhaps predominantly, postmodernity is associated with dispersal and dissensus, with the "celebration of difference and diversity." On the other hand, postmodernity is said to be marked by an overvaluation of aesthetics, a tendency to accord "a ubiquity to the aesthetical." This ubiquity exerts a constraining effect on science and morality, and especially on the latter where the "postmodern ethos" shows tendencies toward "a global aestheticism."[14]

To readers familiar with "postmodern" writings, these judgments will appear summary and neglectful of important nuances. Most importantly, they seem to shortchange the innovative contributions of these writings in the fields of metaphysics, ethics, aesthetics, and even politics—contributions that are unlikely to have run their course or to have reached their full fruition. As it happens, Schrag himself does not fully subscribe to postmodernity's demise. Repeatedly (as stated before) he pays tribute to postmodern initiatives in debunking the Cartesian *cogito* seen as a transparent mirror or fixed substance. Occasionally he also enlists individual postmodernists (or thinkers labeled as such) as useful accomplices in his own project of redefining selfhood. This is particularly true of Deleuze and his portrait of the "rhizomatic self." Deleuze's portrait, he writes, is "particularly germane to my own project of devising a sketch of the human subject." To a lesser degree, some affinity is also claimed with the work of Foucault and especially his conception of "self-scripting" (*l'écriture de soi*), a conception that proves helpful "for articulating what is at issue in our depiction of the self in discourse."[15]

Despite these and similar concessions, the book's overall tenor is that of a postscript or epilogue attempting to uncover the self as "subject *after* postmodernity." This aspect may have something to do with a certain restorative tendency of the text, the tendency to bracket the Cartesian *cogito* only by replacing it with a more concretely situated and thus more robust subject. Despite the shift from the "what" to the "who" question, Schrag pays ample homage to the traditional "modernist" notions of self-constitution, self-enactment, and self-actualization. Thus, in discussing the "self in discourse," Schrag presents speaking as a mode of self-discovery, but also and emphatically as a "creative act," an act of "self-constitution." Even the self as storyteller or *homo narrans*, although finding herself in stories already told, basically strives for "a self-constitution by emplotting herself in stories in the making." Likewise, the portrayal of the "self in action" makes ample room for self-enactment and actualization. Despite the need to recognize human finitude and its constraints, action theory—in his view—must pay heed to the "odyssey of self-constitution" and also to the "dynamics of decision-making" where "the who of action is called into being as an agentive subject," for, as Kierkegaard has insistently demonstrated, it is "through the act of choice that the self constitutes itself."[16]

In fairness to Schrag, his retrieval of the subject is not simply a modernist agenda. In his treatment, self-constitution is not simply a Husserlian enterprise where the self constitutes both itself and the other as alter ego; nor is self-enactment equivalent to a Sartrean mode of self-making. Two devices above all protect his approach from this equivalence. One is the emphasis on "embodiment," the notion that the body is not merely an external costume but rather part of the self's very being. The second device is the correlation between action and reaction, or challenge and response. In Schrag's account, the dynamic of human action occurs in the tension span between "an active or originating force and a reactive or responding force"; in this sense, the who of action is "at once agent and patient, an initiator of action and a receiver of action." This positioning of action "*between* autonomy and heteronomy, pure activity and pure passivity," is said to find grammatical expression in the notion of the "middle voice." Despite their importance in the general argument, however, these devices at best modulate but do not really undermine the preeminence of self-constitution. In the case of embodiment, this fact is evident in the focus on "bodily intentionality" (which merely amplifies Husserlian phenomenology). In the case of action–reaction, the correlation is instantly disrupted in the text by the turn to Kierkegaardian decision making where the self "constitutes itself" through the act of choice.[17]

The real break with self-constitution occurs only in the last chapter devoted to "self in transcendence." Here selfhood in all its embodied robustness is suddenly beleaguered and assaulted by nonself, by a combination of Kierkegaardian religiousness B and Levinasian radical alterity. At initial glance, this change of perspective seems to involve an inconsistency or contradiction (or perhaps another Kierkegaardian "paradox"). At a closer look, however, the change amounts only to a reversal, a look at the other side of the (same) coin. Just because the self was never really dislodged or "decentered" from its traditional interiority, self-transcendence requires as its supplement recourse to a radical exteriority; just because agency in earlier passages was persistently linked with self-constituting autonomy, its antidote must now be found in heteronomy. In the text, this terminology is largely borrowed from Levinas. Reacting critically to the Husserlian constitution of the other, Schrag sides solidly with Levinas's approach "from the other." On this point, he notes, "it is prudent to side with Levinas rather than with Hegel, avowing an original asymmetry within the self–other relation. The radical exteriority of the other as other needs to be acknowledged, attested, and asserted to."[18]

Here one may wonder, first of all, how a radical or absolute exteriority—say a rock on the moon—can have ethical relevance for the self. More to the point, Levinasian terms place considerable pressure on Schrag's earlier presentation that continuously resisted any leap "outside." To recall again a quoted passage: The human self is "neither a sovereign and autonomous self whose self-constitution remains impervious to any and all forces of alterity, nor a self caught within the constraints of heteronomy, determined by forces acting upon it." To the extent that a connection exists between heteronomy or exteriority and heterogeneity (as seems plausible), one is also reminded of Schrag's earlier rebuke of Lyotard. Criticizing the latter's postmodernism, he writes that a recognition of diversity and multiplicity "does not warrant claims for heterogeneity"; the multiple does not necessarily imply something that is "radically 'other,'" as is suggested in the use of *heterogeneous*." Most important, the accentuation of an exterior otherness upsets the intricate balance between action and reaction, between acting and suffering which served as the hallmark of the action chapter. The same or similar problems beset the endorsement of Kierkegaardian religiousness B. Kierkegaard's radical distinction between a "religion of immanence" and a "religion of transcendence" seems to go counter to the main thrust of Schrag's earlier arguments that precisely sought to dislodge and surmount metaphysical binaries (like those between mind and body, inside and outside, immanence and transcendence).[19]

The virtues of Kierkegaardian (and Levinasian) nonreciprocity are illustrated by Schrag with the help of two examples: gift-giving and friendship. Echoing Kierkegaard, his text finds a deep paradox in the giving of a gift, a paradox that is not properly grasped by anthropologists who placed their emphasis on exchange. To be genuinely a gift, it must be presented without any expectation of a "countergift" or a return. To this extent, he writes, the gift remains necessarily "outside, external to, the economy of production and consumption, distribution and exchange" and hence "radically transcendent to the requirements of reciprocity." Here some critical discernment seems called for. Nonmutuality certainly deserves a hearing to the extent that gift-giving is meant to be shielded from commercial or market transactions, from the inroads of "distribution and exchange." However, reciprocity is not necessarily restricted to these mundane or instrumental forms of interaction but may also operate in more subtle ways. As it appears, this subtler type of reciprocity seems also to be at work in gift-giving. Although shunning the expectation of a countergift, a gift must surely be received by the beneficiary "*as*" a gift, to be properly understood and assessed as such. The giving of a gift would certainly misfire if the receiver (say a police officer or public official) took it to be a bribe or if the recipient mistakenly assumed that it involved an item the giver had previously borrowed. Thus, gift-giving, to function as such, inevitably involves some mutuality of understanding and discernment.[20]

Perhaps the most prominent type of nonreciprocal giving, according to the text, is friendship. Close attention here is paid to Kierkegaard, and especially to the latter's *Works of Love*, which celebrates "a love that loves for the sake of loving," a "nonpossessive love" that "expects nothing in return." As Schrag recognizes (following Kierkegaard), this type of loving bears indeed a resemblance to the Aristotelian notion of friendship (*philia*) seen as a dedicated mutual engagement. However, in the wake of Christian teachings of *caritas* and *agape*, Kierkegaardian loving transcends or "leaps beyond" classical Greek insights. In Schrag's words, "It is the Augustinian view that brings into relief the limitations of Aristotle" whose idea of friendship remained "rooted in the requirements for reciprocity" and who saw *philia* as possible "only between equals."[21] Here, again, the critical reader may remonstrate on several grounds—first of all, by pointing to the "as" character even of loving. Even the most gracious and nonpossessive *agape* is liable to misfire if it is seen by the beneficiary as a mode of condescension or paternalism. More importantly, the contrast between *agape* and Aristotelian friendship seems overdrawn in several respects. *Pace* Kierkegaard, Aristotelian *philia* is not mundanely instrumental but nonpossessive in character—as is evident from his repeated statements that genuine friendship means loving the friend "for the friend's sake." The connection between *philia* and equality is, of course, undeniable; but its significance is misconstrued. The point is not that *philia* presupposes equality but rather that it is an agent effectively equalizing unequals, especially those unequal in rank, age, or gender. It is for this reason that Aristotle saw *philia* as the equalizing bond in political regimes, including democracy—whereas the accent on inequality and asymmetry has dubious (if any) democratic credentials.

Apart from its intrinsic quandaries, the turn to nonreciprocity has detrimental effects on two of Schrag's most fruitful and appealing insights: his plea for practical wisdom and his emphasis on "transversality." Critiquing a certain postmodern concern with desire, Schrag argues that the "self in action" displays a "praxis-oriented reason," bringing into view "a dynamics of discernment, an economy of practical wisdom" that carries its own weight without requiring the sanction of "pure cognition and pure theory." It is this kind of practical moral discernment which allows the "self in community" to respond properly to other selves, thus providing the contours for an "ethic of the fitting response"—which in many ways is close to Aristotle's notion of *phronesis* seen as preeminent practical virtue. The problem that arises here is the compatibility of these statements with unilateralism, that is, with a resort to "radical alterity" or a Kierkegaardian "leap of faith." Clearly, practical discernment is not instantly acquired but, like piano playing, needs to be assiduously practiced; as Aristotle has taught (correctly), *phronesis* and all practical virtues need to be steadfastly cultivated. By contrast, on a certain reading of Levinas, ethics seems to be suddenly bestowed on the self by a radical exteriority—apparently without the need for self-care and the practice of virtues. Even more explicit, Kierkegaard's radical fideism cancels or disavows practical discernment, relegating it to a "lower" ethical realm.[22]

Nonmutuality is even more damaging to the notion of transversality—perhaps the most significant contribution of Schrag's text. As previously mentioned, the notion is invoked chiefly as a means of correlating or "unifying" the different culture-spheres of modernity and more generally the multiplicity of diverse life-forms. In Schrag's presentation, transversality is meant to replace the traditional notion of an abstract "universality," namely, by shifting the accent from a finished result to an ongoing dynamic process of unifying by correlating. As he writes, "Transversal unity is an achievement of communication as it visits a multiplicity of viewpoints, perspectives, belief systems, and regions of concern." The problem here is the conflict between this aspect of processual correlation and the simultaneous emphasis on transcendence and alterity seen as an exodus from reciprocity. By definition, such alterity/ exteriority is placed outside or beyond the concrete labor of transversal interactions. As Schrag comments with reference to Kierkegaard's religiousness B, "It is this radical alterity that supplies the standpoint for an external critique of the four culture-spheres." Seen from this angle, religiousness B has already achieved—through a radical leap—that superior standpoint through which all "immanent" perspectives are transgressed and relativized, seemingly without the need of lateral engagement.[23]

Social and Political Lessons

Having voiced these critical observations, it seems appropriate to return to the mode of friendly engagement. After all, these observations were offered precisely in a transversal spirit honoring mutuality. What seems desirable, by way of conclusion, is to highlight aspects of the broader social and political significance of Schrag's arguments, especially as they are applicable to our age of consumerism and ethnic cleansing. Here I wish, first of all, to applaud Schrag's sense of public awareness and responsibility, his self-interpretation as an academic philosopher shouldering the task of a public intellectual. As he writes in the preface to his book, in our time of growing specialization the responsibility placed upon the intellectual is considerable; for he/she is called upon "to forge lines of communication across several academic disciplines" and to explore the relevance of arguments "for citizens of a public world." Schrag at this point evokes the long history of the involvement of philosophy and public life in the development of Western civilization since its beginning. "We need but to recall the Athenian Socrates," he notes, "who at the dawn of Western philosophy exemplified the life of philosophical inquiry in dramatic manner by mingling with the citizens of Athens in the local marketplace, engaging them in conversations about the achievement of self-knowledge." The steady rise of scientific and technological expertise in our time lends a new sense of urgency to the Socratic example. Without eliding their academic functions, public intellectuals today need also to reconstrue their philosophical task: "along the lines of a rhetoric of inquiry directed *to* the public and crafted *for* the public."[24]

Eminently accessible to nonacademic readers, *The Self after Postmodernity* clearly fulfills Schrag's self-imposed task. The publicity of the text, however, is manifest not only in its style but also in many of its substantive arguments. An example is the recuperation of practical wisdom seen not as an inventory of abstract principles but rather as an ongoing responsible life-praxis. "The ethical," Schrag notes (distantly echoing Heidegger), "has to do with *ethos* in its originative sense of a cultural dwelling, a mode or manner of historical existence, a way of being in the world that exhibits a responsibility both to oneself and to others." In this context, one may wish to take a leaf from the work of Julia Kristeva, a professional linguist and psychoanalyst who has also shouldered the role of public intellectual and political theorist. Particularly significant in the latter respect is Kristeva's conception of a "politics of marginality" that seeks to enlist the agency of sidelined or subaltern groups for purposes of political transformation. In her view, given the postmodern decentering of the subject, emancipatory politics can no longer rely on grand ideological schemes entrusted to a collective agent, but must instead operate in the interstices of prevailing constellations (that is, on the level of Foucault's micropowers). As Schrag writes, crediting Kristeva, "The most effective resources for social change are found in the interventions of marginal groups, after one has become duly suspicious of the grandiose aims of collective political programs."[25]

Even more timely and significant on a global scale is the text's endorsement of transversality. Schrag is eloquent in castigating traditional conceptions of unity and universality for relying on centralized command structures and totalizing metaphysical premises. "In the traditions of both the ancients and the moderns," he states persuasively, "unity has fraternized with identity, and in concert unity and identity have waged war against plurality and difference." Against this background, postmodernity's merit resides precisely in its accent on difference and multiplicity—provided this accent is not transformed into an atomistic "foundationalism," into a doctrine of radically isolated substances. It is here that transversality comes into play with its emphasis not on a fixed or pregiven unity but on the open-ended search for self-transgressing horizons and correlations; ranging freely across and between domains of life, the transversal quest proceeds as "an open-textured gathering of expanding possibilities." Seen in this light, transversality bears a close resemblance to Jean-Luc Nancy's notion of an "un-managed or inoperative community" (*communauté désoeuvrée*), a phrase that means to defy both a pre-arranged synthesis and an antisocial heterogeneity. In Nancy's portrayal, community of this kind involves neither a totalizing metaphysics nor a compact empirical presence, but rather something like a calling, an advent or perhaps a promise.[26]

Amplified by Nancy's insights, transversality inserts itself—as a calling—into contemporary global politics by challenging both hegemonic global power structures (often parading as "universal") and the traditional anarchy of states and societies. Wedged *between* universalist arrogance and forms of particularistic (ethnic, religious, or cultural) belligerence, transversal communication invites individuals and societies to participate in open-ended encounters geared toward neither appropriation nor exclusion. Seen in this light, transversality opens an arena for what Schrag describes as a lived practical ethics—now projected onto the global scale. As in the case of personal relations, global interactions urgently need the cultivation of an ethics of the "fitting response," where responding responsibly involves both a mutual learning experience and an element of "praxial critique." In the final pages of his book, Schrag himself points to the global or cross-cultural significance of his argument by referring to Christian-Buddhist encounters, and especially to the affinities and divergences between Christian and Buddhist understandings of love and compassion (the latter illustrated by the writings of Keiji Nishitani). What transversality contributes to such encounters is the promise of a responsive engagement that resolutely stops short of a totalizing or coercive synthesis, thus "letting difference be." As Schrag concludes, "This is what I have named *transversal communication*, striving for convergence without coincidence, conjuncture without concordance, seeking to understand within the context of difference."[27]

Notes

1. Calvin O. Schrag, *The Self after Postmodernity* (New Haven: Yale University Press, 1997), 61. For some of Schrag's earlier writings see especially *Communicative Praxis and the Space of Subjectivity* (Bloomington, Ind.: Indiana University Press, 1986), and *The Resources of Rationality: A Response to the Postmodern Challenge* (Bloomington, Ind.: Indiana University Press, 1992). For a detailed review of the latter book see my "Splitting the Difference: Comments on Calvin Schrag," *Human Studies*, 19 (1996): 229–38.

2. *The Self after Postmodernity*, xii, 4. The reference is to Gilbert Ryle, *The Concept of Mind* (New York: Barnes and Noble, 1949).

3. *The Self after Postmodernity*, 8.

4. *The Self after Postmodernity*, 8–9, 25, 28.

5. *The Self after Postmodernity*, 5–7. Schrag adds that against the backdrop of our explorations, it would appear "that the culture-spheres of science, morality, and art cannot be that facilely divided. There is more of an inmixing of the constative or descriptive, the normative or prescriptive, and the expressive or aesthetic across the domains of science, morality, and art than the framers of the modernity problematic are wont to acknowledge" (32). In his discussion of Habermas, Schrag seems to overestimate the integrative function of "communicative rationality," since Habermas repeatedly insists on the separate trajectories or "logics" of science, morality, and art.

6. *The Self after Postmodernity*, 12–13, 16–17, 19–20.

7. *The Self after Postmodernity*, 22, 26, 29–30, 35, 38.

8. *The Self after Postmodernity*, 42–43, 46, 48–49, 54–55.

9. *The Self after Postmodernity*, 56, 59, 62-63, 66–67, 70. Regarding the notion of the "middle voice" see Suzanne Kemmer, *The Middle Voice* (Philadelphia: John Benjamins, 1993) and John Llewelyn, *The Middle Voice of Ecological Conscience* (London: Macmillan, 1991).

10. *The Self after Postmodernity*, 77, 79–80, 83–84. The reference is to Emmanuel Levinas, *Totality and Infinity*, trans. Alphonso Lingis (Pittsburgh: Duquesne University Press, 1996), chap. 3.

11. *The Self after Postmodernity*, 86–88, 91–92, 96–99. The reference is to Joseph Butler, *The Works of Joseph Butler*, vol. 2: *Fifteen Sermons on Human Nature* (Oxford: Clarendon Press, 1986).

12. *The Self after Postmodernity*, 111–16, 118–21. The reference is chiefly to Søren Kierkegaard, *Philosophical Fragments or A Fragment of Philosophy*, trans. David Swenson (Princeton: Princeton University Press, 1936), and *Concluding Unscientific Postscript*, trans. David Swenson (Princeton: Princeton University Press, 1941).

13. *The Self after Postmodernity*, 124–29, 134, 137, 139–46.

14. *The Self after Postmodernity*, 27, 67, 69, 75.

15. *The Self after Postmodernity*, xii, 38, 56. At other points, however, Schrag is quite critical of Foucault and especially of his "read on the Stoic ethics," which "tends to blur the distinction between ethics and aesthetics" (38). In a later context, he basically concurs with Richard Rorty's "swipe" at Foucault and other current French philosophers (29).

16. *The Self after Postmodernity*, 16, 19, 26, 56–57, 60–62, 84, 95.

17. *The Self after Postmodernity*, 54, 59, 62, 100.

18. *The Self after Postmodernity*, 100, 137.

19. *The Self after Postmodernity*, 30, 59, 120. Why Kierkegaard's bifurcation of types of religiousness should have "nothing to do" with "the distinction between the finite and the infinite, the temporal and the eternal" (Schrag, 135–36), thus setting aside "traditional metaphysical binaries," remains obscure. The obscurity deepens in the face of Kierkegaard's statement quoted in the same passage that "God does not exist, he is eternal." See Kierkegaard's *Concluding Unscientific Postscript*, 296.

20. *The Self after Postmodernity*, 93, 139–40.

21. *The Self after Postmodernity*, 141–42. Further accentuating Kierkegaard's distinction, a recent (Augustinian) scholar writes, "I want to suggest, hesitantly but firmly, that a Christian ethic ought to recognize the ideal of civic friendship as essentially pagan, an example of inordinate and idolatrous love." See Gilbert C. Meilaender, *Friendship: A Study in Theological Ethics* (Notre Dame, Ind.: University of Notre Dame Press, 1981), 75. Schrag himself cites approvingly A. N. Whitehead's statement that "religion is what the individual does with his own solitariness"—probably one of Whitehead's more dubious propositions. See his *Religion in the Making* (New York: Meridian Books, 1960), 16; Schrag, *The Self after Postmodernity*, 89, n. 7.

22. *The Self after Postmodernity*, 57, 97–98, 135. The passage occurs in Kierkegaard's *Concluding Unscientific Postscript*, 296.

23. *The Self after Postmodernity*, 126, 129–33, 147–48.

24. *The Self after Postmodernity*, ix–x.

25. *The Self after Postmodernity*, 40–41, 99, 101. The reference is to Julia Kristeva, *Revolution in Poetic Language*, trans. Margaret Waller (New York: Columbia University Press, 1984), and "The System and the Speaking Subject," in *The Kristeva Reader*, ed. Toril Moi (New York: Columbia University Press, 1986), 24–33. For Heidegger's notion of ethics as "*ethos*" see his "Letter on Humanism," in *Martin Heidegger: Basic Writings*, ed. David F. Krell (New York: Harper and Row, 1977), 233–35.

26. *The Self after Postmodernity*, 129. See also Jean-Luc Nancy, *The Inoperative Community*, ed. Peter Connor, trans. Peter Connor et al. (Minneapolis: University of Minnesota Press, 1991), xxxviii–xxxix, 29–31. For a closer review of Nancy's work see my "An 'Inoperative' Global Community? Reflections on Nancy," in *Alternative Visions: Paths in the Global Village* (Lanham, Md.: Rowman & Littlefield, 1998), 277–79.

27. *The Self after Postmodernity*, 146–47. Regarding Keiji Nishitani see his *Religion and Nothingness*, trans. Jan Van Bragt (Berkeley: University of California Press, 1982); also my "Nothingness and *Sunyata*: A Comparison of Heidegger and Nishitani," *Philosophy East and West* 42 (1992): 37–48, and "*Sunyata* East and West: Emptiness and Global Democracy," in *Beyond Orientalism: Essays on Cross-Cultural Encounters* (Albany, N.Y.: State University of New York Press, 1996), 175–99. To be sure, the encounter with Nishitani, and with Asian Buddhism in general, may involve a greater challenge to Schrag's argument than he realizes—given the Buddhist emphasis on emptiness and no-self. See in this regard Joan Stambaugh, *The Formless Self* (Albany, N.Y.: State University of New York Press, 1999).

~

CHAPTER SEVEN

Border Crossings:
Bernhard Waldenfels on Dialogue

Un pied en un pays,
l'autre pied en un autre. . . .

           —René Descartes

Despite its grander ambitions, philosophy also inhabits the world—if only through its ties to ordinary language communities. In contemporary Western philosophy, it is customary to distinguish between "analytical" and "Continental" versions of philosophizing—where the latter version comprises a broad cross-national smorgasbord of ideas ranging from Nietzsche to Martin Heidegger, Jacques Derrida, and Gianni Vattimo. This smorgasbord approach is surprising in light of a central theme in contemporary Continental thought: the theme of "difference" or "otherness" which militates against any facile homogeneity. Clearly, to remain faithful to this theme, it is necessary to descend from panoramic overviews to the level of situated life-worlds, that is, from the spectatorial to the plane of engaged participants. Among contemporary thinkers on the Continent, no one has been more persistently attentive to cross-national differences than Bernhard Waldenfels, a German philosopher who—although reared in Husserlian (German-speaking) phenomenology—has held his sights constantly aimed across the border toward French intellectual developments. Several of his major publications have dealt with this crossroads or border crossing. Having presented, in 1983, the main strands of "French phenomenology" to a German audience, Waldenfels more recently has come forward with a larger book on this theme, titled

German-French Paths of Thought (*Deutsch-Französische Gedankengänge*)—a book that serves here as springboard for my discussion in this chapter.[1] As the title of his study indicates, Waldenfels is concerned with paths or pathways of thought, and not simply with fashion trends or intellectual fads. Exploring pathways of thought requires patience and diligent scrutiny, which is at odds with rapid appropriation and consumption. With a glance across the Atlantic, Waldenfels speaks at one point of ideas that are "rapidly carried to market" and then suffer equally rapid obsolescence. Such rapidity, he notes, fosters forms of "postism" or beyondism which awkwardly resemble the perennial "revolutionary changes" in consumer goods. Luxuriating "particularly in the United States," such postism in his view constitutes a distinct form of "rapid digestion" of European traditions, giving rise to labels like post-structuralism, post-Marxism, post-philosophy, and the like. Waldenfels's nonmarketing approach is evident in his manner of presentation, which throughout remains on a level of high intellectual intensity. Glancing again across the Atlantic, this approach offers in many ways a refreshing change of pace. To a large extent, American reception of Continental thought has oscillated between bland dismissal and panegyrical praise. While demoted (especially by analytical philosophers) to the status of "mere" literature, Continental texts are often celebrated by their partisans in a style befitting mystery cults. Deviating from both types of reception, Waldenfels soberly speaks of the "labor" of thought, and also of the labor involved in transforming inherited forms of thought. Only such labor, he writes, can prevent new intellectual impulses from being reduced to mere "fashion waves."[2]

Faithful to this discriminating approach, Waldenfels's book offers a careful review of leading figures in German–French interactions during this century—but without suggesting a bland synthesis or ready fusion of horizons. Remembering Descartes's motto (about having "one foot in one, the other in another country"), Waldenfels accentuates the border between philosophical idioms—although a border that is not impermeable. "The other land," he writes, "is and remains other in irremediable alterity. By planting our feet in one and then another country we take our position on one side and do not hover neutrally over both. In this way, we are located both *on this side and beyond* the boundary," that is, both "here and elsewhere."[3] With these comments, Waldenfels intimates a border zone which is not a form of convergence but a mode of complex interlacing and dialogue (possibly of an agonal kind): the border zone between self and other, self and foreign. Although focused on German–French relations, this "between zone" in many ways is the red thread weaving itself through successive chapters and signals the broader significance of the text in contemporary Western thought. In this chapter I shall:

1. Highlight some major arguments of the study, especially as they emerge in the treatment of selected thinkers on both sides of the Rhine.
2. Next, I shall sharpen the focus of discussion by concentrating on two thinkers whose relation appears crucial to Waldenfels's own preferred perspective: Maurice Merleau-Ponty and Emmanuel Levinas.
3. To conclude, I shall try to draw together the diverse facets of the text and offer some of my own critical comments.

German–French Paths of Thought

Waldenfels opens his text with a number of general considerations meant to serve as "entry points" or guideposts for his presentation. On the whole, these considerations are marked by a cautiously tempered élan. Foremost among the book's entry wedges is the nexus between self and other, sameness and difference. As he notes, the relation between self and other—including that between German and French thought—has the character of a dash or "border sign" which can be read both as hyphen and caesura: "If things were not separated, there could be no possible linkage. On the other hand, if things were wholly separated, linkage could not gain a foothold." Relying on a number of authors—Edmund Husserl, Merleau-Ponty, Helmuth Plessner, and Norbert Elias—Waldenfels speaks in this context of a complex form of interlacing, criss-crossing, *enjambement*, and chiasm. As he writes, "Self and other originate together, and this means (in Hölderlin's words) that one's own must be learned just as much as the alien." Linkage with the other here is neither an external fate nor a matter of sheer choice, because "one chooses the other as much and as little as one chooses one's own body." In comments like these, Waldenfels clearly distances himself from more extreme views, especially the polar opposites of a placid consensualism and a radical atomism or separatism (favored by some "postmodernists"). This distancing move is a kind of *leitmotiv* which Waldenfels carefully sounds in the preface of his book:

> Whatever gains its distinctness by differentiating itself in a specific manner from others and by deviating from a common level, does not aim at mere consensus. For how could a figure be merged with its ground? Conversely, deviation here does not aim at dissensus either; for it signals a genuine mode of differing and not a perverted form of consensus.[4]

The relevance of this *leitmotiv* extends from general self–other relations to the distinct realm of cross-national or cross-cultural interactions. In this respect, Waldenfels's argument pits itself both against a melting-pot type of globalism and a Balkanizing strategy of fragmentation; in his words, the pathways of his book move in a philosophical idiom that "refuses the alternative of particularism and universalism" in favor of a nonconvergent style of dialogue or exchange. Such an exchange, he writes, does not involve concurrence but rather a "laboring from two sides where one may perhaps meet in a common field—but a field where points of departure and orientations never coincide." In this regard, he adds, the encounter between peoples and cultures resembles a dialogical exchange "where question and response, speech and counter-speech follow each other without being sublated jointly in a unified *telos*." Unsurprisingly (to students of phenomenology) the text at this point invokes Merleau-Ponty's notion of "lateral universalism" where cross-cultural contact is not imposed by a "universalism from above" but rather emerges from mutual interlacing, questioning, and contestation. In Merleau-Ponty's view, what hovers at or beyond the border of any ethnocentric experience is an untamed or "wild region" which can serve as subterranean passageway to other cultures. "The blind spot in one's own culture," Waldenfels comments, "opens a third way which is wedded neither to universalism nor an (abstract) culturalism" but which also does not remain glued to the "collective selfhood" or self-centeredness of one's own culture or nation.[5]

The cited *leitmotiv* is connected with a number of other entry points or guideposts which include prominently the status of modern reason, the role of subjectivity or subjective agency, and the meaning of history and tradition. Entering the dispute surrounding the "dialectic of Enlightenment," Waldenfels delineates a position which is located neither squarely inside nor simply outside the confines of modern rationality. As he notes, modern Enlightenment culminated in the postulate of a universal reason anchored in a *cogito* which itself was universalizable (or sublated into reason). Echoing Nietzsche and Theodor Adorno, he finds in this postulate a domineering strand, a sign of the "tyranny of *logos*" or the "dominance of reason," evident in reason's attempt to expurgate everything nonrational or else to appropriate everything into its rational order. For better or worse, Nietzschean suspicion has unmasked the "presumptuousness" of this outlook. In the wake of this unmasking several strategies have been adopted to cope with modernity's dialectic. One such strategy is the attempt to salvage the "project of Enlightenment" through a further desubstantialization of reason, a move associated chiefly with the work of Jürgen Habermas and recent critical theory. In this move, reason is sublimated into a string of transempirical and transsubjective validity claims—but at the price of being reduced to a formalized grid. Another prominent strategy consists in the stark disavowal or "dissolution" of modern reason, a disavowal often choosing the method of radical reversal. Pursuing this method of reversal, Waldenfels writes, one can no doubt "oppose multiplicity to unity and difference to identity"; but one neglects how thoroughly a purely "reactive thinking" remains prisoner of the perspective it tries to undermine.[6]

In lieu of the strategies of retrieval and dismissal Waldenfels opts for the path of a transformation of reason (and its underlying subjectivity). "I am convinced," he states,

> that much (though not everything) that has happened in French philosophy since the 1930s can be understood as such a transformation and, moreover, that transformative efforts in this sense have been linked more or less closely with phenomenology—even where the latter is combated or transmuted.

To a large extent, efforts of transformation in the French context have been linked with the notion of an embodiment of reason, an approach that subsequently was further intensified in the direction of an enlargement and dissemination of reason. Taken singly or in combination, efforts of this kind were not equivalent to dismissal. In Waldenfels's view, the endeavor of transformation at no point served as a cloak for "the denial of reason, for irrationalism." Rather, the endeavor signaled a progressive radicalization intent on opening reason to its other (or otherness) and thus to curb its domineering or imperialist ambitions. Reason's transformation also entailed a rethinking of (constitutive) subjectivity and subjective agency. It is in this domain that "postmodern" rhetoric has gained a dubious notoriety, by replacing traditional humanism with antihumanism and by boldly proclaiming the "death of man" or "death of the subject." For Waldenfels it is important to distill the sensible point of this rhetoric. Expressed in "less mythical language," he states, the notion of the death of man refers to "the end of an anthropocentric outlook which elevates humans in diverse forms to masters and proprietors of all things, including themselves." What recent philosophical developments render untenable is the assumption of a foundational subject (functioning as *subiectum* of the world). However, transgressing the "principle of subjectivity" leaves room for many options, including the "patient transformation of what used to be called 'subject.'"[7]

Coupled with the displacement or decentering of the subject is inevitably a rethinking of history—which can no longer be viewed as the progressive fulfillment of human objectives and purposes. Together with a linear historical *telos* this rethinking also calls into question the notion of a pristine origin which simply unfolds in history and which can always be rationally retraced and recuperated. What takes the place of such teleology is neither a blind fatalism nor the sway of arbitrary whim but a view of history as continuous renewal where purpose and nonpurpose are closely entwined. Relying on important strands in recent French philosophy, Waldenfels speaks in this context of a "primal past" (*Urvergangenheit*) meaning a "past that was never present," and of a "primal history" (*Urgeschichte*) evolving through steady reconstitutions and reworkings. Historical memory from this vantage always implicates a *temps perdu*, and self-recollection a mode of other-recollection. What this means, for Waldenfels, is that historical time is neither "up for grabs" (to be appropriated by futuristic ideologues) nor a comfortable refuge (for traditionalists). As he writes, tradition is not a secure foundation "upon which our collective experiences and ideas could come to rest"; rather, it is something "from which every renewal deviates"—though not in the mode of rejection but of a "coherent reworking." Waldenfels returns at this point to his accent on laboring and transformation, seen as antidotes to a bland retrieval or dismissal. Countering again the vogue of "postism" he critiques the belief in a "free disposal" over time, the assumption that there is "only the alternative between an *insistence* on tradition and a *liberation* from tradition"—and not also the possibility of "a laboring on and reworking of tradition which opens new pathways."[8]

The guiding themes sounded in the opening pages of the book are fleshed out and amplified in subsequent chapters—now in close dialogue and confrontation with leading German and French thinkers. In the present context, a few selected highlights must suffice to indicate the general drift of the argument. The dialogue opens in the form of two chapters devoted to the founder of modern phenomenology: Edmund Husserl. In contemporary discussions—especially in the ambiance of postmodernism—Husserl is often sidelined as a simple "subjectivist" or modern rationalist completely obtuse to the "dialectic of Enlightenment" and unaware of the interlacing or *enjambement* of self and other. Without denying Husserl's modernist side (as founder of a constitutive and "transcendental" phenomenology) Waldenfels is intent on alerting readers to profound ambivalences in Husserl's project, to fuzzy border zones where constitution of self and the world is overshadowed or invaded by traces of otherness. In his words, the "sober reticence" characterizing Husserl's work ultimately had to come to terms also with the situation "where the alien appears *as alien*." At this point, the "*logos* of phenomenology" had to prove itself as a "*logos* of otherness" (*Logos des Fremden*). As is well known, Husserl wrestled with this issue in his deliberations on intersubjectivity (in *Cartesian Meditations* and elsewhere). Without in any way resolving the problem, his writings at least pointed to a whole new field of questions—which subsequently became guideposts for French phenomenology.[9]

The questions intimated in Husserl's work were pursued with rigor by several French phenomenologists, usually in the direction of a decentering of intentionality in favor of the "*logos* of otherness." Waldenfels's book turns right away to some early writings of Jacques Derrida—writings marked by an intense engagement and wrestling with Husserlian "egology" and linguistic "idealism." As Waldenfels notes, these writings demonstrate a philosophical sobriety which belies Derrida's reputation (in some quarters) of literary frivolity. Contrary to his detractors, Derrida knew and had studied what he was "deconstructing"; to this extent, he does not belong to "those adepts of 'postism' who pretend to have gone simply 'beyond.'" In one of his earliest writings, Derrida took up a suggestion formulated by Husserl himself regarding a "genetic phenomenology," pushing this suggestion to the very boundary of a subjective constitution of meaning—though without abandoning Husserl's vocabulary. The confrontation was deepened and radicalized in *Speech and Phenomena*, devoted to a critical step-by-step analysis of Husserl's theory of signs (as found chiefly in *Logical Investigations*). As Derrida tried to show, subjective meaning constitution is closely linked with language—but a language which, contrary to Husserl, is not reducible to transparent speech but always implicated in a structure of significations recalcitrant to intentional semantics. Borrowing in part from Saussurean semiotics, Derrida resolutely embedded *logos* in sign systems—without, however, opting for a bland empiricism. In Waldenfels's words, Derrida "did not replace Husserl's transcendentalism with a placid worldliness conforming to existing orders through linguistification and socialization. Rather, he discovered in that transcendence an 'ultra-transcendental' dimension . . . fostering a 'transcendental ferment or unrest.'"[10]

Waldenfels's book does not pursue the later development of Derrida's thought, especially his intense encounters with Nietzsche and Levinas. Instead, the text turns to a detailed critical examination of the evolving *oeuvre* of Merleau-Ponty—a topic I will discuss at a later point. In terms of detailed scrutiny and attentiveness, the Merleau-Ponty chapters are matched only by those devoted to Emmanuel Levinas (whose consideration I likewise postpone). Among other French thinkers, more limited attention is given to the works of Cornelius Castoriadis, Francis Jacques, and Jean-François Lyotard—of which the first two are only distantly related to the orbit of Husserlian phenomenology. In the case of Castoriadis, Husserl's legacy is replaced in large measure by Kant's Third Critique, amplified by elements of existentialism and psychoanalysis. The faculty of imagination, thematized in the Third Critique, is elevated by Castoriadis into a power of creation, extending from individual human life to the "imaginary institution" of society. While appreciating the dynamic quality of this approach, Waldenfels distances himself from an abstract "creationism" that, by virtue of its emphatic self-constitution, would be obtuse to the demands of otherness and intersubjectivity. In the case of Francis Jacques (relatively unknown in the United States), phenomenological motives cede pride of place to linguistic analysis, discourse theory, and elements of "transcendental pragmatics" (as articulated by recent Frankfurt theorists). Although applauding Jacques's intersubjective turn, Waldenfels takes exception to his tendency to formalize discourses, a tendency bent on leveling dialogue into a preordained logical formula.[11]

Critical concerns of a different, nearly opposite character surface in the chapter on Lyotard, and also in the discussion of Michel Foucault (to whom a somewhat longer middle section of the book is devoted). In the case of Lyotard, the accent on linguistic phrases and discourse formations leads to the assumption of a radical divergence between phrases, a divergence which resists neutral settlement and only permits integration into a hegemonic discourse. What this means—Waldenfels notes—is that ethical self–other relations are either stranded between discourse formations or else elevated into an abstract "appeal" without content. A more complex philosophical panorama is presented in Foucault's writings, in their evolution from an early "structuralism" to a later, more nuanced (or post-structural) analysis. What Lyotard pinpointed with the labels "phrase" and "phrase families," Foucault's early writings tended to thematize under the rubric of "knowledge formations" (or structures of *episteme*) which, as "hegemonic formations" in a given period, were closely linked with power or domination. Subsequently, at least since *Archaeology of Knowledge*, these formations were translated into the vocabulary of "discourses" or discursive statements; still later, discursive structures and prevailing power constellations were amplified by forms of individuation or "subjectivation" in given periods. For Waldenfels, the central question here concerns the relation between structures and especially Foucault's ability to negotiate their difference—an issue that (he argues) was not properly addressed and ultimately consigned to the status of a recessed aporia.[12]

Interlacing and Separation

As indicated before, the most extensive discussions in the book deal with the "pathways of thought" of two thinkers who, in different ways, were profoundly shaped by Husserlian phenomenology: Merleau-Ponty and Emmanuel Levinas. In several of his previous writings, Waldenfels had commented in detail on key themes in Merleau-Ponty's work, including the notions of *monde vécu*, intercorporeality, and the "flesh" of the world. By comparison, attention to Levinasian arguments seems to be of somewhat more recent date.[13] As is well known, the reception of Levinas—especially in the American context—has tended to be fervent, occasionally bordering on a "conversion" experience. Against this background, Waldenfels's rapprochement with Levinas—though intense—appears cautious and circumspect and marked more by respectful engagement than pliant surrender; although replete with signs of appreciation and even admiration, his Levinas chapters are evidence of sustained, sometimes critical interrogation. To a large extent, Waldenfels's own perspective is located somewhere at the crossroads of his two chosen mentors. This search for a "between" path or *entre-monde* colors the book's overall presentation of contemporary German-French pathways of thought.[14]

The discussion of Merleau-Ponty is a model of sustained analysis, of a scrutiny which allows texts to speak without granting them doctrinal status. Waldenfels right away focuses on a crucial aspect of the former's phenomenology, and especially his theory of language: the problem of linguistic "expression" (*Ausdruck*). Following one of Husserl's suggestions, Merleau-Ponty repeatedly calls expression a riddle or "miracle," having to do with the fact that language tries to say "something" that does not speak by itself and that may vanish when captured in expression. In Waldenfels's reading, this riddle or "paradox" of language is closely related to Merleau-Ponty's move beyond intentionality toward the "*logos* of otherness." Once subjective constitution is left behind, expression can no longer be viewed as pure activity or intentional creation—just as little as it equals pure passivity or imitation. The riddle of expression also impinges on the problem of "truth"—likewise one of his lifelong preoccupations. Bracketing traditional theories of correspondence and coherence, Merleau-Ponty's writings with growing intensity centered on the notion of a creative truth or "*vérité-à-faire*" (truth-in-the-making)—where *making* is not a synonym of fabrication and actually is closer to the adequacy of a "fitting" response. This notion of creative truth was exemplified in Merleau-Ponty's interpretation of painting, especially his critique of the linear panorama of classical painting in favor of the embroilment of multiple (and "incompossible") visions in recent art. On the whole, Merleau-Ponty's work emerges in these chapters not as a closed system but as an "interrogative thinking"—where questioning always calls the questioner into question."[15]

A similarly attentive approach characterizes also the chapters devoted to Levinas. As in the case of Merleau-Ponty, Waldenfels focuses his discussion on a number of key themes in Levinas's work, particularly the themes of singularity, self-responsibility, and other-responsibility (*Fremd-verantwortung*). As he emphasizes, singularity for Levinas designates not simply a constitutive subjectivity nor individual uniqueness, but a self-hood formed through self-transcendence toward the other—a transcendence resisting any totalizing homogeneity and resulting at best in an asymmetrical plurality. In Waldenfels's words, "Singularity in the plural arises only through *self-transgression* of one's own, which means that the self's uniqueness is more and other than itself." Viewed in this sense, singularity presupposes not just any difference, but the "concrete difference between own and alien or foreign (*fremd*), between own-ness and foreignness." For Levinas, exposure to otherness carries deeply ethical connotations, in the sense that the alien other approaches us not as a neutral bystander but as someone who calls upon and lays claim to us (*Anspruch*). This claim or demand escapes the lure both of consensual reciprocity and of a temporal synchrony or repetition; the stark edges of divergence are only tempered, but not removed in a broader social context where the "face" of all others requires something like an equal justice (among singulars). Responsiveness to a claim or call, in Levinas's account, entails inescapably an ethical responsibility, first of all in the form of "self-responsibility" (*Selbstverantwortung*). What is involved here, Waldenfels states, is not a subject in the traditional sense but a genuine "respondent" who becomes "who he/she is in the response." Levinas extends this kind of responsiveness to the difficult concept of "other-responsibility"—which means not just a shared responsibility but a radical "responsibility for others" where one "substitutes" oneself for others by accepting the role of culprit, hostage, and victim.[16]

The Levinas chapters are rounded out by a section specifically devoted to the relation between Merleau-Ponty and Levinas, under the heading "Interlacing and Separation." According to Waldenfels, both thinkers were deeply indebted to Husserl's legacy, yet both tried to "deconstruct constitutive phenomenology from within"—though in very different, only partially overlapping ways. The similarities/divergences between the two thinkers are explored in a number of thematic areas: including those of intercorporeality (illustrated by the handshake), self–other contacts, gender relations, and residual ontology versus "primary" ethics. For Merleau-Ponty, intercorporeality meant basically a kind of "co-perception," a bodily appresentation permitting "other-experience" (*Fremderfahrung*). This view was exemplified in Merleau-Ponty's treatment of the handshake, a treatment stressing the differential relatedness of active and passive-receptive components, of touching and being touched. It is in this area that an initial divergence surfaces—with Levinas charging Merleau-Ponty with promoting a facile harmonization, a privileging of the active-perceptual element. For Levinas, the lure of harmonization can only be banished by the assumption of a radical otherness or foreign-ness (*Fremd-heit*) which exceeds any type of perception or cognition and which resists "being transformed into *phenomena*." Levinas at this point introduces the idea of a "radical separation" of hands and bodies as an antipode to inter-corporeality, a separation culminating in the formula of the "nakedness of the alien face" as the origin of a primary ethics.[17]

Divergence also surfaces in the field of gender relations where Merleau-Ponty preferred to speak of a differential relatedness—with male and female being profiled against each other in intercorporeality—while Levinas insisted on the separation of genders even in the "community of sensation." In the discussion of these and related themes, the respective positions of the two thinkers are progressively sharpened and tested against each other, in the mode of reciprocal contestation (*Auseinandersetzung*). In the course of this testing Waldenfels's own perspective also begins to take shape. In the opening rounds of the confrontation, Waldenfels repeatedly takes the side of Merleau-Ponty, defending him against spurious or ill-considered accusations. On several occasions, his book takes exception to a certain "impatience" or summary bluntness in Levinas's approach, which accounts for the fact that his criticisms of Merleau-Ponty often miss their target. In the same vein, Waldenfels protects Merleau-Ponty against charges of fostering a bland coincidence or totalizing synthesis. As he writes, such charges bypass the complexity of Merleau-Ponty's thought by simply privileging the "motif of separation" over the "motif of interlacing"—when one has to ask whether the one "can at all be operative without the other." While acknowledging the emphasis on relatedness in Merleau-Ponty's thought, Waldenfels finds sufficient countervailing evidence making it possible to speak of an "asymmetrical interlacing" which eludes the tentacles both of synthetic holism and atomistic fragmentation, pointing instead to a complex "between-world" (or *intermonde*). As if happens, these preferential accents noticeably shift in the course of the presentation, yielding in the end nearly the opposite evaluation. Returning to Levinas's reversal of "logocentrism," Waldenfels concedes that phenomenology of almost every kind is unhinged by the alien other's ethical demands. These demands tend to be muted by interlacing of any kind. For Waldenfels, what needs to be acknowledged at this point is the reality of separation and even rupture (*Riss*) between self and other, a rupture that happens from "outside" and can never be recuperated in any interlacing (of body or meanings).[18]

Decentered Dia-logue

Waldenfels's text evidently pursues a double aim: first, to give a balanced overview of German-French intellectual pathways, and next (and more importantly), to articulate through commentary his own preferred perspective. On both counts, he deserves to be applauded and rewarded by a wide audience of readers. To be sure, congruent with his own approach, Waldenfels would not welcome an uncritical audience—which provides me with leeway to add some of my own critical comments. On a somewhat superficial level, readers may question the selectivity and organizational structure of the book. In a text devoted to German-French interactions, one may be surprised to find only two German authors singled out for treatment: Husserl and Friedrich Nietzsche (whose discussion is tagged on almost as an afterthought at the end). Readers might have expected some chapters on Heidegger and perhaps on one or the other representative of the Frankfurt School. On the French side, the choice of Castoriadis and Francis Jacques appears puzzling, as is the omission of such figures as Sartre and Luce Irigaray (not to mention the later Derrida). Yet, given the overall quality of the text, such matters shrink into minor quibbles.

More significant, in my view, are questions relating to Waldenfels's own perspective on self–other relations. As indicated before, this perspective is subtle and in many ways tensional. At the conclusion of his book—in a chapter titled "Dispersed" or "Decentered Dialogue"—Waldenfels offers some additional comments on his own pathway of thought. Somewhat surprisingly, the chapter speaks of a "birth of philosophy out of the spirit of dialogue." A thinking inquiring into its own ground, we read, "exposes itself to the labor of dialogue"—although the latter has to be seen as a "dia-logue" where the gathering principle of "*logos*" is continuously exposed to the hazard of division and dispersal among participants. Efforts to negotiate this intrinsic tension have produced a number of models or formulas in the history of Western philosophy. Prominent among these formulas is the Platonic ideal of dialogue where sublimation into a shared *telos* is given primacy over the danger of relativizing disjunction. To effectuate this goal, the Platonic model—which is said to resonate still in Hegel, Husserl, and recent hermeneutics—relied on a series of premises or guideposts, such as "knowledge is recognition," "knowing means participating in a (cosmic) whole," and "dialogue is (a version of) soliloquy." A different model was developed by Kant who substituted for the Platonic *telos* a "grounding law" pinpointed in "apriori conditions of possibility." With this move—still reverberating in Habermasian discourse ethics and "universal pragmatics"—dialogue is trans-

formed into argumentation before an impartial judge, specifically the "tribunal of reason" located ideally in everyone's conscience. Although no longer
animated by a substantive purpose, this tribunal replicates the gathering
power of *logos* by expunging critique of the adjudicating norms.[19]

For Waldenfels, both models are flawed and inherently vitiated by their
necessary (though unacknowledged) incompleteness; just as the unified classical *telos* cannot comprehend or exhaust the (cosmic) whole, the modern
conception of a "grounding law" cannot be part of its own rule system. What
is basically missing in both formulas is recognition of the decentering of *logos*, and especially of the dis-orderly and innovative character of self-other
encounters as evident in genuine "dia-logue." In Waldenfels's words, a questioning which proceeds not on the basis of a pre-given order but rather "inaugurates and transforms such order" is not a mere subsumable instance but
rather a *"key event (Schlüsselereignis)* which opens up a discursive field while
precluding other possibilities." Seen as part of this inaugural event, dia-logue
exceeds coincidence and, in effect, is decentered and dispersed into a "plurality of *logoi*," into a multiplicity of discursive frames which is not so much
a peaceful as an "agonistic" (*kämpferisch*) multiplicity where the pursuit of
some possibilities excludes or frustrates others. The only way this multiplicity can escape randomness and fragmentation is through the linkage of question and response, and especially through an understanding of response as
"responsiveness" and responsibility. Such responsiveness, Waldenfels notes,
implies a "reply to the other" which in its uniqueness exceeds the range of
repetition and recollection.[20]

What is admirable in these passages is the attempt to formulate a notion of
dia-logue—and of self–other relations more generally—which escapes the
tentacles both of a totalizing *logos* and of utter divisiveness and isolation. To
this extent, Waldenfels's "postmodernism"—if this label is at all appropriate—
clearly differs from fashionable versions which celebrate randomness for its
own sake. As it seems to me, Waldenfels's approach offers indeed a promising
way of coming to terms with contemporary multiculturalism and with the
challenges facing Western thought in the aftermath of Eurocentrism and Orientalism. The main question I want to raise here is whether his approach does
not perhaps overaccentuate the *dia* over the gathering function of *logos*—or to
put matters in terms of the *agon* between Merleau-Ponty and Levinas,
whether he does not at points overly favor Levinasian "separation" over Mer-
leau-Pontyan "interlacing" (including "asymmetrical interlacing"). This
weighting of scales seems to me neither required not warranted—even as a
(desirable) countermove to a homogenizing reason. Surely there must be a
middle path between a logically predictable response (such as the question

"What is two plus two?") and a radically disjointed response (which, perhaps "creatively," misses the question). In common parlance, we call this middle path a "fitting" response, characterizing responsiveness as such—while unfitting responses are considered either pointless or else offensive or rude. Waldenfels himself, of course, is quite aware of the pitfalls of sheer disjointedness and, on several occasions, tries to guard against it. Still, the solution offered in the concluding pages—that of a pure "responsiveness" seemingly without content—comes uncomfortably close to the *interrogatio pura* criticized at another point.[21]

Following in large measure Levinasian teachings, Waldenfels ties responsiveness closely, perhaps indissolubly, to the claim or demand of the other which disrupts any placid soliloquy. Here again, questions can be raised regarding the quality and status of this claim, especially its determining, commanding, or merely soliciting character. In the United States, Levinas's "face of the other" has often been read and greeted in a near-fatalistic fashion. Although offering a much more nuanced account, Waldenfels's text is not entirely free of this submissiveness, as is evident in his tendency to absolve the other's claim from any reciprocity and thus from any need to justify its rightness or propriety. To the extent that this is the case, the pitfall of an active "creationism"—criticized in the work of Castoriadis—is matched by the opposite pitfall of a reactive passivity. Moreover, devoid of semantic meaning, the notion of a radical claim comes uncomfortably close to an ethics of abstract postulates—to which Lyotard is said to succumb. Reluctant to move in this direction, Waldenfels remonstrates, "Pure imperative sentences which command nothing in particular and are addressed to no one in particular, are a practical chimera."[22]

One needs to recognize, of course, that Lyotard's discourse is not identical with that of Levinas. As Waldenfels ably shows, Levinas's discourse is of a special or peculiar kind—in the sense that "singularity" carries for him a transitive connotation and that nonreciprocity hence retains a certain perceptual linkage. Nevertheless, precisely in light of this peculiarity, one cannot help being chagrined by a distinctively one-sided Levinasian vocabulary (exteriority, heteronomy, and the like)—a vocabulary that in large measure has shaped his reception abroad. At a minimum, one can question the usefulness of this vocabulary that seems to undercut any transitivity in favor of rigid antithesis. In the same fashion, the opposition between "totality" and "infinity" (or transcendence) seems to replicate traditional two-world formulas that have been rendered dubious at least since Nietzsche. One may readily grant that the "other" is not simply inside or part of the same (or self), but this does necessarily render it "external"—provided decentering is taken seriously enough to disclose the self's otherness to itself. Waldenfels repeatedly stresses the embroilment of self and other, inside and outside—but without making this into a problem for Levinas. As he writes at one point, philosophy—despite the lure of logocentrism—is always inhabited by "its own otherness" (*Fremdheit*). Elsewhere, again in reaction to Lyotard, he presents "excess" (or transcendence) as not external to what it exceeds, for "the one is *nothing without the other.*"[23]

The accent on exteriority is closely linked with another troubling issue: that of force and violence. Clearly, if self and other are radically separated, the other's claim can reach me only in the form of violent irruption or disruption. Following in large measure Levinas's lead, Waldenfels's text is replete with references to force and violence (*Gewalt*) seen now as complements of self–other disjunction and the contingent selectivity of choices. Thus, his discussion of creative expression underscores its agonistic or "struggling" (*kämpferisch*) character that always carries with it "elements of violence" or streaks of "violent irruption." This accent is heightened in the Levinas chapters that document the nearly imperceptible transition from the superiority of the other's claims to an "excess of alien violence." As indicated before, the comparison between Merleau-Ponty and Levinas culminates in the stress on rupture (*Riss*), through which every relatedness is forcefully "exploded, torn asunder."

Several comments are in order at this point. First of all, the undeniable selectivity of choices surely can lead to a different, nearly opposite conclusion: precisely the absence of one correct framework would seem to impose on choosers the need for moderation and self-limitation (including the limitation of violence). As regards *rupture*: the term appears meaningless unless it tears apart what belongs together (rather than indifferent elements)—not to mention the painfulness of any *"Riss"* that seems to call for healing. On a more general level—and quite apart from Waldenfels's text—I find disturbing a pervasive "rupturing" tendency in contemporary Continental thought. In an age ravaged by unbelievable and unprecedented violence and brutality, can one be sanguine about the proclivity of many philosophers to muse about the benefits of *"Gewalt"*?[24]

Mitigating rupture obviously entails implications for ethics and ethical relations. One can readily concur with the Levinasian notion that "obligation happens," meaning that we are "always already" ethically obligated without deliberate choice. Thus, we are inevitably obligated to our parents and siblings (and perhaps to the world at large) from the time of birth, independently of intent. This, however, tells only part of the story. Clearly, understanding the nature of the obligation and meeting it appropriately requires ethical preparation and cultivation on our part. To this extent, acknowledgment of the "happening" of obligation does not at all dispense with the personal cultivation of virtues and the labor of character formation. According to traditional teachings, these virtues include temperance, courage (in the face of oppression), prudence, and a disposition for justice. Implicit in the notion of prudence (and other more "theoretical" virtues) is a kind of thoughtfulness—which militates against a presumed "primordiality" of ethics beyond philosophical reflection. It is the same kind of thoughtfulness, in my view, which has prompted the collective wisdom of humanity to shun the extremes of self- or other-centeredness in favor some version of the Golden Rule. It is the same Golden Rule that seems to reverberate in the end also in Waldenfels's view of "asymmetrical interlacing," as culled from Merleau-Ponty. Rather than pursuing my critical queries, I want to conclude with a passage which ably reflects Waldenfels's nuanced perspective at multiple crossroads:

> Interlacing as an asymmetrical linkage of self-transgressing elements precludes both holism and atomism. The non-coincidence of myself with myself and others prevents integration of myself and others into a totalizing whole. . . . Conversely, the non-difference between myself, the world and others militates against a process of isolation where a single being would congeal in its separateness. The double negation implicit in non-coincidence and non-difference preserves single beings from dissolving in the whole, and it preserves the whole from splintering into radical fragmentation. Constituted by this double "no," interlacing diverges from both total fusion and particularistic dispersal.[25]

Notes

1. Bernhard Waldenfels, *Deutsch-Französische Gedankengänge* (Frankfurt-Main: Suhrkamp, 1995), hereafter cited as *DFG*; see also his *Phänomenologie in Frankreich* (Frankfurt-Main: Suhrkamp 1983). Among his other publications, compare *Der Spielraum des Verhaltens* (Frankfurt-Main: Suhrkamp, 1980), *In den Netzen der Lebenswelt* (Frankfurt-Main: Suhrkamp, 1985), *Ordnung im Zwielicht* (Frankfurt-Main: Suhrkamp, 1987), *Der Stachel des Fremden* (Frankfurt-Main: Suhrkamp, 1990), and *Antwortregister* (Frankfurt-Main: Suhrkamp, 1994). *Ordnung im Zwielicht* has recently been translated by David J. Parent as *Order in the Twilight* (Athens, Ohio: Ohio University Press, 1996). For an English-language introduction to this thought see my "On Bernhard Waldenfels," *Social Research*, 56 (1989): 681–712, and also my foreword to *Order in the Twilight*, xi–xv. For a list of English-language essays by Waldenfels see *Order in the Twilight*, 167–68.
2. Waldenfels, *DFG*, 45, 48–49.
3. *DFG*, 50. He adds, the aim is not to produce a "German–French or French–German" melange, but rather to articulate one idiom in the other and to think it together with the other (11).
4. *DFG*, 7, 9–10.

5. *DFG*, 7, 27, 31. See also Maurice Merleau-Ponty, "From Mauss to Claude Lévi-Strauss," in *Signs*, trans. Richard C. McCleary (Evanston: Northwestern University Press, 1964), 114–25.

6. *DFG*, 18–20, 29, 39.

7. *DFG*, 20–21, 40, 42.

8. *DFG*, 24–25, 48–49. Compare in this context Paul Ricoeur's recent book *La mémoire, l'histoire, l'oubli* (Paris: Seuil, 2000).

9. *DFG*, 51, 79–80.

10. *DFG*, 84, 91. Compare also Jacques Derrida, *Speech and Phenomena, and Other Essays on Husserl's Theory of Signs*, trans. David B. Allison (Evanston: Northwestern University Press, 1973). In his reading of this text, Waldenfels comes close to the interpretation of Rudolphe Gasché in *The Tain and the Mirror: Derrida and the Philosophy of Reflection* (Cambridge, Mass.: Harvard University Press, 1986). Waldenfels, however, also raises some critical reservations regarding Derrida's text, by calling into question an exclusively "phonocentric" construal of Husserl's argument and by insisting on a closer interpretation of time (speech) and space (writing) and of self-other relations in speaking and hearing.

11. *DFG*, 190, 193–94, 261–63, 293, 296, 300.

12. *DFG*, 211, 240, 274–76. In the case of Lyotard, Waldenfels refers chiefly to his *The Differend: Phrases in Dispute*, trans. Georges Van den Abbeele (Minneapolis: University of Minnesota Press, 1988). See also Michel Foucault, *The Archaeology of Knowledge*, trans. A. M. Sheridan Smith (New York: Pantheon Books, 1972). Regarding Foucault, it is important to note that Waldenfels's comments do not at all coincide with Habermas's critique, which opposed to Foucault's "dispersal of reason" a universal meta-discourse animated by universal validity claims. As Waldenfels writes, we have no reason "to fetishize the name of Foucault. But what cannot at all be avoided is the question how we can and shall philosophically proceed if it is true that the anthropological centering of reason is no longer defensible and if the centrality of 'man' was not so much thought but invented" (*DFG*, 216). Compare also Jürgen Habermas, *The Philosophical Discourse of Modernity: Twelve Lectures*, trans. Frederick Lawrence (Cambridge, Mass.: MIT Press, 1987).

13. As one may note, the chapter on Levinas in *Phänomenologie in Frankreich* was not written by Waldenfels himself but by S. Strasser (218–65).

14. A similar kind of *Auseinandersetzung*, involving Merleau-Ponty and Derrida, has recently been initiated in the United States. See in this context M. C. Dillon, ed., *Ecart and Différance: Merleau-Ponty and Derrida on Seeing and Writing* (Atlantic Highlands, N.J.: Humanities Press, 1997).

15. Waldenfels, *DFG*, 109–11, 119–20, 131–34, 148, 151, 168–69.

16. *DFG*, 309–10, 314, 316, 326, 328–30, 334–35.

17. *DFG*, 346, 349–50, 352, 354–57.

18. *DFG*, 353–54, 357, 362–65, 370–71, 375, 380–81.

19. *DFG*, 426–33. For Waldenfels, the main innovation of Habermas's pragmatics is the replacement of the Kantian monologue of reason or conscience by an intersubjective "communication" in which every participant functions as judge. The main flaws of this approach are found in the infinite regress of rules (for rule-governance) and in the deficit

of moral motivation (433). Despite his generally critical comments, Waldenfels concedes the limitations of his portrayal and the possibility of retrieving something like an "other Plato" and an "other Kant" (429, 434).

20. DFG, 434–37.

21. DFG, 168, 244. As one should note, however, Waldenfels' text repeatedly departs from "pure" responsiveness. Thus, we read at various points about the appropriateness and cogency (Triftigkeit) of a response and also about a "responsive rationality" that seeks to "meet" a question, thereby avoiding empty chatter (134, 139). One also needs to recognize that Waldenfels has developed a very complex panorama of possible responses in Antwortregister.

22. DFG, 274–75.

23. DFG, 118, 282. In my view, terminological aporias also beset the notion of "otherwise than Being" or "beyond Being"—a notion which quickly tends to land one in the dilemmas of "being and nothingness" (familiar from Sartre). In my view, it is preferable to follow Heidegger by using being "under erasure."

24. DFG, 120, 138, 342, 381. On the political level, the Levinasian accent on separateness seems uncomfortably close to the dominant climate (in the West) of antisocialism and of a certain libertarianism which condemns any human togetherness as "totalitarian" aberration. As one may also note, a combination of Levinasian disjunction with Carl Schmitt's "friend–enemy" formula has led some political thinkers to an endorsement of willful decisionism (harking back to Hobbes). Compare, for example, Ernesto Laclau, "Deconstruction, Pragmatism, Hegemony," in Deconstruction and Pragmatism, ed. Chantal Mouffe (London and New York: Routledge, 1996), 47–67.

25. DFG, 330, 364–65.

CHAPTER EIGHT

Distancing the Other: Jacques Derrida on Friendship

Omni tempore diligit amicus. . . .

—Proverbs

For a considerable time now friendship has been under siege. Over a period of many centuries, self has been steadily removed or distanced from other selves, with the result that ancient notions like "concord" (*homonoia*) or "communion" (*consensio*) have been increasingly problematized if not entirely eclipsed. Several factors have contributed to this process in Western civilization. The rise of Christianity introduced a strong vertical thrust into human orientation, an accent on salvation or "man–God" relationship, sometimes to the detriment of interhuman bonds. Modern Western philosophy—as articulated chiefly by Descartes—erected the thinking ego into a bulwark of inner self-certainty, a bulwark segregated from the "external" world comprising both nature and other selves. Subsequent liberal theory—from Thomas Hobbes to utilitarianism—centerstaged the category of self-interest as the chief engine in politics and market economics, despite occasional (and narrowly circumscribed) concessions to interhuman sympathy and fairness. Even Kantian philosophy—arguably the noblest form of modern liberalism—sidelined or downgraded friendship and affection in favor of impartial rules of justice and the demand of rational respect. The same weighting of accents still continues in the most prominent Western ideology or paradigm today—procedural democracy—a paradigm privileging abstract and neutrally administered procedures over concerns with interhuman sympathy and lateral solidarity.[1]

The plight of friendship is particularly manifest in the area of (what is called) civic or political friendship. In classical philosophy—as articulated chiefly by Aristotle—friendship was treated as the ethical bond holding together a city or public regime, while its decay was seen as the harbinger of civil war and/or tyranny. Adapting this thought to a specifically republican constitution, Cicero extolled the political significance of friendship, while simultaneously castigating a Stoic retreat into solitude as irresponsible and care-less (devoid of *cura*). Here again, Christian theology brought serious complications. Although valuable as an antidote to corrupt politics, St. Augustine's distinction between two cities also entailed a distinction between two kinds of citizenship and hence between two kinds of friendship: the one purely "spiritual" and quasimonastic, the other this-worldly and mainly defective or sinful.[2] Despite its secularizing bent, modern philosophy largely preserved this division by further internalizing and privatizing friendship (and ethical life in general), while abandoning the public domain to the dictates of individual self-interest. Thus, while celebrating his intimate and "perfect" friendship with Etienne de la Boëtie, Michel de Montaigne consigned social relations to the level of mere humdrum acquaintances, a level unable to generate genuine moral obligations. In a similar vein—though closer to a Kantian-style distance of respect—Ralph Waldo Emerson remarked a few centuries later, "I chide society, I embrace solitude, and yet I am not so ungrateful as not to see the wise, the lovely, and the noble-minded as from time to time pass my gate," adding, "In strictness, the soul does not respect men as it respects itself. In strict science all persons underlie the same condition of an infinite remoteness. . . . What a perpetual disappointment is actual society, even of the virtuous and gifted!"[3]

The point here, to be sure, is not to relate a one-dimensional story of social decline, which would grossly truncate the intricate complexity of the process. The Christian and later modern turn to inwardness signaled also a deepening of human experience and of (what some call) personal "authenticity"; as liberals are liable to stress, the same process also meant a growth of individual freedom, especially among previously submerged segments of the population. More importantly, the distantiation between human agents also entailed the possibility of a stronger recognition of the autonomy and separate integrity of other selves (although this point was hardly ignored by classical philosophical arguments). In the meantime, all these issues have gained a new and sharper profile by recent developments in Western philosophy, especially by the stirring of self-critique occurring in the very bosom of modernist thought. In the wake of Edmund Husserl's relentless inquiries into self–other relations, a number of Continental thinkers have further problematized and "decentered" the Cartesian ego (or subjectivity), thereby also placing friendship (including civil or political friendship) in a novel way on the intellectual agenda. Among these thinkers, Jacques Derrida deserves special attention, both because of his trenchant intellectual verve and because of his determined effort to rethink the meaning of friendship, including political friendship. The results of this rethinking surfaced mainly in two texts: an essay titled "The Politics of Friendship" (1988) and a book-length study called *Politics of Friendship* (1994/97). In the interest of brevity and manageability, my focus will be placed here initially and mainly on Derrida's more succinct essay, although his longer book will also be invoked throughout in a supplementary fashion. In addition to the value of succinctness, the initial focus also allows me to comment on an instant rejoinder to the essay formulated by Thomas McCarthy. The presentation proceeds in three steps:

1. The first section recapitulates and gives a condensed overview of the main lines of argument of "The Politics of Friendship."
2. The second part recalls some of the central points of McCarthy's rejoinder (written largely from the vantage of Habermasian critical theory).
3. In conclusion, I assess the cogency and significance of Derridean friendship in terms of both contemporary political philosophy and of political praxis.

The Politics of Friendship

Derrida opens his essay (and also his book) by citing an apocryphal statement attributed by Montaigne to Aristotle: "O my friends, there is no friend." The aporetic character of this statement—its invocation of friends whose lack is simultaneously affirmed—provides in many ways the keynote or tenor of the entire argument. In opening his argument with this phrase (one quickly detects) Derrida seeks to center the light of attention not so much on its source, Aristotle, but rather on Montaigne whom he describes as "another reader of the country I come from."[4] Apart from frequently repeating, almost ritualizing, Montaigne's phrase or quotation, the essay ascribes to Montaigne a pivotal role in the Western understanding of friendship. This role emerges clearly toward the end of the essay when Derrida offers what he calls a "history of friendship" (to be sure, a history far removed from any traditional historicism). In many respects, this history resembles the sketch I offered at the beginning of these pages, but it also bears a distinctive Derridean imprint or trademark.

According to Derrida, the history of friendship gives evidence of "two major ruptures" or transformative incisions. The first rupture occurred at the end or with the waning of the "Graeco-Roman model," a model that Derrida describes as being shaped or marked "by the value of *reciprocity*, by homological, immanentist, finitist, and politicist concord." The postclassical incision is highlighted or exemplified by Montaigne who, despite certain borrowings from the past, "breaks the reciprocity" of the classical model and "discreetly introduces, so it seems to me, heterology, asymmetry, and infinity." Derrida at this point raises some rhetorical questions (which seem to call for an affirmative response). "Shall one say," he writes, "that this fracture is Judaeo-Christian? Shall one say that it depoliticizes the Greek model or that it displaces the nature of the political?" A second fracture or rupture, the essay suggests, was introduced later by writers like Nietzsche and Maurice Blanchot, whose treatments of friendship "defy both historicity and exemplarity." In their diverse ways, these and other recent writers "call the friend by a name that is no longer that of a neighbor, perhaps no longer that of a man." Elaborating on the last part of this sentence, Derrida notes that the "who?" of friendship now "moves off into the distance beyond all these determinations"; in its "infinite imminence," it exceeds "the interest of knowledge, science, truth, proximity, even life and even the memory of life." He also quotes Blanchot, who, in an almost Emersonian vein, asserted that friendship involves "the recognition of the common strangeness that does not allow us to speak of our friends but only to them" and that friends "even in moments of the greatest familiarity keep their infinite distance."[5]

Returning to the beginning and the opening phrase of Montaigne (quoting Aristotle), Derrida recalls the immediate occasion of his own essay: an address before a philosophical society to whose invitation he is responding (and whose members may in turn respond to him). Reflecting on this situational context, he asks whether this context has already any bearing on his chosen topic of friendship. "Supposing," he states, "that one can translate these Greek words today by 'friendship,' I still do not know if what exists between us is *philia* or *homonoia*, nor how one should distinguish here among us, among each of us, who together would compose this as yet quite indeterminate 'us.'" Remembering (or rather anticipating) the ending of his essay, one senses already that this contextual "us" or "we" is bound to be very complicated and elusive. Before sorting things out further, Derrida writes that in effect, "we are already caught up in a kind of asymmetrical and heteronomical curvature of the social space, more precisely, in the relation to the Other prior to any organized *socius*, to any determined 'government,' to any 'law.'" Distancing or "rupturing" the classical Aristotelian legacy, Derrida here describes "originary sociality" as a "heteronomical and asymmetrical curvature," that is, as a relation that confounds and disrupts human autonomy and social reciprocity. Taking his bearings again from some recent French literature, he does not hesitate to link this curvature with a kind of "violence" or disruptive force, noting that what is happening is "perhaps just the silent unfolding of that strange violence that has since forever insinuated itself into the origin of the most innocent experiences of friendship or justice." What accounts for the violence or disjuncture is the fact that sociality in the sense of a responsibility to the Other (or to otherness) catches as unawares or by surprise, thus imposing on us a kind of "responsibility without freedom" or autonomy. Derrida elaborates,

> This responsibility . . . assigns us our freedom without leaving it with us, if one could put it that way. And we see it coming from the Other. It is assigned to us by the Other, from the Other, before any hope of reappropriation permits us to assume this responsibility in the space of what could be called *autonomy*.[6]

What emerges in these lines or arguments is the imposing influence of Emmanuel Levinas (whose name curiously remains unmentioned throughout the essay); all the key terms employed in the preceding passages—like *heteronomy, asymmetry*, and responsibility instilled by the *Other*—are borrowed from the arsenal of Levinasian discourse (as articulated chiefly in *Totality and Infinity*). At issue here are the implications of this discourse for the theme of friendship—a point to which Derrida instantly turns. Reiterating his opening line, Derrida presents Montaigne's phrase as a kind of code word or hidden passkey to his chosen theme. On the face of it, the phrase seems to be merely contradictory or to state a "logical absurdity," namely, by joining a vocative apostrophe ("O my friends") with a predicative denial ("there is no friend"). In an effort to unravel this paradox, Derrida construes the apostrophe and indeed the entire phrase as a transformative appeal or appellation, that is, an appeal calling forth a hidden potential: "It resembles an appeal, because it makes a sign toward the future: be my friends, for I love or will love you. . . . Accede to what is at the same time a desire, a request, a promise and, one could also add, a prayer" (where prayer means a performative utterance transgressing predication). Referring to the age-old quandary of whether friendship arises from insufficiency or completeness, Derrida resolutely opts for insufficiency and want: "How could I give you my friendship where friendship would not be lacking, that is, if it already existed—more precisely, if the friend were not lacking?" Friendship here appears as a kind of transcendental-spiritual goal—and Derrida in fact speaks of the "idea of friendship," of the "ideality of its essence or telos" in the name of which we must conclude that, as yet, "there is no friend." Underscoring the futuristic-eschatological accent of this outlook he insists, "Friendship is never given in the present. It belongs to the experience of waiting, of promise, or of commitment" because its discourse "is that of prayer and at issue there is that which responsibility opens to the future."[7]

Yet, futurism does not fully exhaust the theme. Seemingly moving away or sideways from a Levinasian expectancy, Derrida also embeds friendship in an immemorial past. As he writes, "the apostrophe 'O my friends' turns us also toward the past." It does so by alerting us to the "always already" given pre-suppositions of being and discourse, by signaling toward that "which must be supposed so as to let oneself be understood." For Derrida, this presupposed matrix constitutes a kind of "minimal friendship" or "preliminary consent" without which people could not understand each other or be attentive to any appeal. He elaborates,

> Without this absolute past, I could not, for my part, have addressed myself to you in this way. We would not be together in a sort of minimal community . . . speaking the same language or praying for translation within the horizon of the same language . . . , if a *sort* of friendship had not already been sealed before any other contract: a friendship prior to friendships, an ineffaceable, fundamental, and bottomless friendship, the one that draws its breath in the sharing of a language (past or to come).

Remembering at this point the Aristotelian question of "being" (*ti estin* or "what is?")—a question vigorously and relentlessly renewed by Heidegger in our time—Derrida draws a parallel or connection between the fundamental questioning of "philosophy" (rendered as the "love of wisdom," *philein to sophon*) and friendship (*philia*): "The very possibility of the question, in the form of 'what is?,' seems always to have presupposed this friendship prior to friendships, this *anterior* affirmation of being-together in the allocution."[8]

In Derrida's presentation, however, this anterior affirmation (of minimal friendship) is not really operative or effective in the present, but rather strictly immemorial and hence inaccessible. As he insists, the affirmation "cannot be *presented* as a being-present . . . within the space of an ontology, precisely because it opens this space." Hence, friendship construed both as futuristic promise and as immemorial past is not so much an actual experience but rather a limit concept or an infinitely distant horizon. In fact, Derrida locates the "very movement and time of friendship" in "this surpassing of the present by the undeniable future anterior," a surpassing that opens up "the absolute [vista] of an unpresentable past as well as future." In this manner, the "asymmetrical curvature" that was previously detected in Montaigne's phrase is now transferred or transcribed into an asymmetrical temporality which "absolutely" privileges the future anterior and which envelops friendship within "the performativity of a prayer." To elucidate the character of this performativity, Derrida turns to the topic of "response" and responsibility (a topic triggered by his own response to a professional invitation). Following again Levinas's lead, he distinguishes between "three modalities" of response: in the sense that one always answers "for" oneself, "to" a query or challenge, and "before" a larger community or audience. As one can surmise, answering "for oneself" does not imply here a Hegelian "for-itself" and certainly not a self-identity or unity of the "subject" that can never be secured "as an empirical synthesis"; rather, it refers to the evocative quality of the "proper name," an evocation that extends beyond self-presence and, in fact, "beyond even life or presence in general."[9]

The transgressive or transcendental quality of response is even more clearly evident in the other two modalities. "Answering to" involves the need to answer to the "Other," that is, to the Other's request, prayer, apostrophe or appeal. For Derrida, this need is primary and "more original" than the other modalities chiefly for two reasons: first, because answering for oneself always occurs in response to the Other's challenge or insistence; and second, because even the proper name "for" which one answers is always constituted (or co-constituted) by the Other. Hence, "answering to" manifests the asymmetries noted earlier: it preserves the "asymmetrical anteriority" even within the seemingly "most inward and solitary autonomy of reserve," that is, in the heart of freedom. The third modality of "answering before" inserts the second into a broader social context. In Derrida's account, "answering before" indicates the passage to "an institutional instance of alterity"; it is "no longer singular, but is universal in its principle." While "answering to" refers to an Other who is singular and who "must remain so" in a certain sense, "answering before" places the response in relation to "the law, a tribunal, a jury, some agency (instance) authorized to represent the Other legitimately, in the form of a moral, legal, or political community." The source of this distinction is again unmistakable (though it remains again unnamed); it parallels directly Levinas's distinction between the singular encounter with the "face" (of the Other) and the dimension of general or universal "justice" in which the face is bracketed or submerged. Derrida's comments on the topic seem almost transcribed from Levinasian texts:

> Of these two dimensions of the relation to the Other, the one maintains the absolute singularity of the Other and of "my" relation to the Other. . . . But the relation to the Other also passes through the universality of the law. This discourse

about universality which can find its determination in the regimes of morality, law, or politics, always appeals to a third party, beyond the face-to-face of singularities.[10]

Despite the clear division between the two dimensions—the stark opposition between singularity and universality—Derrida also acknowledges a certain interrelation or mutual implication of the two domains. In a move that perhaps oversteps the Levinasian model, he asks whether the two relations ("to" and "before") do not "imply each other at the moment they seem to exclude each other?" For does not the universality of the law in effect "command me to recognize the transcendent alterity of the Other?" As it appears, however, the mutual implication of the two domains goes deeper than these comments suggest. The relation to the Other does not only "pass through" the universality of the law but shares with the letter a crucial trait: the remoteness of relationship (if that term is still applicable). Both the singular face-to-face and the general law are predicated not on close proximity or any kind of "presence" but rather on respect, indeed on the infinite distance of respect. Paraphrasing and in part modifying Kantian insights, Derrida describes answering "to" and "before" as "two forms or two dimensions of the respect implied by any responsibility," a description that also carries over into the very "heart of friendship." One of the enigmas of friendship, he elaborates, "comes from this distance or this respectful separation which distinguishes it, as a feeling, from love," and he calls at this point for "a rigorous rereading of the Kantian analysis of respect in friendship," for "there is no friendship without 'respect of the Other.'"[11]

Venturing into broader historical-philosophical reflections, Derrida associates answering "to" and "before" with the legacy of traditional binaries or oppositions—such as those between singularity and universality, private and public, apolitical and political domains—oppositions that in his view have always divided "the experience, the concept, and the interpretation of friendship." On the one hand, he writes, from the angle of private singularity, friendship seems to be "essentially foreign or unamenable to the res publica" and thus "could not found a politics." But on the other hand, the "great philosophical and canonical discourses on friendship"—from Plato, Aristotle, and Cicero to Kant and Hegel—have tended to link friendship "explicitly to virtue and to justice, to moral reason and to political reason." Noting both the porousness and the remarkable resilience of traditional binaries, Derrida remarks that the latter tend to dominate "the interpretation and the experience of friendship in our culture: a domination which is unstable and under internal stress, but therefore all the more imperious." After providing some examples of the stubbornness and prejudicial character of traditional binaries (such as the exclusion of friendship between women and between man and woman), Derrida finally turns to the "history of friendship" mentioned before, a history that revolves basically around a progressive rupturing and destabilization of traditional models. To repeat the point made previously, the "Graeco-Roman model" is portrayed as being marked specifically by reciprocity and the emphasis on politics ("politicist concord"), an emphasis that is later "fractured" by Judeo-Christian thought, which "depoliticizes the Greek model" or else "displaces the nature of the political." This displacement is continued and deepened by Montaigne in early modernity with his introduction of asymmetry and "infinity," and later further radicalized by Nietzsche, Blanchot, and others (presumably including Derrida), who call the friend by a name that is "no longer that of the neighbor, perhaps no longer that of a man."[12]

Deconstruction and Critical Reason

At the meeting of the particular philosophical society, Derrida's observations on responsiveness did not fall on deaf ears, but elicited instantly a response from one of its members, Thomas McCarthy. In his comments, McCarthy did indeed "respond" to Derrida's address—though not by submitting simply to its appeal (or apostrophe), but by marshalling the resources of an alternative intellectual framework: that of modern critical reason. Basically, in terms of general orientation, McCarthy was less intent on rupturing than on preserving a certain continuity of modern critical, especially Kantian, philosophy—though minus some of the latter's deeper "metaphysical" premises. As he noted, Derrida's address exemplified a distinctive "postmetaphysical" approach that enlists a "deconstructive strategy" located "at the level of metaphysics in order to disrupt and displace it." By contrast, attention to recent sociology and critical theory yielded "other, less metaphysically motivated, ways of thinking about social relations," possibly also about friendship. By pursuing this line of thought it was possible to maintain critical alertness while avoiding deconstruction's rupturing bent. Hence, for McCarthy, a "better way of being postmetaphysical in ethics, law, and politics" is to focus on concrete social relations and to "stop doing metaphysics, even of a negative sort, when thinking about them."[13]

Among recent social and critical theorists, McCarthy's response gave pride of place to George Herbert Mead and Jürgen Habermas. Echoing distinctly Kantian teachings as filtered through Hegel's dialectics, Mead emphasized the parallelism of individual and society, and hence also of the processes of individuation and socialization. To this extent, McCarthy was able to endorse (at least in part) Derrida's notion of a "minimal friendship" or an immemorial insertion of humans in the "curvature of social space"—a notion that seemed not so far removed from the phenomenological (and Habermasian) concept of the ordinary "lifeworld." However, contrary to Derrida's allegation, this lifeworld was not distantly recessed and unpresentable, but rather readily available in everyday life and continuously taken for granted; moreover, far from being elusive, it exhibited distinct structural features, including the features of an (embryonic) social agency and mutual accountability. As McCarthy writes (following Mead), "At the level of our everyday interactions we normally believe ourselves to be, and take others as being, knowledgeable subjects confronted by real choices, for which we and they will be held accountable." What is important to remember is that, for Mead, the network of social structures and expectations—what he called the "generalized Other"—was intimately connected with individuation or the rise of individual agency. Against this backdrop, Derrida's accent on "asymmetry" was mistaken or at least greatly exaggerated, as was his emphasis on the disjuncture between face-to-face relations and the universality of law. In McCarthy's words,

> It is not only in friendship, but in social interaction generally that the "singularity of the Other" is intimately interconnected with the "generality of the law" (here: normative expectations). And although the individual is related "asymmetrically" to the *generalized* Other, which is always "anterior," the socially generalized patterns of behavior the latter comprises are themselves typically structured as relations of reciprocity with *individual* Others.[14]

Given this view of self-other relations, Meadian social theory could readily serve as a stepping-stone in the formulation of an ethical perspective, particularly one indebted to basic Kantian teachings. Strictly construed, McCarthy noted, the immemorial grounding or matrix of social ties should not be termed a "minimal friendship" as rather a "minimal ethics of reciprocity and accountability," one in which concern with personal integrity and identity is closely interwoven with the societal fabric of mutual recognition. This dual emphasis on individual dignity and societal norms has actually been always at the heart of "traditional moralities"—whose intuitive insights have been further refined and elaborated by modern philosophical ethics. In the Kantian tradition, in particular, respect for individual integrity has been grounded in the equal freedom or "autonomy" of agents, while societal (and universalizable) morality has been tied to the "impartiality of laws" which can be freely accepted by all participants. These Kantian accents have recently been both revived and reformulated by Jürgen Habermas, who replaced Kant's "noumenal" reflexivity with the stress on communicative rationality. Thus, in Habermasian discourse ethics, norms can be validated only by discursively testing their claims in the medium of the "informed, uncoerced, reasoned agreement" of all individuals subject to their rule. In this (neo-Kantian) construal of the "moral point of view," the principle of equal respect is reflected in the requirement of "rationally motivated agreement" freely entered into by individual agents, while the concern for societal (and universalizable) norms is captured in the requirement of "general and reciprocal perspective-taking" where each agent takes "the situations of others into account" and grants them "equal weight."[15]

Proceeding along these lines, McCarthy finds it possible to accommodate even one of Derrida's more unique and emphatic claims: that of the "futurism" of friendship or the status of friendship as a future promise (encapsulated in Montaigne's apostrophe). Stripped of deconstructive hyperbole, the claim can readily be translated into the Kantian notion of a "regulative idea"—a notion, he writes, that exhibits the same sort of "promise" and "responsibility to the future" that Derrida finds in "friendships that are 'the most perfect of their kind.'" In the Kantian tradition, regulative ideas are never fully actual and hence not "present" or "re-presentable" in themselves, but they are effective in guiding our practices. In a similar vein, Habermasian communicative rationality is not empirically given, but must be "counterfactually" assumed in the validation of moral standards. Summarizing his observations, McCarthy locates the (limited) merit of Derrida's approach in its effort to counterbalance universalist abstractions—which are often "unheeding of difference and in violation of singularity"; to this extent, Derridean thoughts on friendship provide "an instructive antidote to the levelling, difference-denying tendencies of much moral and legal theory" (including the Kantian variety). Yet, properly construed, moral universalism—especially when couched as "fairness"—is necessarily also "respectful of the Other and tolerant of difference." Thus, even the limited benefits of Derridean deconstruction are in large part endemic to modern moral philosophy (reasonably interpreted); such benefits in any case cannot outweigh deconstruction's considerable disadvantages. The alternative outlook sketched in his rejoinder—McCarthy concludes—centers around the thesis that "the curvature of social space" is not fundamentally "asymmetrical and heteronomical" and that minimal friendship or "originary sociality" is marked as well "by relations of symmetry, reciprocity, and mutual recognition." In any concrete social context, conduct of such relations belongs to "the repertoire of competent social actors," which in turn implies an "intuitive mastery of the moral point of view."[16]

A Solitary Friendship?

The above exchange of views—the sequence of "response" and counter-response—is instructive and revealing in its profiled contrasts. In large measure, the encounter between McCarthy and Derrida illustrates and exemplifies the encounter between a basically "modernist" perspective wedded to Kantian (or quasi-Kantian) premises and a loosely "postmodern" or deconstructive outlook bent on rupturing these (and all other) premises. While demurring on the issue of metaphysics, McCarthy's arguments clearly preserve the continuity with earlier philosophical teachings; by contrast, Derridean formulations often are couched in a manner signaling a break with or exit from philosophical traditions. Despite their instructive counterpoint, however, the opposition of views is circumscribed by several limiting factors. First of all, on a number of points, the two protagonists seemed to misunderstand or simply talk past each other. Thus, McCarthy's reference to individual integrity and its dialectical relation with generalized otherness (or normativity) seemed to bypass the Derridean (and Levinasian) meaning of "singularity"—a term denoting a more radical uniqueness located beyond definition and hence also beyond the correlation of particular and universal. Likewise, McCarthy's invocation of the "lifeworld" seemed to refer to a realm of mundane everydayness, a realm far removed from the originary arche-space opened up by minimal friendship. Finally, despite undeniable points of contact, the linkage between Derridean "promise" and Kantian "regulative ideas" should probably not be overstated. While Kantian ideas are postulates inherent in reason, Derrida's notion of promise or appeal appears to be more resolutely transgressive or eschatological in character, invoking coming events possibly located beyond reason.

Beyond such matters of detail, the encounter is limited, however, by another factor: a subtle and nearly subterranean collusion of perspectives. As indicated above, both thinkers appeal explicitly and repeatedly to Kantian philosophy—though from different angles and for different purposes. McCarthy identifies morality, along Kantian lines, as the cultivation of "equal respect for individuals" predicated on reciprocal autonomy. Derrida's essay places respect in the very heart of friendship, interpreting and equating respect with interhuman "distance" or a "respectful separation" sharply distinguished from "love" as a feeling. Thus, both thinkers clearly pay tribute to the Kantian privileging of respect over feeling or sympathy, and both construe respect as a kind of good will across distance (in one case between singularities, in the other between individual agents). This feature is closely linked with another, still more prominent convergence: their shared rejection or distantiation from the classical legacy, especially the Aristotelian conception of friendship as a social-political bond (*homonoia*) buttressing the common good. Habermas, whom McCarthy invokes, is well known for his dismissal of Aristotelian or neo-Aristotelian perspectives and for his staunch defense of the primacy of "right over good" (that is, of moral principle over ethical goodness). Although acknowledging possible ties of fellowship or solidarity on the lifeworld level, such ties are entirely subsidiary to normative rightness and the operation of quasi-contractual public procedures. In turn, although quoting an apocryphal saying (reported by Montaigne), Derrida leaves no doubt about his critical stance toward Aristotle whose legacy represents for him pretty much the essence of Western metaphysics. Thus, after citing (mostly without comment) some passages from *Nicomachean Ethics*, Derrida's essay concludes with his staccato narrative whose trajectory revolves basically around the rupturing exit from Greece and Rome. To repeat again the core of the indictment: the classical legacy is said to be marked "by the value of reciprocity, by homological, immanentist, finitist, and politicist concord."[17]

As illustrated by both critical theory and Derridean deconstruction, distantiation from Aristotle is surely a hallmark of modern Western thought (since the time of Descartes and Hobbes), and unquestionably, his legacy is not immune from criticism or contestation. When, in the following, closer attention is given to Aristotle's arguments, the point is not to revive or rehabilitate his philosophy *in toto*, but simply to allow his voice to re-enter the dialogue about friendship—especially political friendship—on a more equal footing. As one may concede (and as I certainly would concede), there is probably no way in our time to embrace a full-fledged Aristotelian metaphysics, especially an emphatic notion of "substance" or "natural teleology." On a political level, the same would hold for conceptions of commonality or the "common good" seen as implying compact uniformity. Still, what seems questionable to me is that critique of Aristotle can proceed without close textual engagement, that is, through a simple mode of rupturing or exodus. From this angle, Derrida's repeated invocation of his apocryphal motto seems at least puzzling—given the abundance of quotable phrases in Aristotle's texts. Among many others, the following passage seems eminently worthy of reflection: "If people are friends, they have no need of justice, but if they are just they need friendship in addition; and the justice that is most just seems to belong to friendship."[18] Close exegesis of this and similar phrases might guard against reductionism and against a certain dismissive attitude prevalent in modern philosophy, and also in Derrida's rupturing indictment. For how—without reductive simplification—can one equate the classical legacy with such labels as "homological, immanentist, finitist"? Clearly, terms like "immanentist" and "finitist" bank on the metaphysical dichotomies between immanence/transcendence and finitude (or totality) and infinity, dichotomies that, in Derrida's own account, were introduced by the "Judeo-Christian" rupturing of classical thought, with the result that the latter (antedating the rupturing) cannot possibly be identified with one side of these polar opposites.

Still more difficult and problematic is the ascription of "homological" to classical thought—a term whose meaning is not further elaborated in the essay (beyond its counterposition to "heterology"). Derrida's later book offers some clues regarding its sense or connotation. According to these hints, classical thought as a whole—and its conception of friendship in particular—approached everything from the vantage and in terms of the self or self-same and hence invariably ended up by reducing the "other" to sameness. This proclivity is said to be clearly evident in the case of Cicero, whose treatment of friendship, according to Derrida, "leans sharply to one side—let us say *the same* side—rather than to the other—let us say *the other*" and who consequently reduced the friend to a replica of the self or to "our own ideal image." The discussion of Aristotle in the book is more round-about and diffuse, but the finding is basically similar: by according primary emphasis to "loving" over "being loved," Aristotle is claimed (or intimated) to have incorporated the loved one into the inclination of the lover and hence to have truncated the calling or apostrophe of the "other" in favor of the lover's activity (or *energeia*). Although posited as a premise of rupturing, this charge of "homology" appears dubious and unpersuasive. What seems neglected in this charge is the self-transcending quality of friendship in classical thought: the aspect that real or "complete" friendship means to love the other basically for the other's sake. This aspect is clearly underscored by Aristotle when he writes that "those who wish goods to their friend for the friend's sake are friends most of all; for they have this attitude because of (or for the sake of) the friend and not coincidentally." Cicero seems to make a similar point when he comments that genuine friendship is to be desired not for any extraneous advantage but "because the whole of its profit consists in love only" and that those who only calculate their selfish utility "are destitute of that most beautiful and most natural friendship which is desirable in itself and for its own sake."[19]

Most problematic and difficult to disentangle is the charge of "reciprocity" seen as a major failing of classical thought, standing in contrast to asymmetry and heteronomy. Here one may note first of all a certain asymmetry or disjunction in Derrida's own presentation between the "asymmetrical curvature" of originary or immemorial sociality and the "asymmetrical anteriority" of responsibility to the Other. Given that immemorial sociality (or friendship be-fore friendship) seems to precede the very emergence of self and other, its asymmetry (if such it is) appears to be of a different sort than that between distinct singularities.[20] More important in the present context is the postulate of asymmetrical heteronomy viewed as basic moral yardstick. Although one may readily grant that the self is not "self-constituting" in the sense of modern philosophy, the turn to "other-constitution" seems to perform a reversal fraught with equally troubling results. For one thing, the postulated primacy and anteriority of the "Other" seems to reduce the self to a purely ancillary passivity—perhaps to passive subordination and even victimization. On a more strictly philosophical plane, the very notion of the "Other" and of the Other's radical "exteriority" seems to presuppose, as its condition of possibility, the correlative notion of the self and the self's radical "interiority." Thus, the radical turn to otherness seems to conjure up the very pitfall of self-enclosure which it is meant to redress.[21]

Returning to classical thought, the "charge" of reciprocity is of course un-deniable—but it can be vindicated or defended on numerous grounds. According to Aristotle (as well as Cicero), friendship cannot simply be equated with unilateral good will or respect proceeding either from the self or the other; rather, it requires a mutuality of caring and affection of which friends are reciprocally aware. As he writes, "Friendship is said to be reciprocated goodwill (*eunoia*). And perhaps we should add that friends are aware of the reciprocated goodwill." Aristotle also adds that friendship usually involves a sharing of preferences as well as a sharing of practices or activities (a point to which I shall return later). The kind of distant respect extolled in Derrida's essay thus seems to fall short of friendship in several ways; apart from lacking the needed affection, respect can be extended to worthy people in far-off places and also to remote historical figures—with whom one could not claim to be linked through ties of friendship. The notion of reciprocity is also important for implying or suggesting a measure of equality among friends—although such equality should by no means be collapsed into sameness or uniformity. Aristotle speaks of friendship among unequals, such as friendship between parents and children or between people of higher and lower status—but insists that care must be taken not to allow the distinction to decay into radical asymmetry or disjuncture. Guarding against such decay requires the cultivation of a "proportional" mode of loving and being loved, a proportionality sustained by the shared bond of love: "This above all is the way for unequals as well as equals to be friends, since this is the way for them to be equalized." By contrast, rupturing of the bond through radical separation conjures up ill will and discord, and above all the social-political evils of tyranny and slavery: "In a tyranny there is little or no friendship, for where ruler and ruled have nothing in common, they have no friendship, as they have no justice either. . . . Nor is there any towards a horse or cow, or towards a slave, insofar as he is a slave" (although friendship persists "to the extent that a slave is a human being").[22]

To repeat: the point here is not a wholesale retrieval of classical philosophy, but a caveat against its reversal. To all intents and purposes, Derrida moves in the opposite direction from that of Aristotle. His essay places the accent on separation and disjuncture, and also on a "strange violence" inhabiting human relations (or non-relations); it eventually affixes the term "friend" to a figure that is "perhaps no longer that of a man" (thus to a figure exiting the human condition, perhaps in the direction of a god or "overman"). The accent on separation is still further expanded and radicalized in the book, *Politics of Friendship*. There, drawing primarily on Nietzschean teachings, Derrida stresses the "incommensurability" between self and other, between "lover" and "beloved," and also the unilateral asymmetry prevailing among singularities. Opposing the symmetry of virtue postulated in Aristotle's "complete" friendship, he writes, "How can we reconcile this first imperative, that of primary friendship, with what we have begun to uncover: the necessary unilaterality of a dissymetrical *philein* and the terrible but so righteous law of *contretemps*" (the temporal rift "disjoining the presence of the present"). Relying specifically on Nietzsche's *Human All Too Human*, the book removes friendship from any sort of ready familiarity or commonality— asking whether friendship (meaning the "friendship to come") does not lend itself "inevitably, maddeningly, to madness?" The kind of friendship that emerges here, Derrida notes, is a relation "without proximity, without presence, therefore without resemblance, without attraction, perhaps even without significant or reasonable preference." To the extent that the term is still applicable, friends are here basically "the friends of solitude," people who "share what cannot be shared: solitude." What comes into view are "friends of an entirely different kind, inaccessible friends, friends who are alone because they are incomparable and without common measure, reciprocity or equality"—in Nietzsche's words: "jealous friends of solitude." Essentially heterogenous, these "friends" are necessarily "dissociated, 'solitarized,' singularized, constituted into monadic alterites"; they remain solitary, although they may "ally themselves in silence within the necessity of keeping silent together—each in his own corner."[23]

This notion of a solitary or inaccessible friendship carries over (perhaps surprisingly) into the political domain, animating Derrida's views on what he calls the "politics of friendship." In his essay of that title, one may recall, clas-

sical thought was charged with favoring a "politicist concord," while successive rupturing breaks were said to "depoliticize the Greek model" or else to
"displace the nature of the political." Yet, displacement in the essay was still
far from complete. Thus, in his discussion of "answering before," Derrida
noted that "one answers before the law," that is, before an agency "authorized to represent the Other legitimately, in the form of a moral, legal, or political community." Largely under Nietzsche's influence, displacement in the
book takes a much more radical form, affecting the very meaning of "the political" and "political community." Once human beings are seen as singular,
solitary, and separate, the classical association of politics with concord
(*homonoia*) and community becomes apocryphal or untenable. Opposing this
classical legacy, Derrida explicitly advances his critique "in the name of another politics." Given the stress on interhuman distance, the "other" politics
"to come" can only denote a "community of solitary friends," inaugurating
what he emphatically calls "community without community, friendship
without the community of the friends of solitude. No appurtenance, nor resemblance nor proximity." What the friends of the coming politics insist on
denouncing is a central traditional mistake: namely, "the contradiction inhabiting the very concept of the *common* and the *community*"—a mistake
challenged in the name of "the incalculable equality of these friends of solitude, of the incommensurable subjects, of these subjects without subject and
without intersubjectivity." Derrida in this context advances the notion of a
new "anchoritic community," a network of those "who love in separation (or
love to be separate)," and also the concept of a "good friendship" replacing
Aristotle's primary type. Such good friendship "supposes disproportion. It demands a certain rupture in reciprocity or equality, as well as the interruption
of all fusion or confusion between you and me. By the same token it signifies
a divorce with love, albeit self-love."[24]

    With its accent on disjuncture and non-communion, Derrida's argu-
ment—despite its rupturing efforts—inserts itself into a long tradition of
Western thought, a tradition that has tended to privilege transcendental ver-
ticality over lateral, interhuman bonds. As previously indicated, this tradition received powerful impulses from Augustinian Christianity with its separation of earthly from spiritual forms of citizenship and friendship (captured
theologically in the subordination of *eros* and *philia* to *agape*). Seen in this
light, Derrida's notion of an "anchoritic community" is distantly reminiscent
of quasi-monastic ideals, while his celebration of jealous solitude seems to
align itself both with Pascalian antihumanism and (in a more secular vein)
with the remote (non)communion of New England transcendentalists. No
doubt, in our late modern (or postmodern) era, there are good and weighty

reasons speaking in support of this non- or anticommunitarian stance. In an age of rampant consumerism and commodification when primary attention everywhere is focused on commodity production and appropriation, nothing seems indeed more urgent than the insistence on a certain human nonavailability, that is, on the prohibition to treat humans (and the world at large) as simple commodities or means to ends. In many ways, this insistence runs counter to a powerful strand in modern metaphysics that construes the entire world as the target or "project" of a designing and infinitely appropriating (individual or collective) subject—a construal undergirding modern processes of industrialization and capital accumulation. Derrida is eloquent in denouncing this metaphysics. Postulating a "new justice" beyond calculation and equivalence, he asks readers to envisage an equity placed "beyond proportion, beyond appropriation." Taking a leaf from some pages in Nietzsche's *Gay Science* he elaborates,

> This "disappropriation" would undoubtedly beckon to this other "love" whose true name, says Nietzsche in conclusion, whose "just name" is *friendship*. . . . (T)his little two page treatise on love denounces, in sum, the *right to property*. This property right is the claim of love (at least, of what is thus named). The vindictive claim of this right can be deciphered throughout all the appropriative manoeuvers of the strategy which this "love" deploys. It is the appropriating drive (*Trieb*) par excellence. "Love" wants to possess; it wants the possessing. It is the possessing—cupidity itself (*Habsucht*).

As opposed to this "drive," friendship as noncommunity challenges "the very value of proximity, the neighbor's proximity as the ruse of the proper and of appropriation." Its goal is "not to give in to proximity or identification, to the fusion of you and me," but rather "to place, maintain or keep an infinite distance within 'good friendship'."[25]

Although appreciating the denunciation of instrumental appropriation or *Habsucht*, one can still wonder about the extreme character (and hence the justice) of Derrida's proposed antidote. For clearly, friendship may be jeopardized not only by egocentric appropriation but also by a radical "disappropriation" celebrating interhuman remoteness and infinite distance. As experience teaches, retreat into solitude may occasionally lead to "vertical" or spiritual enrichment, but it may also, and perhaps more frequently, be the gateway to an unabashed narcissism (which is the most prominent character flaw of our age). In the case of Derrida's presentation, one may puzzle, how can noncommunicative remoteness at all be reconciled with the postulated (Levinasian) responsibility or responsiveness to the "Other"? How can self-transgression happen or how can self at all be transformed without the steady and "timely" intervention of an "other," that is, without the difficult labor involved in undergoing the challenge or "apostrophe" of an "other" located concretely in time and space? These and similar considerations are prone to introduce at least some question marks into the celebration of solitude and splendid aloofness—question marks that classical writers abundantly attached to this theme. As is well known, Aristotle saw friendship as a remedy for isolation and solitary life; he even argued that very good and "blessedly happy" people still cultivate friendship and, in fact, "desire to spend their days together, since a solitary life fits them least of all." Following Aristotle's lead, Cicero likewise presented humans as sociable beings whose character development is likely to be impeded by solitude. Turning against certain Greek philosophers who rejected social ties as a threat to inner peace, Cicero chided their aloofness or self-security (*securitas*) as a moral failing, stating,

> Wonderful wisdom indeed! For they seem to take the sun from the sky who withdraw friendship from life. . . . For what is that freedom from care or caring (*cura*) they talk about? In appearance it is flattering, but in truth it is in many cases to be disdained . . . For if we fly from care, we must fly from virtue also.[26]

What is troubling here is not the praise of solitude as such (which remains valuable in many respects), but rather its contemporary social-political context: the upsurge to undisputed global dominance of the ideology of liberal individualism (or libertarianism) in its conjunction with market imperatives. This upsurge can be traced back to the dismantling of the Soviet Union (and perhaps still further to the aftereffects of 1968). Since the time of these events, all the major intellectual trends in the West have tended to conspire to one end: the debunking of any social commonality or "community"—terms resonating loosely with socialism and communism—in favor of the celebration of individual separateness or the nonrelation of singularities. As a corollary of these trends, notions like the "common good" or public concord (*homonoia*) have tended to be summarily dismissed as crippling or restraining (forgetful of the possibly empowering effects of public life). Despite obvious differences of accent, this dismissal or at least devaluation is shared by a number of theoretical perspectives, from traditional liberalism to recent critical theory and deconstruction (notwithstanding that separation proceeds sometimes from the self, sometimes from the primacy of the other). The costs or negative side effects of this dismissal—thematized under such labels as "anomie," "world-alienation," and "*trahison de tous par tous*"—are not entirely ignored, and occasionally even deplored, but without any effect on the general orientation.[27]

A major drawback of this orientation, especially with regard to *political* friendship, is the lack of praxis or shared social practices. On this point, of course, classical writers were emphatic, insisting that friendship in the proper sense had to be shown not only in words (or the inner mind) but in deed. Aristotle, as indicated, held that even happy people still like to "spend their days together," adding that friendship ultimately amounts not only to a sharing of views but a "sharing of life" manifest in the willingness to "share the friend's distress and joy." In turn, Cicero emphasized the broad range of friendship, extending from enjoyment of ordinary pleasures to mutual character formation to practices in the public realm. Importantly, for both writers friendship—although initially preferential and intimate—was destined to spread or fan out into public life (hence their shared concern with public or political friendship).[28] Viewed against this background, Derrida's postulate of remoteness and the perennial absence (or nonpresence) of friends appears oddly disabling—and also humanly implausible. (Michel Montaigne, so frequently invoked in his writings, seems to have happily ignored the postulate when enjoying the company of Etienne—although he did not allow his fondness to percolate into the larger community.)

Similarly disorienting is Derrida's persistent critique of steadfastness, and especially of Aristotle's emphasis on the need of friends to remain faithful and reliable (*bebaios*) to each other. But how—without a measure of faithfulness and reliability—can friendship at all be cultivated and even conceived? How, without attentive care and reliable helpfulness—a help often required promptly or "presently"—can friendship be kept from deteriorating into a chance encounter or simply a mode of self-indulgence? Can one still speak of friendship if "friends" are always safely elsewhere, promising something in the indefinite future (perhaps on a transcendental plane)? At this point, if may be helpful to invoke some biblical passages (an apostrophe not unprovoked by some "messianic" allusions in Derrida's texts). One such passage is the story of the "good Samaritan"—a story, one may recall, where the vertical spirituality of some priests is put to shame by the instant helpfulness of a stranger passing by. Another pertinent passage are some lines from Micah (6:8), where the prophet—in succinct terms and without rhetorical flourishes—summarizes basic rules of human conduct: "He has shown you what is good; and what does the Lord require of you but to do justice, and to love kindness, and to walk humbly with your God?"

Notes

1. This account is no doubt sketchy and simplified in many ways—though the general direction of the development can scarcely be doubted. Some facets of this direction are

well pinpointed by Gilbert Meilaender when he writes, "There can be little doubt that friendship was a considerably more important topic in the life and thought of the classical civilizations of Greece and Rome than it has, for the most part, been within Christendom. With the possible exception of the literature of monasticism, friendship has never been a central concern of Christian thought. . . . It would be difficult, if not impossible, to find a contemporary ethicist—whether philosophical or theological—who in writing a basic introduction to ethics would give friendship more than a passing glance. Indeed, having been for a time in the modern period the province of essayists (such as Emerson), friendship now appears to have fallen to a still lower estate: A book on friendship now means, quite often, a collection of little sayings, attractively illustrated, meant as a gift, and sold in a drugstore." Meilaender is also quite emphatic about the difference between modern liberalism and classical friendship: "There is a qualitative difference—a moral difference perhaps—between the liberal understanding of politics as activity necessary simply to leave the individual free for his or her private concerns, and the ideal of a participatory-communal polity" (anchored in friendship). See Gilbert C. Meilaender, *Friendship: A Study in Theological Ethics* (Notre Dame, Ind.: University of Notre Dame Press, 1981), 1, 70–71.

2. An illustrative example of this division can be found in the booklet on "Spiritual Friendship" by the Cistercian abbot Aelred of Rievaulx (about 1150) who sharply distinguished between pure or "spiritual" friendship, on the one hand, and merely "carnal" or "worldly" forms of friendship on the other. See Michael Pakaluk, ed., *Other Selves: Philosophers on Friendship* (Indianapolis: Hackett Publishing Co., 1991), 129–45. Accentuating and further radicalizing the abbot's point, Meilaender writes: "I want to suggest, hesitantly but firmly, that a Christian ethic ought to recognize the ideal of civic friendship as essentially pagan, an example of inordinate and idolatrous love" (*Friendship*, 75).

3. In his essay "Of Friendship," Montaigne had written: "Common friendships can be divided up: . . . but this [true] friendship that possesses the soul and rules it with absolute sovereignty cannot possibly be double. . . . A single dominant friendship dissolves all other obligations." On his part, Emerson in his essay on "Friendship" asserted: "It is foolish to be afraid of making our ties too spiritual, as if so we could lose any genuine love. . . . Let us feel if we will the absolute insulation of man. We are sure that we have all in us." See Pakaluk, ed., *Other Selves*, 195, 221–22, 224, 231. On the other hand, though largely sharing Emerson's outlook, Henry David Thoreau expressed more sociable sentiments. "A base friendship is of a narrowing and exclusive tendency, but a nobler one is not exclusive; its very superfluity and dispersed love is the humanity which sweetens society, and sympathizes with foreign nations; for though its foundations are private, it is, in effect, a public affair and a public advantage, and the friend more than the father of a family, deserves well of the state." See Thoreau, "Friendship," in *A Little Book of Friendship*, ed. Joseph Morris and St. Clair Adams (New York: George Sully & Co., 1925), 109–10.

4. Jacques Derrida, "The Politics of Friendship," *Journal of Philosophy* 85 (1988): 632.

5. "The Politics of Friendship," 643–44. The reference is to Maurice Blanchot, *L'Amitié* (Paris: Gallimard, 1971), 326–27; trans. by Elizabeth Rottenberg as *Friendship* (Stanford, Calif.: Stanford University Press, 1997).

6. Derrida, "The Politics of Friendship," 633–34. (As published in the *Journal of Philosophy*, the essay uses *homonomia* as a translation of "concord," which is clearly a mistake. The Aristotelian term is *homonoia*.)

7. "The Politics of Friendship," 635–36. See also Emmanuel Levinas, *Totality and Infinity: An Essay on Exteriority*, trans. Alphonso Lingis (Pittsburgh: Duquesne University Press, 1969).

8. "The Politics of Friendship," 636–37. The notions of future and anterior friendship are further elaborated in Derrida, *Politics of Friendship*, trans. George Collins (London: Verso, 1997), 235–37.

9. "The Politics of Friendship," 637–38. See also *Politics of Friendship*, 250–52.

10. "The Politics of Friendship," 639–41.

11. "The Politics of Friendship," 640–41. For Derrida's ambivalent relation to Kant see also *Politics of Friendship*, 253–62.

12. "The Politics of Friendship," 641–44.

13. Thomas McCarthy, "On the Margins of Politics," *Journal of Philosophy*, vol. 85 (1988), 645, 648.

14. "On the Margins of Politics," 645–46.

15. "On the Margins of Politics," 646–47. Compare in this context Seyla Benhabib and Fred Dallmayr, eds., *The Communicative Ethics Controversy* (Cambridge, Mass.: MIT Press, 1990).

16. "On the Margins of Politics," 647–48. Somewhat more extensive concessions to Derridean deconstruction, as an antidote to universalist abstractions, have recently been made by other thinkers equally indebted to Habermas. See especially Axel Honneth, "The Other of Justice: Habermas and the Ethical Challenge of Postmodernism," in Stephen K. White, ed., *The Cambridge Companion to Habermas* (Cambridge: Cambridge University Press, 1995), 289–323.

17. Derrida, "The Politics of Friendship," 644. For Habermas's critique of Aristotelian or neo-Aristotelian views see, for example, "Discourse Ethics: Notes on a Program of Philosophical Justification," in Habermas, *Moral Consciousness and Communicative Action*, trans. Christian Lenhart and Shierry Weber Nicholson (Cambridge, Mass.: MIT Press, 1990), 98–108; for his privileging of the "right" over the "good" see "Morality and Ethical Life: Does Hegel's Critique of Kant Apply to Discourse Ethics?" in the same volume, 195–215. Compare also my "Kant and Critical Theory," in *Between Freiburg and Frankfurt* (Amherst: University of Massachusetts Press, 1991), 105–31.

18. Aristotle, *Nicomachean Ethics*, 1155a25; trans. Terence Irwin (Indianapolis: Hackett, 1985), 208 (Book VIII, 9.11).

19. Derrida, *Politics of Friendship*, 4, 7–10; Aristotle, *Nicomachean Ethics*, 1156b10, trans. Irwin, 213 (Book VIII, 9.35); Cicero, *On Friendship and the Dream of Scipio*, ed. and trans. J. G. F. Powell (Warminster: Aris and Phillips Ltd., 1990), 43 (IX: 31), 63 (XXI: 80). The charge of the reduction of friends to sameness is particularly strange in the case of Cicero whose friend Atticus was in so many ways unlike him (he abstained from politics and leaned toward Epicureanism).

20. The first anteriority might perhaps be called ethical or "ontological," while the second pertains to the field of morality. It is perhaps not accidental that the discussion of immemorial friendship ends with a long footnote devoted to Heidegger and to (what Derrida calls) the "incessant meditation on friendship in the path of Heidegger's thought." See "The Politics of Friendship," 637, n. 5. For more critical comments on Heidegger, chiding him for an insufficient break with Aristotle, see *Politics of Friendship*, 240–44.

21. Some of these points have been cogently articulated by Paul Ricoeur in *Oneself as Another*, trans. Kathleen Blamey (Chicago: University of Chicago Press, 1992), 188–89. For a fuller discussion see the next chapter.

22. Aristotle, *Nicomachean Ethics*, 1155b30, 1159a35, 1161a34–b10, trans. Irwin, 210 (Book VIII, 9.22), 223 (Book VIII, 9.53), 229 (Book VIII, 9.66). Aristotle also includes in radical separation the process of divinization where a person is elevated above human beings to become a "god"; for as a god "he will no longer have friends." *Nicomachean Ethics*, 1159a5–10 (Book VIII, 9.52). Aristotle's views are echoed by Cicero when he writes: "This is indeed the life of tyrants where undoubtedly there can be no good faith, no affection, no steady confidence of another's goodwill; all is perpetual mistrust and vexation—there is no room for friendship. . . . It is of the greatest importance in friendship to treat inferiors as equals. . . . This conduct should be adopted and imitated by all, so that if a person has attained to any outstanding quality, either in character or intellectual gifts or wealth, he should communicate and share it with his friends." See Cicero, *On Friendship and the Dream of Scipio*, 53 (XV:52), 59–61 (XVIII:69–70).

23. Derrida, *Politics of Friendship*, 10, 14, 23, 28–29, 35, 54–55.

24. *Politics of Friendship*, 6, 35, 37, 42–43, 62. In stipulating a "community without community," Derrida deliberately radicalizes and moves beyond the more moderate notions of an "unavowable community" or of an "inoperative (or un-managed) community" proposed respectively by Maurice Blanchot and Jean-Luc Nancy. As he writes (48, n. 15): "There is still perhaps some brotherhood in Bataille, Blanchot, and Nancy, and I wonder . . . if it does not deserve a little loosening up and if it should still guide the thinking of the community, be it a community without community, or a brotherhood without brotherhood." That classical thought established a parallel between other-love and self-love is, of course, undeniable—but also plausible and defensible (seeing that people who hate or corrupt themselves do not usually qualify as friends). On this point, Paul Ricoeur seems on the mark when he writes that "between the two extremes of the summons to responsibility, where the initiative comes from the other, and of sympathy for the suffering other, where the initiative comes from the loving self," friendship appears as "a midpoint where the self and the other share equally the same wish to live together." See *Oneself as Another*, 192.

25. Derrida, *Politics of Friendship*, 64–65. The reference is to Nietzsche, *The Gay Science*, trans. Walter Kaufmann (New York: Vintage, 1974), 1, 14.

26. Aristotle, *Nicomachean Ethics*, 1157b21, 1169b18, trans. Irwin, 216–17 (Book VIII, 9.44), 257 (Book IX, 11.64); Cicero, *On Friendship and the Dream of Scipio*, 51 (XIII:47). At another point, Cicero presents even the majestic beauty of the universe as stale and

insipid unless it is shared in company: "Thus nature leaves nothing solitary and, as it were, always reaches out to something as a support—which in the dearest friend is most delightful." See 67 (XXIII:88). Somewhat annoyed with the extreme subtlety of some philosophers, Cicero adds: "We must not, then, listen to persons who overflow with self-indulgence when they argue about friendship, of which they have no real knowledge either in theory or in experience." See 53 (XV:52).

27. Derrida's verbal artistry is, of course, part of his acclaim. In addition to postulating a "community without community," his book also advances such notions as "decision without decision (or decisionism)" and an "enmity without enmity" (or an exchangeability of friend and enemy—which, of course, can only happen if both are equally respected and esteemed). See *Politics of Friendship*, 58–59, 67–68, 249. The labels "anomie," "world alienation," and "*trahison de tous par tous*" (betrayal of all by all) are associated respectively with the names of Emile Durkheim, Hannah Arendt, and Gabriel Marcel.

28. See Aristotle, *Nicomachean Ethics*, 1157b22, 1166a7, 1172a1, trans. Irwin, 216–17 (VIII, 9.44), 245 (IX, 11.11), 265 (IX, 11.92); Cicero, *On Friendship and the Dream of Scipio*, 73 (XXVII:103). Despite his own accent on a rarified anchoritic (non)relation, Derrida repeatedly criticizes both Aristotle and Cicero for their stress on the rarity of close or genuine friendship, charging them with fostering a kind of preferential oligarchy (*oligophilia*); see *Politics of Friendship*, 3, 71. This criticism, however, neglects the lateral extension of friendship into social and political life. Thus, Aristotle regarded friendship as a cornerstone of politics and wrote: "Certainly it is possible to be a friend of many in a fellow-citizen's way, and still to be a truly decent person." Even more emphatically Cicero states: "Among the good a liking for the good is, as it were, inevitable. . . . But the same kind of disposition extends also to the multitude; for virtue is not inhuman or cruel or arrogant, being accustomed as she is to watch over whole peoples and to provide the best measures for their well-being—which assuredly she would not do did she shrink from the affection of the many." See Aristotle, *Nicomachean Ethics*, 1160a22, 1171a17, trans. Irwin, 225 (VIII, 9.62), 263 (IX, 11.73); Cicero, *On Friendship and the Dream of Scipio*, 53 (XIV:50).

∿

CHAPTER NINE

Oneself as Another:
Paul Ricoeur's "Little Ethics"

Both in theory and in practice, ethics today is in disarray. In the famous opening pages of *After Virtue*, Alasdair MacIntyre depicted a grim scenario of devastation where ethical memories—especially the great ethical teachings of the past—had been obliterated by a debacle akin to a nuclear holocaust. Although perhaps overly dramatized, the scenario seems not far off the mark. On the level of social practice, an age marked by genocide and ethnic cleansing cannot credit itself with a high degree of ethical sensibility. Partly as a result of the practical malaise, ethical theorizing in many ways presents a babel of tongues, with protagonists of the most diverse paradigms competing for attention.[1] To some extent, the clamor of voices can be simplified or streamlined by turning attention to the presumed source of moral norms, a source located either in the individual or in society or a public community. In this respect, the recent Cold War still throws its long (and disorienting) shadow over contemporary debates, by pitting champions of individual freedom against socialists and social communitarians. While the former exalt private autonomy—sometimes to a point indistinguishable from license—the latter accentuate social obligations (which often turn out to be obligations to a dominant regime or ruling doctrine). The demise of the Cold War has only rearranged and broadened these intellectual front lines. Today liberal defenders of the "free world" (meaning the West) are confronted by the upsurge of numerous nonindividualistic cultural traditions in the rest of the world—which demonstrates that ethics today has necessarily a global or cosmopolitan cast.

Venturing into the thicket of contemporary ethical debates requires courage and intellectual stamina; attempting to make headway in that thicket also demands sobriety and a good dose of fair-mindedness—qualities that nowadays are in short supply. Fortunately, our age is not entirely devoid of guideposts or guiding mentors; one of the more reliable guides is Paul Ricoeur. Although frequently sidelined by changing "fashion trends" in his native France, Ricoeur over the decades has proven himself to be one of the most perceptive analysts of contemporary social-political dilemmas as well as one of the most sober and clear-minded voices in the complex (and often over-heated) controversies of our time. Steeped deeply in "Continental" philosophy but also attentive to Anglo-American "analytical" reasoning, his publications betray a breadth of intellectual scope that militates against any kind of parochialism. In the field of ethics, including public or political ethics, his work stands as an impressive counterexample to MacIntyre's scenario by recollecting and vividly bringing back to life the classical, polis-centered teachings of Aristotle's ethics as well as the modernist "groundwork" of autonomous moral self-legislation celebrated by Kant. By correlating and carefully calibrating these diverse legacies, his approach makes a major contribution (among other things) to the festering "liberalism versus communitarianism" debate and also to the "tradition versus modernity" conundrum.

Nowhere is this contribution more powerfully evident than in Oneself as Another, a chef d'oeuvre of his later years, which will be the main focus of this chapter. My aim here will be to highlight and applaud Ricoeur's accomplishments—but to do so in a critical vein (which alone befits a philosopher); paying him such a critical tribute, in any case, seems to accord well with his own emphasis on "critical solicitude" seen as preeminent form of practical wisdom.[2] The presentation will be tripartite:

1. The first section recapitulates the main arguments regarding ethics and its role in the public domain as presented in Oneself as Another.
2. The second part raises a number of critical queries or reservations.
3. The final section will explore the relevance of Ricoeur's argument for contemporary politics and public life, especially in the context of the emerging "global village" or cosmopolis.

Ethics and Public Life

The theme of ethics and public life is a central concern of Oneself as Another, but it is approached somewhat circuitously through an analysis of "selfhood" in its different modalities. This approach seems to insert Ricoeur's text into the broadly familiar framework of the "subject" seen as the source of moral norms and obligations. This impression, however, is unwarranted. As is well known, and as he himself repeatedly insists, Ricoeur is not a "philosopher of the subject" or of the "cogito," but rather a hermeneuticist—moreover, the proponent of a hermeneutics enriched or amplified by borrowings from linguistic analysis, depth psychology, and post-structuralist efforts to "decenter" the ego. This decentering has been a hallmark of his thought from the beginning. Thus, although a profound student of Descartes and Edmund Husserl, some of his early writings had called into question the foundational role of subjectivity in favor of a notion of situated and embodied selfhood (indebted in many ways to Gabriel Marcel). Somewhat later, his investigation of depth psychology vindicated a complex "hermeneutics of suspicion" as opposed to the straightforward grasp of semantic meanings. Roughly at the same time, his analysis of "willing" and "freedom of will" complicated the linearity of rational intention through recourse to a quasi-mythical "symbolism of evil." Congruent with these precedents, the selfhood invoked in *Oneself as Another* is not a fixed or self-contained ego, but rather a flexible "emergent" being discovering itself in a variety of situated engagements. Reflecting this practical accent, the text examines in sequence these basic questions: "Who is speaking? Who is acting? Who is recounting [narrating] about himself/herself? Who is the moral subject of interpretation?"—thus passing successively in review the speaking, the acting, the narrating, and the moral-ethical self (with the latter serving as a capstone of the entire series).[3]

What renders the theme of ethics and public life central or pivotal in *Oneself as Another* is the fact that only here the "other" or "other-than-self" comes specifically into focus. Although, in Ricoeur's account, selfhood is never devoid of other-relation, this relation only now becomes the distinct target of inquiry. In exploring this relation, Ricoeur's text advances a novel and startling theory of ethics, and of ethics in public life, which is marked both by a circumspect balance and a definite weighting of accents in one direction. In large measure, this weighting derives from the premise of a situated selfhood and the critique of the ego. What this premise renders dubious is the theory of moral self-legislation anchored in "noumenal" consciousness; what it renders attractive is the assumption of an ethical bond preceding and undergirding normative stipulations. Although indicating an order of preference, however, the text does not simply reject or negate the first option in favor of the second. In a manner distantly echoing Hegel, Ricoeur maintains the respective legitimacy of both "morality" and "ethics"—where ethics deals with "the *aim* of an accomplished life," while morality stands for normative legislation characterized by the "claim to universality" and an "effect of constraint." As he adds, the two terms are stand-ins for two traditions of an Aristotelian heritage "where ethics is characterized by its teleological perspective" and a Kantian heritage "where morality is defined by the obligation to respect the norm, hence by a *deontological* point of view." Combining the two traditions with his weighted preference scheme, *Oneself as Another* formulates a series of basic propositions that remain guideposts for the entire study:

> (1) the primacy of ethics over morality; (2) the necessity for the ethical aim to pass through the sieve of the norm, and (3) the legitimacy of recourse by the norm to the aim whenever the norm leads to an impasse in practice. . . . [Thus] morality is held to constitute only a limited, although legitimate and even indispensable, actualization of the ethical aim, and ethics in this sense would then encompass morality.[4]

In line with these propositions, the text moves from a discussion of teleological ethics in the Aristotelian vein via a Kantian or quasi-Kantian deontology to a final recuperation of ethics under the rubric of situated *phronesis* or practical wisdom. Reformulating the respective philosophical traditions, Ricoeur posits as the aim of teleological ethics the achievement of "self-esteem," while deontology is said to obey the principle of "self-respect"; the key category of a recuperative ethical praxis, finally, is found to reside in ethical "conviction," the term taken not in the sense of private opinion but rather in that of a reflective "attestation" bearing witness to competing demands in the public area. Elucidating the meaning of teleological ethics, the text offers a capsule phrase which highlights its central ingredients: ethics on this level, we read, means "aiming at the 'good life' with and for others, in just institutions." Decomposing the phrase into its constituent components, Ricoeur first focuses on the notion of leading a "good life" or "living well." As he notes, goodness along Aristotelian lines is always a "good for us"—not in the sense of an instant possession, but in that of something constantly (and unendingly) yearned or striven for. The question that arises immediately is whether goodness is the mark of a particular action taken by itself, or whether the latter is only a means to a more distant end (which perhaps can never be fully specified). Taking a leaf from the writings of Alasdair MacIntyre, Ricoeur distinguishes between particular actions or practices and broader, more encompassing "life plans" that allow the integration of singular acts into a "narrative unity of life" governed by intrinsic "standards of excellence." By adopting this perspective, goodness can be shown to be the intrinsic measure both of individual actions taken by themselves and of the "good life" taken in the sense of a whole life "lived well"—thus lending credence and support to the teleological argument of Aristotle's *Nicomachean Ethics*.[5]

Ethical goodness, however, cannot be a private monopoly; hence a "good life" is not one lived in isolation, but a life "with and for others." To characterize this aspect of living-with Ricoeur chooses the term "solicitude" (full of Heideggerian resonances). As he emphasizes, just as the "self" should not be construed as an ego, self-esteem as the aim of the good life cannot be divorced from solicitude; in fact, the latter is not "something added on to self-esteem from the outside" but rather an intrinsic quality unfolding "the dialogic dimension of self-esteem." As an emblem of co-being, solicitude is deeply shaped by reciprocity or mutuality—the kind of mutuality which Ricoeur sees as the hallmark of Aristotelian friendship. In Aristotle's account, he notes, (genuine) friendship involves neither an appropriation of the other nor a self-effacement in favor of the other, but rather a balance between self-love or self-care (*philautia*) and a self-transgression where the other is loved "for his or her sake," as "the being he/she is." Akin to friendship, solicitude thus emerges as an interchange between self and other, as "the midpoint of a spectrum" located between "giving and receiving." Arguing against Emmanuel Levinas's privileging of the "other," Ricoeur faults this approach for failing to establish an interhuman relation "to the extent that the other represents absolute exteriority with respect to an ego defined by the condition of separation." In another departure from Levinas, ethical sensibility for Ricoeur extends beyond interpersonal or face-to-face encounters to the field of "institutions," a public domain basically governed by the category of "justice." By institutions the text means structures of shared life, or else "bonds of common mores" permeating a historical community. Like solicitude, justice occupies a kind of midpoint between interpersonal care and the externality of legal constraints; as an ethical category, it involves the proper distribution of shares among members of a community, where shares include not only material goods but also roles, advantages, and forms of life.[6]

Having thus defended the "primacy of ethics" (in a more or less Aristotelian manner) Ricoeur recalls his second basic proposition according to which ethics, or the ethical aim, must "pass through the sieve of the norm," that is, through the sieve of deontological morality. The way in which ethics is tested by morality is chiefly through the principle of "universality" (or universalization) expressed preeminently in the universal maxims of Kantian moral theory. In Ricoeur's account, Kant's categorical imperative is precisely designed to pass the test of universalization—although the different formulations of the imperative give rise to quandaries. The text at this point refers to a number of problems or aporias in Kant's theory—to which it will be necessary to return later, but which can briefly be flagged here. These problems have all to do with the return of a certain moral affectivity (presumably exiled by Kantian self-legislation), giving rise to questions like these: Does the derivation of autonomy from a "fact of reason" not jeopardize the former's purity? Does Kant's admission of radical evil not rebound on the postulated freedom of will? Does the central category of "respect" for others not circumscribe a sovereign self-rule? Pursuing the last point, Ricoeur finds in respect a certain "dialogic structure" which approximates it to solicitude (in teleological ethics) and in any case to the traditional Golden Rule with its demand for reciprocity. Here again, however, a certain tension emerges between respect owed to "humanity" at large and respect owed to persons in their singularity: "The notion of humanity has the effect of lessening, to the point of elimination, the otherness that is at the root of this diversity" (of persons). To round out this discussion of morality, the text turns finally to the theme of justice as seen under deontological or proceduralist auspices. The prime example of the latter approach is John Rawls's *A Theory of Justice* with its blending of Kantian and contractarian premises.[7]

As announced in the third basic proposition, deontological morality cannot stand on its own or have the last word by virtue of its intrinsic dilemmas or limitations, moral reflection is prompted to return to "the initial intuition of ethics"—now under the rubric of "moral judgment in situation" or "practical wisdom." Surprisingly, the return occurs again circuitously through the detour of tragedy or "tragic action." The basic point of the detour is to ward off any thought of a final reconciliation or synthesis, especially a Hegelian-style synthesis in which the preceding steps would be "sublated" (*aufgehoben*). In Ricoeur's words, tragedy—above all Sophocles' *Antigone*—teaches "something unique about the unavoidable nature of conflict in moral life"; it offers viewers a glimpse of "the agonistic ground of human experience," of the "interminable confrontation" of man and woman, individual and society, human beings and gods. The only way to mitigate or mediate these conflicts is through cultivation of practical wisdom (nurtured by tragic wisdom). A major argumentative move here is a reformulation of Hegel's political and ethical philosophy, one that seeks to "shift Hegelian *Sittlichkeit* in the direction Aristotelian *phronesis*." Once this is done, *Sittlichkeit* would no longer denote "a third category, higher than ethics and morality," but would designate "one of the places in which practical wisdom is exercised, namely the hierarchy of institutional mediations through which practical wisdom must pass if justice is truly to deserve the name of fairness." The benefits of a turn to *phronesis* are illustrated by Ricoeur on three levels of public debate. In the case of everyday debates about concrete policies, Aristotle's notion of deliberation warrants and supports the modern-liberal demand for open discussion in a public forum (*Öffentlichkeit*). On the level of debates about preferable regimes or constitutional arrangements, *phronesis* helps to guard against simplistic recipes by appealing to the wisdom of practical experience. Finally, on the level of the basic legitimation of regimes, *phronesis* aids in combating the "crisis of legitimacy" by marshalling the "overlapping consensus" of diverse traditions.[8]

Returning to the theme of respect/solicitude, Ricoeur repeats and sharpens a dilemma he had previously noted in Kantian morality: namely, the tension between respect for humanity at large and respect for singular persons (seen as ends in themselves). For Ricoeur, this is a major area calling for the intervention of prudential judgment. In Kant's formulas, he writes, "respect tends to split up into respect for the [universal] law and respect for persons." Under these conditions, "practical wisdom may consist in giving priority to the respect for persons, in the name of the solicitude that is addressed to persons in their irreplaceable singularity." For Kant, every deviation or exception from universality was necessarily a moral lapse. The situation changes, however, once the demand for respect is radicalized. At this point, "the genuine otherness of persons makes each one an exception"; practical wisdom here means pursuing a course that "will best satisfy the exception required by solicitude"—without arrogantly nullifying universal rules as such. Proceeding, in a final step, to the topic of self-legislation grounded in autonomy, Ricoeur recapitulates some of the quandaries previously alluded to—especially the role of the "fact of reason" and of the pervasive affectivity infiltrating rational obligation. In Ricoeur's pointed words "An autonomy that is of a piece with the rule of justice and the rule of reciprocity can no longer be a *self-sufficient* autonomy." Similar quandaries beset the principle of universality or universalization—which Ricoeur prefers to replace with the standard of "constructive coherence" (as found in judicial reasoning, especially in common-law countries).[9]

In *Oneself as Another*, the discussion of ethics and public life is rounded out by some general comments on the relation, or rather correlation, between universal principles and historical or cultural contexts. As the preceding review has indicated, this correlation is surely a central concern of the entire study—apart from constituting a prominent issue in contemporary ethical and political thought. As Ricoeur himself remarks, all the arguments presented in his text "find an echo and the focal point of their reflection, as it were, in the conflict between universalism and contextualism." The issue clearly impinges on John Rawls's theory of justice, given that a "fair" distribution of social goods depends on historically and culturally shaped understandings of the meaning of "goods"—with the result that "no system of distribution . . . is universally valid." The issue also affects the Habermasian program of a universal discourse morality (or discourse ethics). Without in any way endorsing cultural or historical relativism, Ricoeur detects in these theories the legacy of Kantian dualisms, especially the polarities of reason and inclination and reason and convention. Paralleling his reformulation of Hegelian *Sittlichkeit*, Ricoeur at this point proposes a replacement of the reason/convention dualism by the more subtle dialectic between "*argumentation and conviction*." In this dialectic, argumentation allows itself to be inserted into a multiplicity of different (though not incommensurable) language games, thereby gaining historical and cultural richness and profile. At the same time, social contexts permit themselves to be seasoned by critical reasoning, the latter operating not as the enemy of tradition but as a "critical agency operating *at the heart* of [historically sedimented] convictions." As Ricoeur concludes, "It is just such a reflective equilibrium between the requirement of universality and the recognition of contextual limitation affecting it that is the final issue in situational judgment" or the exercise of practical wisdom.[10]

Some Critical Reservations

Having followed the book's intellectual journey, the reader is likely to be stunned by the vastness of its scope and the subtlety of its insights. Placed in its own context, *Oneself as Another* surely deserves to be ranked as one of the great philosophical texts of our time. The virtues of the study are too numerous to be fully enumerated, but a few should be highlighted. One of the primary virtues resides in the boldness of the first proposition, which sets the basic tenor of the study: the affirmed "primacy of ethics over morality" (or of the good over the right). With this affirmation Ricoeur sets his face against one of the dominant, but thoroughly disorienting assumptions of modernity and modern political thought: that of a presocial, autonomous human existence outside of community bonds (as postulated by the contractarian tradition from Hobbes to contemporary liberal proceduralism). What this assumption ignores is that being human is not something "given" (by nature or reason), but rather a practical task requiring steady cultivation in social contexts. Differently phrased, human nature or "humanity" is not a fixed endowment but the fruit of a process of "humanization" involving sustained interactive solicitude. Ricoeur on this point is not reluctant to show his cards, that is, his intellectual indebtedness to Aristotle and his notion of "*zoon politikon*." Referring to *Oneself as Another*, he describes it as a study "whose tone is Aristotelian from start to finish." In the same context, he takes a stand against the contractarian doctrine of a state of nature (replete with "natural rights"), stating, "This hypothesis of a subject of law, constituted prior to any societal bond, can be refuted only by striking at its roots. Now the root is the failure to recognize the *mediating* role of others."[11]

To be sure, as indicated, Aristotle is not the sole mentor in the text, but shares the limelight with two prominent figures not usually associated with him: Kant and Hegel. The linkage of Aristotle and Kant, and especially the treatment of Kant as a necessary gateway from Aristotle to a viable modern ethics, is surely a unique and startling idea. Proponents of Aristotle are usually hostile to Kantian teachings, and the reverse holds equally true; hence both sides are disinclined to mutual learning. (Probably one of the weakest parts of MacIntyre's *After Virtue* was his cursory dismissal of Kantian morality.) Here Ricoeur boldly breaks the pattern by giving broad room to Kantian universalism and categorical maxims. What primarily motivates this break is the recognition of Kant as a thinker of human freedom and self-legislation—aspects which our age cannot and should not hastily renounce. The presence of Kant is further complicated by the additional invocation of Hegel testifying to a remarkably tolerant scope of intellectual horizons. In this respect, Ricoeur also breaks some established patterns, especially the fashionable and almost ritualistic denunciation of Hegel as proponent of "totalization" (read: totalitarianism) as found in recent Continental philosophy. As he admits frankly, Hegel's philosophical project "remains very close to my own views, to the extent that it reinforces the claims directed against political atomism"; in this respect at least, the notion of *Sittlichkeit* "has never ceased to instruct us." The remarkable triad of mentors is summed up by Ricoeur in these words:

> This "little ethics" [developed in *Oneself as Another*] . . . suggests that the practical wisdom we are seeking aims at reconciling Aristotle's *phronesis*, by way of Kant's *Moralität*, with Hegel's *Sittlichkeit*. . . . Between the "naïve" *phronesis* of our first pages and the "critical" *phronesis* of our final pages extends, first, the region of moral obligation, of duty . . . and, more particularly, the demand that the suffering inflicted on humans by other humans be abolished. . . . In this way, "critical" *phronesis* tends, through these mediations, to be identified with *Sittlichkeit*. The latter, however, has been stripped of its pretension to mark the victory of Spirit over the contradictions that it itself provokes. Reduced to modesty, *Sittlichkeit* now joins *phronesis* in moral judgment in situation.[12]

Intellectual generosity extends also to some prominent contemporary figures, including Jürgen Habermas and Levinas (though for very different reasons). Although critical of his practical deficit—his sidelining of practical judgment—Ricoeur readily endorses Habermas's "linguistic turn" or his turn to argumentation. In this respect, *Oneself as Another* takes sides against certain contextualist detractors of Habermas who—perhaps too quickly—are ready to abandon broader public horizons in favor of self-enclosed language games. In a very different register, Ricoeur's text grants a hearing to the Levinasian inversion of ethics—provided that the privileging of the "other" is seen simply as an antidote to, or compensation for, rampantly egocentric approaches prevalent in modernity. As an astute reader of Kant, Ricoeur cannot fail to be apprehensive about such Levinasian formulas as radical "exteriority," "dissymmetry," and "heteronomy," suspecting them to be new forms of human self-alienation and authoritarian tutelage. By installing the other as "master of justice," he writes, the self is liable to be reduced to a passive recipient or object; "summoned" to responsibility, "it is in the *accusative* mode alone that the self is enjoined." This means that the summons targets "the passivity of an 'I' who has been called upon." The critique of Levinas is carried forward and expanded in the final chapter or epilogue of the book dealing with the metaphysics (or ontology) of self and other. There, appealing to the dialectic-dialogical character of solicitude, Ricoeur chides both Husserlian "egology" and Levinasian "exteriority" for missing the mediated nexus of self and other.[13]

These critical comments, however, do not amount to complete rejection. Underneath overt denials, there is an undercurrent of complicity, signaling an indebtedness to Levinasian discourse and, more broadly, to post-structuralist accents on "otherness." Sensitive to these accents, Ricoeur is unwilling to subscribe to any unitary metaphysics (or ontology) which would submerge the diversity of particulars to a grand synthesis (or totalization). This aversion colors the reception of his mentors. Thus, in the case of Aristotle, the ethical aim of leading a "good life," both individually and collectively, no longer obeys a unitary formula, but is decentered into different types of goodness (which sometimes are in tragic conflict). In the case of Kant, the maxim of treating human beings as ends is decomposed into respect for humanity in general and for persons in their singularity, with a distinct preference given to the second formulation. The most resolute decentering, however, affects Hegelian philosophy where "*Geist*" is subordinated to *phronesis* and *Sittlichkeit* transformed into practical judgment in concrete situations. Apart from its philosophical importance, this decentering clearly has far-reaching political implications—to the extent that Hegel's philosophy is seen as a bulwark of the modern "state." Ricoeur is adamant on this point. What he finds "inadmissible" in Hegel's work is the concept of the "objective mind" and, as its corollary, "the thesis of the state erected as a superior agency endowed with self-knowledge." As a recipe for "demystifying the Hegelian state" he recommends the turn to "political practice" in concrete contexts (although the point is not further pursued). Basically, what these comments suggest is a turn from the "state" to the domain of "civil society"—the latter seen not so much (or not only) as an arena of economic competition but as a space for the unfolding of different "life plans" on the part of individuals and groups.[14]

Having highlighted some—by no means all—of the fruitful and promising features of *Oneself as Another*, it is time to make room for "critical solicitude." Reservations arise at a number of points—one being precisely the treatment of Hegel. A central motive behind Ricoeur's critique of the Hegelian state derives from the horrible experiences of our time. As he writes, people who have moved through "the monstrous events of the twentieth century tied to the phenomenon of totalitarianism" can no longer be sanguine about the state; when social community is perverted "to the point of feeding a deadly *Sittlichkeit*," only recourse to heroic individuals (perhaps imbued with Kantian morality) can bring relief. Here one may wish to remonstrate against the equation of the Hegelian state with political perversion or corruption. *Pace* Karl Popper, the Hegelian state is a rational-ethical "idea" and as such not reducible to contingent, empirical structures; by the same token, a "deadly *Sittlichkeit*" can no longer count as ethical but precisely as "*unsittlich*." What this means is that Hegelian thought probably cannot be criticized, and certainly not be dislodged, by purely empirical rejoinders pointing to the "way of the world." Fittingly for a philosophical discourse, a basic theoretical or metaphysical idea can only be countered by a "better argument," that is, by the development of a more adequate or more nuanced idea. In its main tenor, *Oneself as Another* precisely pursues such a course, namely by articulating the notion of a decentered or nonunitary *Sittlichkeit* illustrated by respect for persons in their singularity and by pursuit of the "good life" in different modalities.[15]

Next to Hegel, the treatment of a number of other figures elicits critical qualms. Among more contemporary thinkers, Charles Taylor deserves brief mention. As students of Taylor surely will have noticed, there are multiple parallels linking him with Ricoeur's arguments. Prominent among these are the privileging of the "good" over the "right," the reconstruction of "selfhood," and the remolding of Hegel's legacy in the direction of a viable public ethics in our time. Despite some furtive compliments, however, the Canadian receives only scant attention in the text; occasionally he is linked with "communitarians" disdainful of universal rights—in neglect of Taylor's own complex mediation of universalism and historical context on the ethical plane.[16] Probably the least persuasive treatment in the text is accorded to Martin Heidegger—whose voice meanders intermittently through its pages, but receives distinct contours only in the final epilogue. Despite the clear connection between "solicitude" and Heidegger's notion of "care" (*Sorge*), the relation is initially left unexplored and only tackled in the epilogue, in a somewhat roundabout way. The Heidegger that emerges in the conclusion is basically the interpreter and adapter of Aristotle, with *Being and Time* said to perform three central interpretive moves: namely, from Aristotelian *praxis* to "care"; from Aristotelian *phronesis* to "conscience" (*Gewissen*); and from Aristotelian *energeia* to being-in-the-world as "facticity." Leaving aside the aspect of conscience, these alleged moves clearly involve a narrowly "ontic" reading of Heidegger's work, neglecting the more recessed (ontological) dimensions of that work—a narrowness evident in the treatment of *praxis* as action (versus passion) and also in Ricoeur's own preferred re-styling of *energeia* as "*conatus*" (a term borrowed from Spinoza's metaphysics of life and power).[17]

The mention of Heidegger brings into view an aspect that is perhaps the most problematical feature of *Oneself as Another*: namely, Ricoeur's preference for detours and byways in lieu of a genuine rethinking or reformulation of basic issues. As it happens, this feature is a long-standing trait of his opus. Thus, his *Conflict of Interpretations* chided Heidegger for taking a "short route" in blending hermeneutics with phenomenology—in contrast to a recommended "long route" leading through the detours of epistemology and (transcendental) reflection. Similarly, his *Rule of Metaphor* charged Heidegger with leaping head-long into poetic metaphor instead of pursuing the longer path through conceptual/speculative discourse.[18] In *Oneself as Another*—explicitly self-styled as a "philosophy of detours"—the argument tends to proceed in quasi-Hegelian fashion from one side to the opposite side, with practical wisdom finally brought onto the stage as *deus ex machina*. Surely, one may ask how two questionable positions can yield a viable theory. In the case of Aristotle, given a multiplication of goods, how much of teleology remains standing? In the case of Kant, does the enumeration of paradoxes and aporias—from the "fact of reason" to the inroads of affectivity and radical evil—still permit recourse to deontological morality as a necessary detour?[19]

The preference for detours takes its heaviest toll in the domain most central to the book's concerns: the relation of self and other. Here detour may precisely mean derailment; for clearly, if the "other" is merely a detour on the road from self to self (presumably from naïve self to reflective self), the book's announced theme of "oneself *as* another" is foiled. This problem is not obviated by Ricoeur's distinction between two types of selfhood, *idem-* and *ipse-*identity—the former referring to a stable self-nature, the second to authentic singularity—because the road to *ipse*-selfhood still remains circuitous.[20] This circuitous approach is glaringly manifest in the epilogue dealing with the "ontology" of self and other. Here, Ricoeur steers a precarious course between Husserl and Levinas, that is, between a constitution of the other by the self and a constitution of the self by the other's summons. However, the basic tenor of the entire discussion is closer to Levinas, in that the "other" remains in principle "other than the self" and thus is experienced as an inroad in the mode of "passivity." The conclusion discusses this other-experience under three headings, labeled the "triad of passivity and hence, of otherness." There is, first of all, the passivity represented by "the experience of one's own body" (or one's own "flesh"), where the body appears as a kind of alien agent. Next, there is the "otherness of other people," that is, passivity involved in the relation of self to the "foreign" or "other (than) self." Finally, there is the "most deeply hidden passivity" located in the relation of the self to itself, a relation disclosed in "conscience" (*Gewissen*). Thus, there are for Ricoeur "three great experiences of passivity" undergone by the self at the hands of otherness—but nowhere (or so it seems) an experience of "oneself *as* another."[21]

Ricoeur and Political Praxis

Having made room for critical reservations, it seems appropriate to conclude these pages on a note of solicitude. There are many aspects of Ricoeur's work that deserve praise; some have been mentioned before. Overshadowing all other features in importance is the asserted primacy of the "good" over the "right," that is, the affirmation of a basic goodness of life prior to any "rights" talk and also prior to any theoretical formulation of ethics or metaethics. In Ricoeur's (plausible) formulation, deontology "provides at best the formalization of a sense of justice that it never ceases to presuppose." This, to be sure, leaves open the question of how to proceed from a primary sense to a viable theoretical conception—a question that raises again the vexed problem of "detours," that is, the progression from teleology via deontology to practical *phronesis*. In a certain sense, even the notion of detours may be justifiable, provided the term does not signal a zigzag movement between opposite positions, but rather the path of a complex learning process involving trials and errors (and also *Holzwege*). Clearly, for inhabitants of modern Western societies, none of the great episodes of modernity—from Renaissance and Reformation to Enlightenment and industrialization—can be simply expunged. This means that even staunch opponents of Enlightenment still have to come to terms with, or offer a response to, developments they reject.[22]

In terms of contemporary public life, one of Ricoeur's most incisive contributions resides in his resolute effort to move beyond the stale oppositions between liberalism and communitarianism, and also between universalism and contextualism. As indicated, one of the central aims of *Oneself as Another* is to find a "reflective equilibrium" between "the requirement of universality and the recognition of contextual limitations"; a crucial thesis advanced in this respect is that an open political arena demands the maintenance of both claims, the universalist and the contextualist, "each in a place" without amalgamation or mutual exclusion. It is here that Ricoeur's argument regarding multiple kinds of goodness reveals its current political significance. Clearly, in an age marked by multiculturalism or the upsurge of multicultural diversity, the maintenance of a public space requires both the cultivation of (individual or group) differences and the "solicitous" search for a shared framework, perhaps an "overlapping consensus," through interactive dialogue and contestation. In this contemporary situation, older ethical paradigms—like restrictive communitarianism stressing a unitary goal or liberal contractarianism focused on narrow self-interest—are no longer persuasive. What Ricoeur's public ethics recommends, instead, is a tolerantly open public space encouraging respect for persons or groups in their "singularity" without losing sight of the requirement of justice or a rule of law. Such an ethics maintains a shared horizon of "truth" and "goodness" but allows for multiple, even conflicting interpretations of these terms—without lapsing into a debilitating relativism. It honors a sense of universalism which Ricoeur at one point (too briefly) describes as "universals in context" or else "potential or inchoate universals."[23]

The contemporary salience of this public ethics is particularly manifest in light of the unfolding global scenario, that is, the emergence of a global community differentiated along multiple (cultural, ethnic, religious) lines. What this scenario clearly requires is cultivation of respect for difference, for the diversity of cultures and traditions—without succumbing to particularistic myopia anchored in self-enclosed language games. *Oneself as Another* remonstrates strongly against the latter type of relativism: against the claim, as Ricoeur says, that "cultures are ultimately multiple" and incommensurable—where "culture" is taken in a narrowly ethnographic sense "far removed from that of instruction in the ways of reason and liberty" (favored by modern *Bildung*). At the same time, the goal of *phronesis* would not be served by a simple neglect of cultural diversity—an issue that is well illustrated by the controversy surrounding the alleged "ethnocentrism" of supposedly "universal" human rights. As Ricoeur notes, such rights—enshrined in the Universal Declaration of Human Rights (of 1948)—have in fact been ratified or endorsed by the vast majority of countries in the world. Yet, "the suspicion remains that they are simply the fruit of the cultural history belonging to the West, with its wars of religion, its laborious and unending apprenticeship of tolerance." In this situation, *phronesis* demands a complex negotiation of claims that steers clear both of hegemonic universalism and contextual incommensurability:

On the one hand, one must maintain the universal claim attached to a few values where the universal and the historical intersect, and on the other hand, one must submit this claim to discussion, not on a formal level, but on the level of the convictions incorporated in concrete forms of life. Nothing can result from this discussion unless every party recognizes that other potential universals are contained in so-called exotic cultures. The path of eventual consensus can emerge only from mutual recognition on the level of acceptability, that is, by admitting a possible truth, admitting proposals of meaning that are at first foreign to us.[24]

A highly intricate and erudite work, *Oneself as Another* thus reveals itself in the end as a major contribution to reflective political praxis (in the best Aristotelian, post-Hegelian, and Arendtian sense). Ricoeur is by no means a novice or a stranger to the political domain. In several of his previous writings, he had shown himself as both an astute observer of, and engaged participant in, the political agonies of our age. Thus, his *Political and Social Essays* (written during the decades following World War II) articulated a vision of politics or public life combining two central demands: first, creation of an open public space permitting the free pursuit of different modes of goodness (along broadly "liberal" lines), and second, cultivation of social solidarity and a sense of social responsibility, especially for the fate of underprivileged or disadvantaged groups. The yearning for social justice, he emphasized, cannot be divorced today from "solidarity with the most underprivileged fraction of humanity, with the misery of the underdeveloped peoples." Pursuing this line of thought Ricoeur also commented on the process of globalization, on the emergence of a "planetary consciousness," highlighting both its promise and its perils. While potentially fostering greater solidarity and shared respect among humanity at large, this globalizing process—especially under the rubric of "mondialization"—can also lead to increased uniformity and streamlining of cultures under the pressure of economically and technologically hegemonic powers.

In this context, a commitment to social democracy, projected onto the global scale, implies resistance to the division of the world into "haves" and "have-nots," into North and South, and to the systematic exploitation of one part of humanity by another. Nothing less is demanded by distributive justice and by the reflective equilibrium of *phronesis*. As Ricoeur writes more recently and engagingly in *Oneself as Another*, "the 'good life' is for each of us [and hence for humanity at large] the nebulus of ideals and dreams of achievements with regard to which a life is held to be more or less fulfilled or unfulfilled." What we are summoned to think here is the idea of a highly complex "finality" (*telos*) of humankind which can and should never cease to be the "internal mainspring" of human praxis.[25]

Notes

1. For an overview of ethical theories in our time see Steven M. Cahn and Joram G. Haber, *Twentieth Century Ethical Theory* (Upper Saddle River, N.J.: Prentice-Hall, 1995); T. Henderich, ed., *Morality and Objectivity* (London: Routledge & Kegan Paul, 1985); William D. Hudson, *Modern Moral Philosophy* (Garden City, N.Y.: Anchor Books, 1970); also my "Introduction" to Seyla Benhabib and Fred Dallmayr, eds., *The Communicative Ethics Controversy* (Cambridge, Mass.: MIT Press, 1990), 1–20. Compare also Alasdair MacIntyre, *After Virtue: A Study in Moral Theory*, 2nd ed. (Notre Dame, Ind.: University of Notre Dame Press, 1984), 1–2; and John D. Caputo, *Against Ethics: Contributions to a Poetics of Obligation with Constant Reference to Deconstruction* (Bloomington, Ind.: Indiana University Press, 1993).

2. Paul Ricoeur, *Oneself as Another*, trans. Kathleen Blamey (Chicago: University of Chicago Press, 1992), 273.

3. *Oneself as Another*, 16. He emphasizes: "The philosophy that comes out of this work deserves to be termed a practical philosophy" (19). For some of Ricoeur's earlier writings see *Gabriel Marcel et Karl Jaspers* (Paris: Temps Present, 1948); *Freud and Philosophy: An Essay on Interpretation*, trans. Denis Savage (New Haven, Conn.: Yale University Press, 1969); *Freedom and Nature*, trans. Erazim Kohak (Evanston, Ill.: Northwestern University Press, 1966); *Husserl: An Analysis of His Phenomenology*, trans. Edward G. Ballard and Lester E. Embree (Evanston, Ill.: Northwestern University Press, 1967); *The Symbolism of Evil*, trans. Emerson Buchanan (New York: Harper & Row, 1967); *The Conflict of Interpretations*, ed. Don Ihde, trans. Willis Domingo et al. (Evanston, Ill.: Northwestern University Press, 1974); *Time and Narrative*, 3 vols., trans. Kathleen McLaughlin and David Pellauer (Chicago: University of Chicago Press, 1984–1988).

4. *Oneself as Another*, 170. Ricoeur adds, "There will thus be no attempt to substitute Kant for Aristotle, despite a respectable tradition to the contrary. Instead, between the two traditions, I shall establish a relation involving at once subordination and complementarity, which the final recourse of morality to ethics will ultimately come to reinforce" (170–71).

5. *Oneself as Another*, 172–77.

6. *Oneself as Another*, 180–83, 188–90, 194, 197, 200.

7. *Oneself as Another*, 204–7, 209, 212–19, 222–23, 229. See also John Rawls, *A Theory of Justice* (Cambridge, Mass.: Harvard University Press, 1971).

8. *Oneself as Another*, 243, 256–61. Ricoeur elaborates: "There is nothing better to offer, in reply to the legitimation crisis . . . than the memory and the intersection in the public space of the appearance of the traditions that make room for tolerance and pluralism, not out of concessions to external pressures, but out of inner conviction, even if this is late in coming. . . . If, and to the extent that, this 'good counsel' does prevail, Hegelian *Sittlichkeit* . . . proves to be the equivalent of Aristotle's *phronesis*: a plural, or rather public, *phronesis* resembling the debate itself" (261).

9. *Oneself as Another*, 262, 265, 269, 275–77, 280. At this point, Ricoeur comments critically on the model of "discourse morality" as propounded by Jürgen Habermas and Karl-Otto Apel.

10. *Oneself as Another*, 284–88.

11. *Oneself as Another*, 281.

12. *Oneself as Another*, 254–55, 290. Regarding denunciations of Hegel in recent French philosophy, see my "Effective History: Hegel's Heirs and Critics," in Dallmayr, G. F. W. *Hegel: Modernity and Politics* (Newbury Park, Calif.: Sage, 1993), 233–38. Compare also Karl Popper, *The Open Society and Its Enemies*, 5th ed. (London: Routledge and Kegan Paul, 1966).

13. *Oneself as Another*, 189, 281, 284, 331, 336. As Ricoeur recognizes, this critique is primarily addressed at Levinas's *Totality and Infinity*. He also comments, however, on a subsequent radicalization, in *Otherwise than Being*, whereby the recipient subject is transformed hyperbolically into a hostage. "The paroxysm of the hyperbole seems to me to result from the extreme—even scandalous—hypothesis that the Other is no longer the master of justice here, as is the case in *Totality and Infinity*, but the offender who, as an offender, no less requires the gesture of pardon and expiation" (338). See Levinas, *Totality and Infinity: An Essay on Exteriority*, trans. Alphonso Lingis (Pittsburgh: Duquesne University Press, 1969); and *Otherwise than Being or Beyond Essence*, trans. Alphonso Lingis (Dordrecht: Kluwer Academic, 1991).

14. *Oneself as Another*, 225, 256. For a development of an argument along these lines see my "Rethinking the Hegelian State" in *Margins of Political Discourse* (Albany, N.Y.: State University of New York Press, 1989), 137–57. Regarding civil society compare especially Jean L. Cohen and Andrew Arato, *Civil Society and Political Theory* (Cambridge, Mass.: MIT Press, 1992), and John Keane, ed., *Civil Society and the State* (London: Verso, 1988).

15. *Oneself as Another*, 256. See G. W. F. Hegel, *Hegel's Philosophy of Right*, trans. T. M. Knox (Oxford: Oxford University Press, 1967), par. 258 (addition), 279.

16. *Oneself as Another*, 179, 181, 280, n. 67. See Charles Taylor, *The Ethics of Authenticity* (Cambridge, Mass.: Harvard University Press, 1992).

17. *Oneself as Another*, 308–17, 348–49. On the question of conscience, Ricoeur in the end wants to mediate between Heidegger and Levinas, stating, "To the reduction of being-in-debt to the strange(r)ness tied to the facticity of being-in-the-world, characteristic of the philosophy of Martin Heidegger, Emmanuel Levinas opposes a symmetrical reduction of the otherness of conscience to the externality of the other manifested in his face. . . . To these alternatives . . . I shall stubbornly oppose the original and originary character of what appears to me to constitute the third modality of otherness, namely *being enjoined as the structure of selfhood*" (354). Compare Heidegger, *Being and Time*, trans. Joan Stambaugh (Albany, N.Y.: State University of New York Press, 1996), esp. 247–77; "Letter on Humanism," in David F. Krell, ed., *Martin Heidegger: Basic Writings* (New York: Harper & Row, 1977), 234–35. Regarding the ethical dimension of Heidegger's thought see also my "Heidegger on Ethics and Justice," in Dallmayr, *The Other Heidegger* (Ithaca, N.Y.: Cornell University Press, 1993), 106–31.

18. See Ricoeur, *The Conflict of Interpretations: Essays in Hermeneutics*, ed. Don Ihde (Evanston, Ill.: Northwestern University Press, 1974), 6–11; *The Rule of Metaphor: Multi-Disciplinary Studies of the Creation of Meaning in Language*, trans. Robert Czerny (Toronto: University of Toronto Press, 1977), 293–312. For critical comments on both studies, see

my *Language and Politics: Why Does Language Matter to Political Philosophy?* (Notre Dame, Ind.: University of Notre Dame Press, 1984), 120–23, 139, 161–65, 179–82. For some earlier comments pointing in the same critical direction, see my "Tale of Two Cities: Ricoeur's Political and Social Essays," in *Twilight of Subjectivity: Contributions to a Post-Individualist Theory of Politics* (Amherst, Mass.: University of Massachusetts Press, 1981), 269: "The predilection for tensions and antinomies sometimes impales arguments on the proverbial horns of dilemmas, while mediations acquire overtones of weak compromise."

19. *Oneself as Another*, 17, 212–18, 223–27, 236–39, 284–85.

20. On this distinction, see Ricoeur, *Oneself as Another*, 2–3, 118–19. The task announced in the title is on occasion lucidly stated, but without serious effect on the overall argument. Thus, we read, "A kind of otherness that is not (or not merely) the result of comparison is suggested by our title, otherness of a kind that can be constitutive of selfhood as such. *Oneself as Another* suggests from the outset that the selfhood of oneself implies otherness to such an intimate degree that one cannot be thought of without the other" (3).

21. *Oneself as Another*, 318, 355. Perhaps some borrowing from Merleau-Ponty would have been appropriate, especially his notions of lateral "reversibility" and "chiasm." Compare Merleau-Ponty, *The Visible and the Invisible*, ed. Claude Lefort, trans. Alphonso Lingis (Evanston, Ill.: Northwestern University Press, 1968), 160, 263. For a more detailed discussion see my "Interworld and Reversibility: Merleau-Ponty," in *Twilight of Subjectivity*, 103–7.

22. *Oneself as Another*, 236.

23. *Oneself as Another*, 274, 288–89. For a similar correlation of universalism and contextualism, effected through the connection of "blind" universal justice and concrete "seeing-eye" justice see my "'Rights' versus 'Rites': Justice and Global Democracy," in Dallmayr, *Alternative Visions: Paths in the Global Village* (Lanham, Md.: Rowman & Littlefield, 1998), 253–76.

24. *Oneself as Another*, 286, 289. In this context, Ricoeur speaks of "those inchoate universals whose genuine moral tenor will be established only by the subsequent history of the dialogue between cultures" (289, n. 83).

25. *Oneself as Another*, 179. See also Ricoeur, *Political and Social Essays*, ed. David Stewart and Joseph Bien (Athens, Ohio: Ohio University Press, 1974), 213, 241.

CHAPTER TEN

~

Resisting Totalizing Uniformity: Martin Heidegger on *Macht* and *Machenschaft*

Outside of Euclidean geometry, linearity is always suspect: straight lines hide their own curvature. This aspect is clearly manifest in the domain of individual human endeavors as well as the arena of public policies and structures. That human beings control their own destiny is good advice to the downcast or apathetic—but it is dubious counsel to the reflective person aware of the complexity of action. As experience teaches, human "projects" or projections are continuously twisted and rechanneled in unexpected, even countervailing directions; their presumed center, the human agent, is uncannily surrounded and contested by nebulae of nonselfhood—by what Paul Ricoeur has called "oneself as another."[1] The paradoxes of agency and intentionality have played themselves out on a larger scale in the history of Western modernity. Although wedded to the steady unfolding of human emancipation and civilized freedom, Western modernity has also spawned colonialism and imperialism and, in the twentieth century, the reign of unprecedented barbarism highlighted by genocide and totalitarian oppression. In the strictly philosophical domain, the paradoxes of intentionality are nowhere as starkly manifest as in the case of Martin Heidegger, one of the century's foremost philosophers. Curiously and uncannily, Heidegger's work is deeply tainted by his complicity with totalitarian (fascist) oppression—despite the fact that his work, in its basic tenor, was always dedicated to "freedom" and resistance to totalizing uniformity.

To be sure, as a subtle philosopher, Heidegger was not unaware of the paradoxes of intentionality or the complex intertwining of meaning and countermeaning; in fact, awareness of this complexity heightened steadily in the course of his intellectual development. In large measure, such awareness can be seen as a major impulse behind the intellectual sea change in his life, the famous "turning" or "*Kehre*." This turning happened both on a recessed ontological and a more mundane political level; as will be shown, a central aspect of the transformation involved a rethinking of the role of power (*Macht*) and violent domination (*Gewalt*). While his early writings before the turning tended to view power in terms of human potency or else a gigantic struggle between human self-assertion and the overpowering force (*Übermacht*) of "Being," Heidegger's middle and late writings came to see the pitfalls and streamlining effects of linear power-seeking and to adumbrate a realm beyond power and impotence, domination and submission, under the rubric of a "power-free" (*machtlos*) dispensation that allows being(s) "to be."

In this chapter, an attempt will be made to trace Heidegger's evolving thought on power and domination by focusing on writings before, during, and after the turning; a major guidepost will be found in recently published lecture courses (of the mid- and late 1930s) that closely link power and manipulative domination, "*Macht*" and "*Machenschaft*." The presentation proceeds in three steps:

1. The first section gives a brief overview of the evolving pathways and byways of Heidegger's thought prior to the *Kehre*.
2. The second part offers a more detailed assessment of his intellectual transformation during the mid- and late 1930s, with particular attention to the significance of his comments on *Machenschaft*.
3. The concluding part seeks to insert these comments into the context of contemporary political philosophy, particularly the ongoing process of globalization.

Freedom and Power

Given its disastrous effects, complicity with totalitarian fascism (or National Socialism) surely deserves condemnation. In the case of Heidegger, some kind of complicity is undeniable—although intense dispute surrounds the duration and character of his engagement. In the eyes of some interpreters—whose verdict has garnered the limelight of attention—his complicity amounted to a profound and lifelong commitment that tainted and basically vitiated his entire opus.[2] That this verdict is puzzling and even paradoxical can be seen by a glance at the evolving trajectory of his thought. In some accounts, the verdict of total commitment is predicated on his (early) "existentialist" pathos, his reliance on the rhetoric of self-projection and "resoluteness" encouraging (it is claimed) a quasi-Nietzschean stance of political elitism. However, the same kind of rhetoric has also been employed profusely by many "existentialist" writers, especially in postwar France, whose works have never been charged with pro-fascist leanings. In other accounts, it is Heidegger's ontological bent, his resumption of the "question of Being," that is held responsible for his lifelong complicity. That the "question of Being" in large measure dominated his entire opus is, of course, incontestable—but it did so precisely as a "question" (not as a doctrine—racial, political, or otherwise). The verdict is particularly puzzling given his association of "Being," or the truth of Being, with "freedom" (Freiheit). As he wrote in an essay of 1929, the human being (Dasein) "ek-sists" or stands out into the ground of Being and this transcendence is the meaning of freedom (in and for the ground). Similarly, the famous essay "On the Essence of Truth" (of roughly the same time) identified the truth of Being and the "being of truth" explicitly with freedom, stating that freedom means the "ek-sistent/ekstatic disclosure which lets beings be. Every type of ek-static/open behavior flourishes in this 'letting be' of beings."[3]

The accent on freedom is not limited to individual essays or lectures, but also marks throughout the magnum opus of Heidegger's early period, Being and Time (1927). As is well known, Heidegger in that work characterizes human Dasein not so much as "animal rationale," but rather as a being that is concerned about and "cares" for the point of its own being (and of Being as such). Moved by such care, Dasein is opened up to its potentiality (to be), to the range of its own possibilities, and in discovering this range it also finds its basic freedom. As Heidegger writes, in anticipating its "own-most potentiality of being," Dasein discovers "the existential and ontological condition of the possibility of being free for authentic existential possibilities." The main incitement for the discovery of freedom as potentiality originates in the "call of conscience" (which also is the "call of care"): for when reached by this invocation, Dasein testifies to its "becoming free for the call, that is, its readiness for the summons of the potentiality of being." Being open to its full potentiality also requires Dasein to face up to the limit of this potentiality, particularly to its own death seen as the possibility of the impossibility (of Dasein)—with the proviso that death here is not an external intrusion but anticipated by Dasein as part of its freedom. "Only this freedom for death," Heidegger writes, "gives Dasein its final goal and thus pushes existence into its finitude." As one should note, the function of care is not restricted to one's own potentiality but includes prominently "care for others" (Fürsorge), which can take a variety of forms. The most authentic kind of Fürsorge is one that allows others to gain their own freedom; this care, we read, addresses the other's very existence and thus "helps the other to become self-transparent in his/her care and hence *free for* it."[4]

Dasein's freedom persists even in a self-inflicted unfreedom. According to *Being and Time*, one of the intrinsic possibilities of *Dasein* is precisely to renounce or flee from its own freedom, that is, to hide or seek shelter in the surrounding world, more particularly in the anonymity of a multitude that Heidegger calls "*das Man*" ("the They"). *Dasein's* proclivity to slide or escape into the inauthenticity of *das Man* is portrayed by Heidegger in numerous eloquent passages. Here is one such passage:

> Submerging oneself in *das Man* means that one is dominated by public opinion (or pre-interpretation). At this point, what is discovered or found appears in a mode where everything is covered over or closed off by chatter, curiosity, and ambiguity. Although openness to beings is not extinguished, it is thoroughly uprooted. Beings here are not completely concealed, but discovered precisely as distorted; they still show themselves—but in the mode of semblance. . . . Because it falls essentially prey to the "world," *Dasein* hovers constitutively in the realm of "untruth."

Once having surrendered itself to *das Man*, *Dasein* finds it difficult to perceive the call of care and of conscience, which now is muted and drowned out by public clamor and the idols of the market (*idola fori*). Being attuned only to "loud idle chatter," Heidegger writes, *das Man* disparages the very possibility of a call, thereby disguising "its own failure to listen and its reduced range of hearing." Surrendering to *das Man* also deeply affects interhuman relations by subjecting *Dasein* basically to anonymous forces or the "powers that be"; to the extent that interhuman concern persists, it survives only in the form of meddlesome intrusiveness and manipulative hostility. The "others" at this point are not distinct fellow-beings but rather an anonymous multitude which has "inconspicuously established its dominion" (over *Dasein*). Yet, under the guise of anonymity, he adds, all kinds of predatory instincts are let loose; under the aegis of *das Man*, "everyone keeps track of the other, watching principally how he/she will behave, what he/she will say to something." Thus, co-being here is not mutual indifference, but rather involves "a tense, ambiguous policing each other, a secretive, mutual listening-in." Hence, "under the mask 'for-one-another,' the 'against-one-another' is at play."[5]

Heidegger's reservations regarding public anonymity and the *idola fori* were not a unique feature of *Being and Time*, but anticipated in many of his earlier writings and lecture courses. In his study *The Young Heidegger*, John van Buren has provided an insightful analysis of many of these writings and courses, with a particular focus on the early Freiburg period (1919–1923). As he shows, the notion of *das Man* (the They) surfaced already prominently in some lecture courses of that period, particularly courses dealing with Aristotle and the "hermeneutics of facticity." Anticipating his later argument, Heidegger in these lectures contrasted genuine existential engagement with the static and anonymous dominion of *das Man*, with the humdrum routines of everyday life; as in *Being and Time*, everyday routines were associated with "averageness," shallow "publicity," "pre-interpretation," and also with a pliant acceptance of the social order, of the established order of "rank, success, position in life (world)." Then, as later, submergence in *das Man* was not simply a negation of freedom, but rather portrayed as a flight from authenticity (still testifying to what it left behind); basically, the flight was an escape from the perils, uncanniness, and anxiety (*Angst*) of existential care into the safety of familiar, habitual routines—an escape characterized at one point as a plunge or "crash" (*Sturz*).

As van Buren indicates, Heidegger at the time associated this plunge with other prominent types of escapism—especially the retreat into abstract metaphysics and into anonymous technology. Both types of retreat, he notes, amount to the replacement of existential care with a fixed system "that is homogeneous, universal, 'at-hand,' and thus able to be calculated and mastered"; both manifest "a will to totalization, closure, and what Heidegger already understood as the 'technization' of being." In the modern era, abstract metaphysics tends to shade over into universal, totalizing "worldviews" or ideologies that solidify the dominion of *das Man*; coupled with the rise of technology, modern culture thus promotes the triumph of calculative rational mastery, stripping *Dasein* of its élan. In van Buren's words (which perhaps too hastily anticipate later Heideggerian concerns):

> In the modern age of technology, the tendency to technization and ideology was raised [for Heidegger] to the second power in metaphysics. Throughout the early twenties, he warned that philosophy must resist its own tendency to technization, that is, its reduction to a "method" in the sense of a "technique" and business (*Betrieb*) consisting of rules that can be mastered. . . . [Heidegger] now asserted a "radical separation" of worldviews and philosophy . . . [and] practiced a kind of ontologically emancipatory critique of all such pretensions and the marginalizing effects of their hierarchical claims.[6]

As one should note, the notions of "technization" and "technique" were not identified at the time with the Greek term "*techne*," which, for Heidegger, signified a creative force or potency (in contrast to calculative rationality). As a result, *techne* in his treatment was not opposed to, but rather closely linked with *Dasein*'s genuine potentiality and resolute engagement with "Being." This feature is clearly manifest in An *Introduction to Metaphysics* (of 1935)—a text that, in other respects, might also be seen as signpost of an impending *Kehre*. Partly under the influence of Nietzschean teachings, *Dasein*'s "ek-static" character, its readiness to burst the confinement of *das Man*, was given a dramatic cast and portrayed as an awesome struggle between human potency or power and Being's "overpowering" might. In struggling with the elements of the sea, the earth, and the rest of nature, human beings do not constitute but discover an uncanny "ek-static" power and capability. By venturing into the realm of the unfamiliar (*unheimlich*) and "overpowering" (*überwältigend*), they first of all discover themselves: namely, their "power/ violence" (*Gewalt*) as creative agents, a force that "breaks out and breaks up, captures and subjugates." It is at this point that Heidegger introduces the Greek term "*techne*," which, he writes, "means neither art nor skill, to say nothing of technique in the modern sense"; rather, "we translate *techne* by 'knowing' (*Wissen*)." In Heidegger's usage, "knowing" here does not mean abstract knowledge, but rather a kind of creative foresight, namely, "the ability to plan and organize freely, to master institutions." More specifically, *techne* as knowing signifies a creative act of transcendence or ek-statsis that "effectuates" (puts into work, *ins-Werk setzen*) the Being of particular beings, that is, establishes the point of their being.[7]

Commenting on the opening chorus in *Antigone*, An *Introduction* brings *techne* in close connection with human uncanniness (*deinon*), because the ek-static act of "putting-into-work" also is powerful/violent (*gewalttätig*). Heidegger at this point introduces another term that later was to assume growing significance: that of "*Machenschaft*" or machination. As ambience of powerful/violent agency, he writes, power/violence (*Gewalt*) refers to "the entire scope of *Machenschaft* (*to machanóen*) entrusted to *Dasein*"—where machination "is not taken in a disparaging sense." Although uncannily potent, human power or *Machenschaft* is not unlimited, but always runs up against a limiting and "overpowering" counterforce. One such counterforce is death, described as "an end beyond all completion, a limit beyond all limits." In a more significant sense, however, the counterforce is Being itself, which reveals its own uncanniness in the form of "justice" or fitting order (*dike*). Seen from this angle, human power or *Machenschaft* finds itself inevitably embroiled in a gigantic struggle (*gigantomachia*), a contest over the very meaning of Being. In Heidegger's words, "Thus the *deinon* as the overpowering (*dike*) and the *deinon* as the powerful/violent (*techne*) confront each other, though not as two separate entities." In this confrontation, "*techne* bursts forth against *dike*, which, in turn, as fitting order (*Fug*) disposes (*ver*-

fügt) of all *techne*." Accordingly, *Dasein's* ek-static venture into the unfamiliar is fraught with immense risks and perils. In the end, this struggle or *agon* can never be stabilized, domesticated, or settled, without eliminating *Dasein's* ek-static openness and hence its ability "to be." Being or "to be" means reciprocal struggle and confrontation.[8]

Machenschaft and Kehre

By the time *An Introduction to Metaphysics* was completed, the situation in Germany had sharply deteriorated. National Socialism was steadily tightening its grip on the country, transforming its initial emergency rule into a long-term totalitarian domination. In this situation, customary language was placed under pressure; for example, terms like "power" and "violence" could no longer be used naively, or even metaphorically, to express *Dasein's* potent opening toward "Being." Having portrayed human *Dasein* distinctly as "being-in-the-world," Heidegger could not for long remain obtuse to these "worldly" developments. As it happens, his writings after *An Introduction* show signs of intense agony and turmoil, giving evidence of a profound intellectual reorientation or *Kehre*. An important signpost of this reorientation were his lecture courses on Nietzsche (stretching from 1936 to 1941) that reveal a growing discomfort or dissatisfaction with Nietzsche's celebration of the "will to power"—although this discomfort remained initially somewhat muted and ambivalent.[9]

Fortunately, the evidence today is no longer limited to the Nietzsche lectures. The past decade has seen the publication of a series of major texts or treatises that—even more clearly than his public lectures—provide clues of the ongoing reorientation. Mainly three texts deserve attention here: *Beiträge zur Philosophie* (Contributions to Philosophy, 1936); *Besinnung* (Mediative Thinking, 1938–1939); and *Die Geschichte des Seyns* (The History of Being, 1939–1940). Of the three, the first is the most voluminous and also the most ambitious, setting forth an entire, detailed trajectory of intellectual and existential transformation (leading from a "pre-view" and "foreplay" to a "leap" and a final new "grounding" in a promised future). The text is challenging and provocative also on a more mundane, political level. As before, Heidegger takes aim again at the reign of worldview-ideologies—but now with a definite slant at National Socialism and its motto of "total mobilization." Such a "total (or totalizing) worldview," Heidegger writes, "must close itself off against the probing of its own ground and the premises of its actions"; it must do so, because otherwise "total ideology would put itself in question." The text also critiques a central pillar of National Socialist ideology: its presumed grounding in

the German "*Volk.*" This grounding, we read, "remains dark and deeply ambiguous—not to mention the entire looseness of the rhetoric of '*Volk.*'"[10]

It is in connection with the critique of worldviews that the term "*Machenschaft*" resurfaces prominently—but now with starkly new connotations. The
rise of worldviews to dominion, Heidegger notes, is a result of modern metaphysics, and in that context "worldview basically means *Machenschaft*"—the
term no longer taken as genuine creativity, but rather as a mode where creativity is replaced by "business" (*Betrieb*) and the hazards of creating are "solidified into the monumentality of *Machenschaft.*" At this point, the term
designates basically the prevalence of "making (*Machen, poiesis, techne*)"—
though not solely as a form of human conduct, but as a distinct (modern)
type of ontological disclosure. In modernity, Heidegger points out, *Machenschaft* is promoted by the sway of science and technology that render everything "makeable" (*machbar*). Under these auspices, the cause-effect nexus becomes "all-dominant," though in varying guises: "Both the mechanistic and
the biologistic worldviews are only consequences of the underlying *machen-
schaftlich* interpretation of Being." Preceded by biblical accounts of creation
(as fabrication), the modern sway of *Machenschaft* was decisively inaugurated
by Descartes' equation of *ens creatum* with *ens certum* (fixed, determined being); subsequently, this approach was further solidified by the rise of mathe-
matical physics and technology (*Technik*). Against his background, Heidegger asks, "What is *Machenschaft?*" and responds, "It is the scheme of the
complete explanatory calculability whereby every being is uniformly equated
with every other being—and thereby alienated (and even more than alienated) from itself." As he further elaborates, calculability and anonymity are
curiously allied in *Machenschaft* with something seemingly very different:
namely, subjective feeling or sentiment (*Erlebnis*). But the contrast is only
apparent because subjectivism and anonymity are only two sides of the same
coin: both testify to the "oblivion of Being."[11]

Jointly with the rethinking of *Machenschaft*, *Beiträge* also offers a reformulation of "power," "violence," and related terms. Departing from an earlier
ambivalent usage (sometimes approaching interchangeability), the text offers a series of definitions with clearly demarcated contours. Closely associated with *Machenschaft* are the two terms "power" (*Macht*) and "violence"
(*Gewalt*). In the new usage, violence (*Gewalt*) signifies the willful but impotent attempt to change things or conditions without ontological foresight or
reflection: "Wherever change is sought ontically (*Seiendes durch Seiendes*),
violence is needed." Power (*Macht*) stands purely in the service of willful
machination; it signifies "the ability to secure the control of possibilities of
violence." In sharp contrast to these terms, *Beiträge* mentions "authoritative

rule" (*Herrschaft*) as a mode of ontological potency deriving its authority from the call of Being. "*Herrschaft*," Heidegger writes, "is the need of freedom for freedom" and happens only "in the realm of freedom"; its greatness consists in the fact "that it has no need of power or violence and yet is more potent (*wirksamer*) than they." Such *Herrschaft* is impossible under the reign of worldviews, especially totalizing worldview-ideologies, which have no room for freedom and subject everything to the uniform rule of *Machenschaft*. Under the latter rule, human beings are streamlined or homogenized into an entity called "*Volk*" (people), an entity whose behavior can be explained, and hence predicted and manipulated, in accordance with empirical sociology. In this case, human beings individually and the people at large are merely fixed resources of *Machenschaft*, and the only issue is the preservation and enlargement of these resources. The only way for *Dasein* and people to live genuinely is through an act of self-transcendence (ek-stasis) that is simultaneously an act of self-finding, highlighted by the term "*Ereignis*." For *Ereignis* means basically a needful encounter where humans need and search for Being or the divine while simultaneously being solicited and needed by "the godhead of the other God" (*die Gottheit des anderen Gottes*).[12]

The critique of totalizing and domineering *Machenschaft* was continued and further sharpened in *Besinnung*. As in the case of *Beiträge*, the text can be read both on a recessed, philosophical and a more mundane, political level—although the two levels are closely interlaced. On the political level, *Besinnung* offers a bold and cutting critique of the *Führer* himself, a critique deriving its point from the surrounding philosophical argument. As before, Heidegger dwells on the meaning of *Machenschaft* and its relation to *Macht* and *Gewalt*. "*Machenschaft*," he writes, "means the all-pervasive and totalizing 'makeability' of everything" and moreover the routine acceptance of this process in such a way that "the unconditional calculability of everything is assured." In pursuing its leveling and destructive path, *Machenschaft* employs violence (*Gewalt*) and the latter is stabilized through the "secure possession of power (*Macht*)" aiming at universal subjugation. In modernity, the aims of *Machenschaft* are promoted and abetted by technology (*Technik*) that reduces human beings to mere empirical resources whose status is assessed purely in terms of utility and productivity. It is against this background that one needs see the attack on Hitler who, in an address to the *Reichstag* in 1939, had made this statement: "There is no stance or posture (*Haltung*) which would not receive its ultimate justification from its utility for the totality (of the nation)."[13]

Reacting to this statement, Heidegger immediately raises a number of questions, such as the following: What is totality or collectivity (*Gesamtheit*) and who instantiates it? How is such totality determined and what are its goals? Further: What is the utility of a stance or posture? Where does one find the standard of utility, and who determines or fixes that standard? Moreover, why should it be utility that provides the yardstick or justification of human behavior? Summing up these and related questions, Heidegger arrives at a general indictment that clearly proceeds from very different premises:

> What is "totality," if not the quantitative expansion of a particular conception of humans as individual egos? What is posture (Haltung)? Does this term capture the basic nature of human Dasein? If not, what sense can one make of the justification of Haltung by the collectivity and collective utility? Does this term "Haltung" not signify the denial of the essential questionability (Fraglichkeit) of human Dasein with regard to its hidden relation to Being? Are humans here not definitively fixated as geared toward the control and mastery of beings (in the midst of abandonment of/by Being, Seinsverlassenheit)? . . . Is not every posture together with the totality of a Volk collapsed into empirical things (Seiendes), insofar as both [without care] merely revolve around themselves?[14]

In addition to and beyond the critique of Machenschaft, Besinnung adumbrates and provides guideposts for something radically "other": namely, the reflective recovery of care for Being, a care completely immune to manipulation. As before, Heidegger carefully distinguishes between power and violence, on the one hand, and "authority" (Herrschaft), on the other. "Apart from exuding dignity," he writes, "Herrschaft means the free potency for an original respect for Being (rather than empirical entities); it signifies the dignity of Being as Being." To characterize this dignity, Besinnung introduces a new vocabulary, by presenting Being (Seyn) as "the power-free (das Machtlose), beyond power and non-power or impotence (jenseits von Macht und Unmacht)." As Heidegger emphasizes, "power-free" does not mean powerless or impotent, because the latter remains fixated on power, now experienced as a lack. From an everyday angle, Being may appear powerless or impotent, but this is only a semblance or illusion resulting from the particular mode of Being's disclosure in our time, the mode of "refusal" (Verweigerung), concealment, or withdrawal. Due to this refusal, Being can never be dragged into human machinations, into the struggles between the powerful and the powerless; but precisely in this Verweigerung it reveals its Herrschaft—a reign that "cannot be matched by any power or superpower because they necessarily ignore the nature of the basically power-free." This reign of the power-free "can never be disempowered (entmachtet)." To be sure, access to this reign is difficult and radically obstructed by the Machenschaft of our age. An important pathway through and beyond these obstructions is precisely "meditative thinking" (Besinnung), which opens a glimpse into the "time-space-play"

(*Zeit-Spiel-Raum*) of Being as *Ereignis*. Such reflective thinking, Heidegger states, can sharpen the sense for a crossroads or parting of ways: a parting that determines "whether *Machenschaft* finally overwhelms humans, unleashing them into limitless power-seekers, or whether Being discloses its truth as a need—a need through which the encounter/counterpoint (*Entgegnung*) of God and humans intersects with the dispute (*Streit*) between earth and world."[15]

Further glimpses into the turning (*Kehre*) experienced during this period are provided in *Die Geschichte des Seyns*, a series of related texts dating from the beginning of World War II. In light of the grim historical context, the language here is even move intense than in the preceding writings and the political references still more pointed and acerbic. Central again to the new texts is the critique of *Machenschaft* defined as a mode of Being that "pushes everything into the mold of 'makeability.'" As before, *Machenschaft* is intimately linked with the glorification of power (*Macht*), and the latter is anchored ultimately in "will" (to power) and in "unconditional subjectivity" (a chief trait of modern metaphysics). To effectuate its rule, power relies on violence (*Gewalt*) as its chief method and instrument. When violence or brutality becomes predominant, matters are starkly simplified; everything is geared toward the "unconditional annihilation (*Vernichtung*) of opposing forces with unconditional means". The end result is annihilation "for its own sake." The unleashing of brutal violence carries in its train the "devastation" (*Verwüstung*) of everything in the sense that it spreads a "desert" (*Wüste*) where nothing can grow any longer—especially not any care for Being or any openness to the call of Being. A particularly vivid and harrowing sign of this devastation is the hankering of violence for warfare—a warfare that, due to the totalizing ambitions of *Machenschaft*, now turns into "total war" (*totaler Krieg*). As an antidote or counterpoise, the texts refer again to the possibility of "authoritative rule" (*Herrschaft*); however, even that term now appears suspect to Heidegger because of its lingering proximity to power. In its bent toward "overpowering" (superpower), he writes, power can never "ground *Herrschaft*" seen as the sway of Being itself. The term *Herrschaft* here means to designate "the *charis* (favor) of Being as Being, the quiet dignity of a gentle bond which never needs to congeal into a desire for power." But in this case, he adds, maybe *Herrschaft* becomes an "inappropriate term which should better be consigned to the realm of power (*Wesensbereich der Macht*)"—with the result that Being emerges not only as "power-free" but also as not "*herrschaftlich*."[16]

The sharpening of the language referring to *Macht* and *Machenschaft* is paralleled in the text by an intensification of political polemics. *Die Geschichte des Seyns* ridicules fascist leaders for their self-glorification as "mighty rulers" (*Machthaber*) whose great achievement was their "seizure of power" (*Machtergreifung*). Leaders, Heidegger writes, are never "possessors of power" (*Machthaber*) but rather puppets in the grip of *Macht* and *Machenschaft*; they cannot "seize" or "possess" power because they are "possessed by it" (in the manner of an obsession). The texts also critique National Socialism directly by ridiculing its chosen terminology. Drawing on his argument that modernity is marked by "unconditional subjectivity," Heidegger comments that "the consequence of this subjectivity is the 'nationalism' of nations and the 'socialism' of the *Volk*." As an outgrowth of subjectivity and hence of *Machenschaft*, both "isms" lead to the relentless struggle for more and more power and hence to "limitless wars (*grenzenlose Kriege*) furthering the empowerment of power." Unsurprisingly, such wars ultimately take the form of "total wars" and "world wars" in the service of an "unleashed *Machenschaft*."[17]

Apart from debunking dominant ideologies, the texts also take aim at a central ingredient of German fascism, its biological racism. In Heidegger's words, "The concept of race (*Rasse*) and the calculation in terms of race derives from the construal of Being as subjectivity" (hence from *Machenschaft*). "Cultivation of race" (*Rassenpflege*) is always linked with power politics and dependent on prevailing constellations of power. As a result, racial doctrines (*Rassenlehre*) are not simply scientific-biological but always geared toward racial "superiority" claims governed by power objectives. Despite the fact that power cannot be "possessed" (as a tool) but operates obsessively, Heidegger does not hesitate at this point to link power and violence with "criminality" (*Verbrechen*). Given the unleashing of *Machenschaft* and unconditional power, he writes, our age also produces "the great criminals" (*die grossen Verbrecher*)—criminals whose deeds far exceed ordinary human standards: "There is no punishment which would be sufficiently great to punish these criminals." Heidegger in this context refers to "global master criminals" (*planetarische Hauptverbrecher*) and adds this comment: "In the most recent period (which renders them possible and even inevitable), these global master criminals can be counted on the fingers of one hand." (Considering the timing of this comment, would the number not necessarily include figures like Hitler, Stalin, and Mussolini?)[18]

In comparison with the intellectual turmoil characterizing the period of the 1930s, Heidegger's postwar writings are marked by greater continuity and steadiness (perhaps serenity). In many ways, his earlier arguments regarding *Macht* and *Machenschaft* are continued in his reflections on technology under the rubric of "*Gestell*" (Enframing). Since these reflections are relatively well known and widely discussed in the literature, brevity seems justified in the present context. In the postwar writings, the term *Machenschaft* appears only infrequently, making room for concern with *Gestell*—for good reasons (a main reason being the misleading closeness of *Machenschaft* and "makeability" to human fabrication and design). In his essay "The Question Concerning Technology" (dating from 1949–1950), Heidegger agrees that technology (*Technik*) may also be taken as a mode of human fabrication, as a means to given human ends. But although "correct" in a certain limited way, this view is by no means adequate or properly "true." To gain a proper grasp of technology, it is important to perceive it as a form of ontological disclosure—but a disclosure (*Entbergung*) in which Being precisely withdraws and shelters itself. Once placed under the aegis of disclosure, technology shows itself not just as fabrication but as the mid-point between constituting and being constituted, between positing (*stellen*) and being positioned or challenged (*gestellt*)—a mid-point captured in the term "*Gestell*." Viewed from the angle of *Gestell*, technology appears not as a random happening but rather as a kind of ontological dispensation or "mission" (*Geschick*)—though one far removed from a confining destiny or mere fate. In Heidegger's words, disclosure is "never the compulsion of a fate; for humans become free precisely by opening themselves up to the 'mission' of Being." To the occurrence of disclosure or truth, he adds, "freedom stands in the closest and most intimate kinship"; for "every disclosure originates in freedom, moves toward freedom, and delivers into freedom."[19]

Heidegger and Globalization

The preceding discussion has attempted to give an overview of Heidegger's evolving thought on *Machenschaft*, especially on the latter's totalizing ambitions evident both in "totalitarian" rule and the pervasive "technization" of human life. To be sure, the overview was limited and condensed, and would have to be supplemented by many additional references (some of which not yet available today). Despite its restricted scope, however, the discussion should have revealed the starkly paradoxical character of the main charge leveled at Heidegger: his complicity with the totalizing worldview-ideology of fascism. As has been indicated, the basic tenor of his work—the "key" to which it was persistently tuned—was freedom, the term taken not as a synonym for license or caprice, but in the sense of a self-opening pointing beyond caprice and compulsion (or necessity). In light of this tenor, his complicity appears deeply puzzling or enigmatic—or else as a sign of naiveté and thorough misapprehension of the prevailing power-play at the time. As has also been shown, this naiveté or misapprehension was progressively shattered in the 1930s, making room for an agonized and steadily deepening turning or *Kehre*, and also for (subtle and not-so-subtle) political polemics. To be sure, one may have wished or expected him to be still more resolute and forthright in his critical statements, but this expectation is easily voiced by hindsight and in the safety of "liberal" procedures, far removed from the omnipresent threats of totalitarian control.

Viewed against this backdrop of totalitarian power, many of Heidegger's statements—both in his lectures and his writings—are remarkable and startling. Particularly startling is his debunking of National Socialism as a world-view-ideology (combining the defects of both "nationalism" and "social-ism"), his direct attack on a major public address of the *Führer*, and his reference to "planetary master criminals" countable on "the fingers of one hand." These statements are surrounded and complemented by a number of other comments of similar import—not all of which were mentioned before. One such comment involves the "deconstruction" of a shibboleth dear to fascist ideology: the idea of *"Kampf"* (struggle, dating back to Hitler's *Mein Kampf*). As Heidegger noted in *Beiträge zur Philosophie*, the age was faced with a stark alternative: whether humans would gain access again to the "truth of Being" or whether human life would deteriorate into violent struggle or *Kampf*. In the latter case, all that was left was *"Kampf* over the naked conditions of survival in gigantic proportions, with the result that worldview and culture become mere props and instruments of *Kampf.*" And if that happens, the essence of human-ness is lost and we witness "the transition to the *technicized animal* which compensates the diminishing instincts through the monumentality of technology." The public Nietzsche-lectures of 1939 bring animalization (in the sense of the "technicized animal") somewhat harshly in contact with Nietzschean metaphysics. The guiding motto of that metaphysics, we read, is *"animalitas (Tierheit)."* In the end, modern subjectivity emerges as "the *brutalitas* of *bestialitas,*" yielding as its central (fascist) doctrine: *"homo est brutum bestiale."* Placed in this context, Nietzsche's word of the "blond beast" was not an "occasional exaggeration," but a predictable outcome.[20]

It would be a mistake, of course, to limit the relevance of Heidegger's argument to National Socialism and its totalitarian rule. Although most directly aimed at fascist domination, the brunt of his argument clearly is addressed at modern and late-modern worldviews in general, all of which are seen as marked—in different ways— by *Machenschaft*, and hence by disdain of the "power-free" and unmanaged dispensation of Being. *Beiträge* offers a longish list of recent and contemporary worldviews, varying from fascism to liberalism. What unites these worldviews despite their differences, Heidegger comments, is the fact that in all of them human *Dasein* is taken as "something already known," as an empirical entity "fixated in its basic nature" that then is integrated and streamlined into ideological designs as an available resource. One of the worldviews repeatedly mentioned by Heidegger in this context is communism, anchored in (what is called) "orthodox" Marxism. In *Die Geschichte des Seyns*, communism is closely linked with *Machenschaft* and absolute "seizure of power" (*Ermächtigung*). "This seizure of power in the form of unconditional *Machenschaft*," we read, is illustrated in "communism"—the term taken neither sociologically nor politically (in a narrow sense). In prevailing opinion, communism signifies the "community of equals," an arrangement where everybody is the same by "working, earning, consuming, and enjoying the same." In its own self-understanding, moreover, communism designates a process of emancipation whereby a previously suppressed class of people is liberated and empowered. A closer look, however, reveals the error of this view. As an ideology geared toward the "seizure of power," communism necessarily entails the organization of a monolithic "party" that then subjugates everything to its absolute rule. Hence, Heidegger comments, rather than liberating and uniting "proletarians around the world," communism first of all produces a mass proletariat by pushing human beings into "the uniformity of collectivity" (stylized as "power seizure by the people"). Thus, *Macht* in the case of communism is a power that "hypnotizes everything into total uniformity"—and by comparison with which the "people" hover in "non-power" or impotence (*Ohnmacht*).[21]

With the demise of the Soviet Union and other regimes of "really existing socialism," Heidegger's comments seem again to have been superseded by historical events; as in the case of fascism, however, this view neglects the range of his arguments. On several occasions, Heidegger includes among totalizing worldviews modern (Western) "liberalism"—despite its seeming bent toward variety. Modern liberal societies, he notes, are assumed to be composed of isolated individuals seen as fixed entities, that is, as agents pursuing their own interests, drives, or desires and obeying only the standard of "interest maximization"—a standard that is the same for all. Nowhere in this ideology, Heidegger remarks in *Beiträge*, is there any room for ek-stasis or self-transcendence, for a reaching out into an "uncharted domain under whose auspices the fixed human entity would become questionable (*fraglich*)." Thus, human self-assurance or self-security (*Selbstsicherheit*) constitutes the "innermost character of 'liberalism.'"[22]

Remembering the intimate linkage of worldviews with calculation and "technization" of life, Heidegger's comments seem particularly pertinent to economic or market liberalism, that is, to liberal capitalism that today is the dominant ideology around the world. Under the aegis of liberal capitalism, all beings are uniformly transformed into commodities of production and consumption, with the exchange of commodities governed by a quantitative and calculable price mechanism. Apart from the yardsticks of price, cost, and profitability, no other considerations can possibly enter the capitalist system of production and consumption without vitiating or spoiling its over- all efficiency. Thus, the effects of the process on human beings, on *Dasein* and its care, are treated simply as "externalities," as random noises negligi- ble from the angle of productivity. Defenders of capitalist production and utility maximization are liable to denounce dissenters as empty dreamers and "utopians," thereby placing themselves in control of "reality." The no- tion of "reality" (*Wirklichkeit*), Heidegger observes in *Besinnung*, is here equated with "efficiency" (*Wirksamkeit*), "workability" (*Wirkendheit*) or "what works"—whereas Being is dismissed as impotent (neglecting its "power-free" status).[23]

Heidegger's comments in this respect are particularly noteworthy given the ongoing process of globalization and the contemporary prevalence of liberal capitalism as global ideology. His writings of the 1930s frequently make reference to globalization seen as a struggle for "planetary" control, a struggle animated everywhere by the imperatives of *Machenschaft*. As we read in *Besinnung*, "One speaks of global or planetary concerns"—and re- veals by this rhetoric "that the seizures of power are no longer 'total' in a restricted sense (tailored to one state or one people) but now extend their reach to the limits of the inhabited earth, and even into the atmosphere and stratosphere"; hence, the planet as a whole is now seen as "a resource of power"—which dictates "the search for a global enemy." *Die Geschichte des Seyns* is even more explicit in its references to the global dangers of *Machenschaft*. "The global (*das Planetarische*)," Heidegger observes there, "means the extension of *Macht* to the entire globe," in such a way that we witness "the dawn of a unique kind of global dominion." This extension, he adds, is by no means accidental or fortuitous but reveals the limitless character of power and the struggle for power—the fact that *Macht* does not acknowledge any competing concerns and ultimately becomes an end in itself. "The fact that *Macht* is globalizing," the text states, "is the reason for the more and more relentless struggle for the possession of 'world power'"—a struggle that demonstrates the nature of power. Viewed against this background, one has to view with suspicion the so-called higher aims of emerging global or superpowers—aims like the promotion of freedom and rights; for, under the auspices of globalization, even "the most sincere struggle for freedom and morality" is inevitably tainted by considerations of *Macht* and its enhancement.[24]

Given the ongoing process of globalization—especially economic and technological globalization—Heidegger's comments surely cannot be dismissed as obsolete; nor can his critique of *Machenschaft* be relegated to a—supposedly banished—totalitarian past. Given prevailing power constellations, the radical dismissal of Heidegger's thought (for political motives) shows itself as short-sighted and counterproductive, as an unwillingness to learn from insights that still may carry significant lessons for our time. To be sure, such unwillingness appears most understandable and legitimate in the case of Heidegger's comments regarding democracy. Paralleled by numerous passages elsewhere, *Die Geschichte des Seyns* raises questions about "democracy," particularly about the possibility for the "people" to be their own rulers. But perhaps passages of this kind should be read in a different sense: not as questioning whether the people *can* be their own masters, but as asking whether they *should* be seen as supreme masters or rulers at all, that is, as functionaries of *Macht* and accomplices of *Machenschaft* with its bent toward uniformity and the technization of life.

At this point, it becomes important to remember Heidegger's distinction between *techne* seen as making or instrumental fabrication and *techne/poiesis* viewed as creative action or praxis (*Schaffen*). Heidegger's later work is sometimes (mis)interpreted as being marked by withdrawal from life into apathy and esoteric contemplation. This construal, however, is disproved by his continued emphasis on creative praxis—taken in the sense neither of ego-expression nor of fabrication but of participation in a disclosure of Being. It is in this sense that one has to read the famous opening lines of the "Letter on Humanism": "We are still far from pondering the nature of action carefully enough. We view action only as causing an effect; and the actuality of the effect is estimated in terms of its utility. But the essence of action is bringing-forth" (*Vollbringen*)—where "bringing-forth" means to unfold something into the fullness of its potential and hence to participate in a nonmanipulative and noncoercive mode of disclosure. Seen in this light, Heidegger's later thought is not withdrawn or reclusive, but testifies to an ongoing commitment to freedom—a freedom that was pledged by some modern "emancipatory" ideologies (like Marxism) but foiled by their own embroilment in *Macht* and *Machenschaft*. Although, given its "fallenness," human life remains always in the shadow of power and powerlessness, genuine praxis—even when struggling against domination—must always honor at least the promise of a "power-free" (*machtlos*) dispensation and hence of a "reign of freedom."[25]

Notes

1. Paul Ricouer, *Oneself as Another*, trans. Kathleen Blamey (Chicago: University of Chicago Press, 1992). In some of his earlier writings, Ricoeur had particularly highlighted the paradox of politics: the fact that politics aims at the common good (or justice), but in the context of a struggle for public power. See his "The Political Paradox," in *History and Truth*, trans. Charles A. Kelbley (Evanston, Ill: Northwestern University Press, 1965), 247–70; also my "Politics and Power: Ricoeur's Political Paradox Revisited," in David Klemm and William Schweiker, eds., *Meanings in Texts and Actions: Questioning Paul Ricoeur* (Charlottesville, Va.: University of Virginia Press, 1993), 176–94.

2. Among the steadily expanding literature on the topic see, for example, Victor Farias, *Heidegger and Nazism*, ed. Joseph Margolis and Tom Rockmore (Philadelphia: Temple University Press, 1989); Hugo Ott, *Martin Heidegger* (Frankfurt: Campus Verlag, 1988); Tom Rockmore and Joseph Margolis, eds., *The Heidegger Case: On Philosophy and Politics* (Philadelphia: Temple University Press, 1992); Richard Wolin, *The Politics of Being: The Political Thought of Martin Heidegger* (New York: Columbia University Press, 1990); Tom Rockmore, *On Heidegger's Nazism and Philosophy* (Berkeley: University of California Press, 1992); Pierre Bourdieu, *L'ontologie politique de Martin Heidegger* (Paris: Minuit, 1988); Hans D. Sluga, *Heidegger's Crisis: Philosophy and Politics in Nazi Germany* (Cambridge, Mass.: Harvard University Press, 1993); Miguel de Beistegui, *Heidegger and the Political* (New York: Routledge, 1998); Johannes Fritsche, *Historical Destiny and National Socialism in Heidegger's "Being and Time"* (Berkeley: University of California Press, 1999). The above presentation does not try to exonerate Heidegger's complicity, but only to question its character. Even if short-lived and perhaps based on misunderstanding, the complicity was still a grave derailment.

3. Martin Heidegger, "Vom Wesen des Grundes," and "Vom Wesen der Wahrheit," in *Wegmarken* (Frankfurt-Main: Klostermann, 1967), 71, 81, 87. In the latter essay, freedom is clearly distinguished both from arbitrary license and from submission to some destiny (*amor fati*). Freedom, we read, "is not the arbitrariness of being able to do or not to do; nor is it the mere readiness to do what is required or necessary." Rather, it is "the engagement in the disclosure of beings as such" (84). For an English version of the second essay see David F. Krell, ed., *Martin Heidegger: Basic Writings* (New York: Harper & Row, 1977), 117–41 (translation here slightly altered). Compare also my "Ontology of Freedom: Heidegger and Political Philosophy," in *Polis and Praxis: Exercises in Contemporary Political Theory* (Cambridge, Mass.: MIT Press, 1984), 104–32.

4. Heidegger, *Being and Time*, trans. Joan Stambaugh (Albany, N.Y.: State University of New York Press, 1996), 115 (part 1, division 1, IV, 26), 179–80 (part 1, division 1, VI, 41), 263–64 (part 1, division 2, II, 58), 351 (part 1, division 2, V, 74) (translation slightly altered).

5. *Being and Time*, 118 (part 1, division 1, IV, 27), 163 (part 1, division 1, V, 37), 204 (part 1, division 1, VI, 44), 273 (part 1, division 2, II, 60) (translation slightly altered).

6. John van Buren, *The Young Heidegger: Rumor of the Hidden King* (Bloomington, Ind.: Indiana University Press, 1994), 138–41, 320–23. He adds, "In its drive toward totalization, homogenization, and technization, [modern] metaphysics not only levels differences,

but rather, like the popular They [*das Man*], actually winds up bringing the flux of *Ereignis* to closure in one of its particular effects and falling into a worldview-ideology" (322). One must appreciate van Buren's perceptive discussion of Heidegger's early writings—even if one may not be willing to embrace his gesture of opposing the "youthful" to the "late" Heidegger (a gesture perhaps too frequently rehearsed in the case of Marx). Heidegger's own comment that some of his youthful ventures might also lead to "injustice" is met by van Buren with (youthful) incomprehension (9). His reference above is chiefly to Heidegger, *Phänomenologische Interpretationen zu Aristoteles* (1921–1922), eds. Walter Bröcker and Käte Bröcker-Oltmans (*Gesamtausgabe*, vol. 61; Frankfurt-Main: Klostermann, 1985), and *Ontologie (Hermeneutik der Faktizität)* (1923), ed. Käte Bröcker-Oltmans (*Gesamtausgabe*, vol. 63; Frankfurt-Main: Klostermann, 1988). For an English translation of the latter text see *Ontology—The Hermeneutics of Facticity*, trans. John van Buren (Bloomington, Ind.: Indiana University Press, 1999).

7. Heidegger, *An Introduction to Metaphysics*, trans. Ralph Manheim (Garden City, N.Y.: Anchor Books, 1961), 13–14, 132–34 (translation slightly altered). See also Heidegger, *Einführung in die Metaphysik*, ed. Petra Jaeger (*Gesamtausgabe*, vol. 40; Frankfurt-Main: Klostermann, 1983), 19, 166–68. As one may recall, Heidegger composed roughly at the same time (1935) his essay on "The Origin of the Work of Art"; see Krell, ed. *Martin Heidegger: Basic Writings*, 149–87.

8. *An Introduction to Metaphysics*, 133–35 (translation slightly altered; deviating from Manheim's translation, I have rendered *Gewalt* and *gewalt-tätig* as "power/violence" and "powerful/violent" because Heidegger's usage in this context seems to oscillate between these connotations). As is well known, *An Introduction* also contains the notorious passage about the "inner truth and greatness" of National Socialism, not to be confused with what was being "bandied about" as its "philosophy" or ideology (166). The passage necessarily gives rise to questions like these: What led Heidegger to think that National Socialism was *not* the kind of totalizing worldview-ideology he otherwise denounced? What prompted him to believe that the movement revealed a creative potency (*techne*) shattering the conventions of *das Man*? In large measure, an assessment of Heidegger's behavior during this period seems to hinge on an answer to these questions. On Heidegger's fascination during the 1920s and early 1930s with "struggle" (*Kampf*) and *polemos* (strife) see Gregory Fried, *Heidegger's Polemos: From Being to Politics* (New Haven, Conn.: Yale University Press, 2000).

9. Heidegger, *Nietzsche*, 2 vols., 2nd ed. (Pfullingen: Neske, 1961). For an English translation see Heidegger, *Nietzsche*, 4 vols., trans. David F. Krell, Frank A. Capuzzi, and Joan Stambaugh (San Francisco: Harper & Row, 1979–1987). According to Hannah Arendt, it is possible to locate Heidegger's turning or *Kehre* in the shift of mood or tone occurring between the Nietzsche lectures of 1936–1937 and the wartime Nietzsche lectures (on nihilism). See Arendt, *The Life of the Mind*, vol. 2: *Willing* (New York: Harcourt Brace Jovanovich, 1978), 172–73.

10. Heidegger, *Beiträge zur Philosophie (Vom Ereignis)*, ed. Friedrich-Wilhelm von Herrmann (*Gesamtausgabe*, vol. 65; Frankfurt-Main: Klostermann, 1989), 40, 42. As Heidegger adds, the reign of worldview-ideologies extends, at least incipiently, "even to the last great philosophy: the philosophy of Nietzsche" (38., This happens because Nietzsche did

not pursue his questioning far enough into the "truth" of Being, but remained content with a (metaphysical) affirmation of the will to "life" (*Leben*) and "will to power" (362–64). For an English translation (not followed here) of *Beiträge* see *Contributions to Philosophy (From Enowning)*, trans. Parvis Emad and Kenneth Maly (Bloomington, Ind.: Indiana University Press, 1999). The critique of worldview–ideologies was continued in "Die Zeit des Weltbildes" (1938) where Heidegger denounced the increasingly virulent "contest of worldviews" (*Kampf der Weltanschauungen*); see *Holzwege* (Frankfurt-Main: Klostermann, 1950), esp. 87. The comments on "*Volk*" in *Beiträge* clearly constitute a self-correction on Heidegger's part when compared with earlier more positive or affirmative uses of the term. Compare, e.g., Heidegger, *Being and Time*, trans. Joan Stambaugh, 352 (Part One, Division Two, V, 74); also Heidegger, *Logik als die Frage nach dem Wesen der Sprache* (1934), ed. Günter Seubold (*Gesamtausgabe*, vol. 38; Frankfurt-Main: Klostermann, 1998), 128–29. See also my *The Other Heidegger* (Ithaca: N.Y.: Cornell University Press, 1993), 103–5.

11. *Beiträge zur Philosophie*, 38, 40, 126–32. As one should note, Heidegger always differentiates carefully between *Erlebnis* (subjective feeling) and *Erfahrung* (which *Dasein* has to shoulder or undergo).

12. *Beiträge zur Philosophie*, 50–51, 140, 282, 319. In Heidegger's words: "*Ereignis* hands over (*übereignet*) God to humans while dedicating/consecrating (*zueignet*) humans to God." Compare also the statement, "A *Volk* is only *Volk* if it receives its history through the discovery of its God, a God who compels it beyond itself. . . . Only in this way can it avoid the danger of revolving around itself and of idolizing contingent conditions of existence as something unconditional/absolute" (398).

13. Heidegger, *Besinnung*, ed. Friedrich-Wilhelm von Herrmann (*Gesamtausgabe*, vol. 66; Frankfurt-Main: Klostermann, 1997), 16–17, 122–23.

14. *Besinnung*, 122–23. Heidegger's language is actually more vivid than the above translation "collapsed" indicates: his expression is "*dem 'Seienden' in den Rachen geworfen*" (thrown into the jaws of beings). The above comment indicates, in any event, that *Kehre* cannot be a mere change of "posture" or a form of "posturing."

15. *Besinnung*, 15–17, 22, 187–88, 191. I am indebted to Krzysztof Ziarek for the felicitous rendering of *machtlos* as "power-free." Heidegger adds, "The struggle between *Entgegnung* and *Streit* is the disclosive *Ereignen* whereby God shadows the earth as sheltered and humans constitute the 'world,' in such a way that world awaits God and earth receives humans (or *Dasein*)" (22). (As will be recalled, the dispute between earth and world was also one of the central themes of "The Origin of the Work of Art.") *Besinnung* again contains several passages distancing meditative thinking from Nietzschean "metaphysics"; for example, "The metaphysical definition of Being as will to power and of being-ness as eternal return is only the end" of a long development of decline; metaphysics reaches its zenith in "the doctrine of the 'will to power' which must be seen as the empowerment of power to a permanent overpowering/superpower (*Übermächtigung*)" (192–93).

16. Heidegger, *Die Geschichte des Seyns*, ed. Peter Trawny (*Gesamtausgabe*, vol. 69; Frankfurt-Main: Klostermann, 1998), 46–48, 50, 64, 69, 76–77.

17. *Die Geschichte des Seyns*, 44, 63, 70, 77–78. For a critique of "leaders" (*Führer*) as supreme technicians compare also Heidegger, "Überwindung der Metaphysik" (1936–1946) in *Vorträge und Aufsätze*, part 1 (Pfullingen: Neske, 1954), esp. 85–88.

18. *Die Geschichte des Seyns*, 180, 209.

19. Heidegger, "Die Frage nach der Technik" and "Die Kehre," in *Die Technik und die Kehre* (2nd ed.; Pfullingen: Neske, 1962), 6–7, 24–25. For an English version (not followed here) of that essay, see Krell, ed., *Martin Heidegger: Basic Writings*, 287–317. For some perceptive discussions of Heidegger's thoughts on technology see, for example, Michael E. Zimmerman, *Heidegger's Confrontation with Modernity: Technology, Politics, Art* (Bloomington, Ind.: Indiana University Press, 1990); Gerhard Glaser, *Das Tun ohne Bild: Zur Technikdeutung Heideggers and Rilkes* (Munich: Maande Verlag, 1983); John Loscerbo, *Being's Technology: A Study in the Philosophy of Martin Heidegger* (The Hague: Nijhoff, 1981).

20. Heidegger, *Beiträge zur Philosophie*, 98; *Besinnung*, 27; *Nietzsche*, vol. 2, 200. For additional "antisystemic" comments in Heidegger's public lectures of the 1930s see my "Heidegger, Hölderlin, and Politics," in *The Other Heidegger*, 140–44. With regard to the notion of *Kampf* one again finds a self-correction on Heidegger's part vis-à-vis earlier uses of the term; see above, note 8.

21. Heidegger, *Die Geschichte des Seyns*, 191–93; *Beiträge zur Philosophie*, 24–25. In the later "Letter on Humanism," orthodox Marxism (or communism) was more closely identified with *Machenschaft* in the sense of technology. To enter into a "productive dialogue with Marxism," we read there, it is necessary "to free oneself from naïve notions about materialism, as well as from the cheap refutations directed against it. The essence of materialism consists not in the assertion that everything is simply matter but rather in a metaphysical determination according to which every being appears as the material of labor (*Arbeit*). Now, the modern-metaphysical nature of labor is anticipated in Hegel's *Phenomenology of Spirit* as the self-propelled process of unconditional production, that is, the objectification of reality through man experienced as subjectivity. The essence of materialism is concealed in the essence of technology, about which much has been written but with little reflection." See Krell, ed., *Martin Heidegger: Basic Writings*, 220. Compare also my "Heidegger and Marxism" in *Between Freiburg and Frankfurt: Toward a Critical Ontology* (Amherst, Mass.: University of Massachusetts Press, 1991), 160–82.

22. *Beiträge zur Philosophie*, 53.

23. *Besinnung*, 187–88. In American academia, intellectual life is in large measure integrated into the production process, with performance being measured in quantitative terms (funding and output).

24. *Besinnung*, 18; *Die Geschichte des Seyns*, 74, 182–83, 187–88. In an uncanny way, the latter text anticipates features of the later "Cold War" by stating that the difference between war and peace is "steadily vanishing," adding: "Peace now becomes only the complete control of all possibilities of war and the attempt to secure their employment. . . . The distinction between war and peace becomes obsolete because both reveal themselves with growing vehemence as equivalent modes of 'totality'" (181–82).

25. Heidegger, "Letter on Humanism," in Krell, ed., *Martin Heidegger: Basic Writings*, 193; *Die Geschichte des Seyns*, 189. Thus, in struggling against *Macht* and *Übermacht*, praxis must always try to shun violence (*Gewalt*), except as a last resort—thus following the path of nonviolent resistance charted by Gandhi and Martin Luther King Jr.

~

Conclusion

With the last chapter, the discussion of self–other relations has returned almost imperceptibly to the topic of globalization. This should not be surprising, given the close connection of the two issues. As has been indicated, the
division of this volume into two parts has been motivated mainly by practical considerations, chiefly the wish to render access easier to readers coming
to the text with different expectations and dispositions. Thus, as I have
pointed out in the preface, philosophically disinterested or disinclined readers may choose to move lightly through part 2 (dealing with self–other relations), while philosophers and other humanists may wish to deemphasize
part 1 (dealing with globalization)—just as long as they remain at least dimly
aware of the interconnections. From my own perspective, of course, things
look different; for me both parts are equally important—which is the reason
for the structure of the volume. Actually, in my view, that structure might
have been—and perhaps should have been—reversed.[1] This is based on a
consideration that might be termed one of the book's chief theses: the notion
that globalization cannot properly be achieved except laterally—that is,
through the cultivation of multiple self–other and cross-cultural encounters.

As the chapters in part 2 should have demonstrated, self–other relations
are immensely complex and cannot be captured or stabilized in a simple
formula. Basically, the task is to find a path between inclusion and exclusion, between predatory appropriation and radical distantiation—a task
pointing to an infinite search. The complexity of lateral relations is carried
over into the process of globalization, into the endeavor to steer a viable

course between parochial localism and abstract globalism, between partic-
ularist contexts and universal aspirations (the themes of part 1). As has repeatedly been stressed, this is a study of "mediations"—and mediations are
roundabout and move in (what some philosophers call) a "hermeneutical
circle." In many ways, a study of mediations is like Penelope's labor—
always beginning, dissolving, and starting anew. This is why mediations de-
pend on practical engagement and seasoned judgment, apart from or in addition to theorizing. It is only through such practical engagement that
coming generations may have a chance to satisfy at least in part the yearning of "achieving our world."

If this study teaches one thing, however, it is that this yearning cannot be
satisfied merely through instrumental construction or social engineering.
Rather, what is needed is a carefully circumspect labor, an engagement nurtured by care (*Sorge*) of self, of fellow human beings, of our natural habitat,
and of all the immanent-transcendent horizons of our "world." Some of the
dimensions requiring care have been specially thematized in this study under
the rubrics of "local–global" and "self–other" relations; other dimensions—
especially those relating to our ecological habitat and to immanence/
transcendence—might be added and fleshed out. The main point is that care
always operates in a complex network, an intricate web of relations where no
part can be isolated or separately active without affecting all the rest.

This means, above all, that change has to proceed cautiously and responsibly—a lesson that is important to remember in our age of rapid globalization wedded to a "permanent revolution" of life-forms (especially life-forms
of the marginalized and dispossessed). It also means—and this may be another major thesis of this study—that every part that radically isolates or seg-
regates itself from the larger network of mediations conjures up the threat of
destruction, by being a harbinger of potential violence. Stated more concretely, with special application to this study, radical separation carries
within itself the seeds of a major derailment of our "being-in-the-world," that
is, the danger of centrifugal or centripetal forms of world-slippage or world
alienation. In our globalizing age, the major enemies of mediation are devotees of "McWorldism," disdainful of ordinary people everywhere, and xenophobic fundamentalists, disdainful of divergent life-forms and beliefs. Practical engagement among friends of this world requires constant vigilance
against these prominent derailments and also sustained efforts to befriend or
extend solicitude to people adrift in our "runaway world."

In many ways, then, this book is written against the grain of current developments. In a world torn apart by multiple forms of violence, there is no
need (I believe) for a writer to add fuel to the conflagration and to stoke fur-

ther the flames of hatred and violent destruction. None of this could plausibly contribute to "achieving our world"—even along the modest and reticent lines suggested in this study. What seems most urgently needed in our time is tolerance, an open mind (or as the Chinese say, an open "heart-and-mind"), a sincere commitment to social justice, and a willingness to struggle against injustice and exploitation in nonviolent ways (following in the footsteps of the Mahatma Gandhi).

To conclude, I would like to cite some statements about our "world," or rather some paeans to the wondrously mediated fabric of the world, taken from both Western and Eastern literature. First, there is this sentence by Hegel, found in a note to his *Philosophy of Right*: "What is the holy? That which binds people together—even if only lightly, like a grass blade binding a wreath." And here are some lines from the great Indian "Song of the Blessed One" or *Bhagavad Gita*: "Let thy aim be the good of all or world maintenance (*loka samgraha*), and thus carry on thy task in life." And here finally some verses from the *Tao Te Ching*:

> Those who would take over the earth
> And shape it to their will
> Never, I notice, succeed.
> The earth is like a vessel so sacred
> That at the mere approach of the profane
> It is marred
> And when they reach out their fingers it is gone.[2]

Notes

1. In an earlier draft of the book, the parts had actually been reversed. I was dissuaded from this arrangement by the consideration that readers might be deterred from further reading if initially confronted with (somewhat difficult) philosophical chapters.

2. See G. W. F. Hegel, *Grundlinien der Philosophie des Rechts oder Naturrecht und Staatswissenschaft im Grundrisse* (Frankfurt-Main: Suhrkamp, 1976), 249 (n. to par. 132); *The Bhagavad Gita*, trans. Juan Mascaró (New York: Penguin Books, 1962), 58 (3/20); *The Way of Life According to Lao Tzu*, trans. Witter Bynner (New York: Perigee Books, 1972), 58 (chap. 29).

Index

~

About the Author

Fred Dallmayr is Packey J. Dee Professor in the departments of government and philosophy at the University of Notre Dame. He holds doctoral degrees from the University of Munich and Duke University. He has been a visiting professor at Hamburg University in Germany and at the New School for Social Research in New York, and a Fellow at Nuffield College in Oxford. During 1990–91 he was in India on a Fulbright research grant. He is the author or editor of numerous books, including *Beyond Orientalism: Essays on Cross-Cultural Encounter*, *The Other Heidegger*, *G. W. F. Hegel: Modernity and Politics*, *Alternative Visions: Paths in the Global Village*, and *Border Crossings: Toward a Comparative Political Theory*.